SLOW READING IN A HURRIED AGE

SLOW READING
in a
HURRIED AGE

David Mikics

THE BELKNAP PRESS OF
HARVARD UNIVERSITY PRESS
Cambridge, Massachusetts, & London, England
2013

Library of Congress Cataloging-in-Publication Data
Mikics, David, 1961–
Slow reading in a hurried age / David Mikics.
pages   cm
ISBN 978-0-674-72472-3 (alk. paper)
1. Reading comprehension.   2. Books and reading—Philosophy.
I. Title.
LB1050.45.M55   2013
372.47—dc23   2013009375

In memory of my father

Contents

SLOW READING IN A HURRIED AGE

Introduction

Why should you read a book? Many millions of people in the world can't read, and of those who can, very few read books regularly. It's easy to fill the day (when you're not working, doing chores, or talking to friends, family, and coworkers) by surfing the Internet, skimming the headlines of news stories, and checking e-mail—not to mention television and video games. None of this activity is reading in the sense I mean. Scanning an e-mail or a text message is fundamentally different from the activity of reading as I will describe it to you. Reading is a craft, a practice. My aim is to provide you with the tools you need to become a better reader.

Reading better means reading more slowly. There is a quiet movement afoot on behalf of slowness: slow cooking, slow thinking, and yes, slow reading. In reaction against the breathless pace of our computer-driven world, writers on social trends have begun to extol the virtues of a more meditative, involved approach to many parts of our lives, and reading is no exception. Faster is not always better. Reading for information is not the same as slow, deep reading, reading for pleasure and understanding. Slow reading is as rigorous as it is full of unexpected delight.

If you've picked up this book, you already love reading—but often you don't have time for it. Too frequently, and especially at the end of a busy day, reading becomes flipping the pages of the *New Yorker* without finishing any of its articles; or glancing at the news on the Web; or checking social media sites. Slow reading is the antidote to such distractions, which increasingly plague us in the digital age.

My point is not to harass, cajole, or threaten you into reading more books. Instead, I want you to get more out of what you read. If you're looking at this book, you already want more from reading; you're committed. You have the chance to live up to that commitment by improving the way you read, making your experience of a book more serious and involved—and, yes, slower.

How you read matters much more than how much you read. And a good book is the only thing that will teach you how to read with a full mind, focused on enjoyment and mental profit. Newspaper articles, tweets, and blogs won't show you what reading is all about. Only a book can do that.

Getting lost in a book—immersed, absorbed, happily abandoned—asks for some preparation. In order to enjoy, you have to know what to look for. The aim of *Slow Reading in a Hurried Age* is to guide you toward greater pleasure in reading, through some simple rules and some enriching discussions of favorite books.

When you have learned slow reading, you will have a secure possession, and an endlessly provocative one. Your attitudes and responses to the world will change in ways you could never have predicted. I can't promise you that slow reading will help you to become a better person, to make more money, or to find true love. But in a subtler way, you will be transformed, and your life will become more interesting as a result. Imagine you had never exercised before, and that you then became a successful athlete, running several miles every day. Slow reading changes your mind the way exercise changes your body: a whole new world will open up; you will feel and act differently, because books will be more alive and open to you.

Slow reading is an active discipline. The more you put into it, the more worthy and absorbing you will find it. The more seriously and actively you read, the more you will be inclined to return to the same books, reconsidering and reevaluating them, and reevaluating yourself too. Walt Whitman wrote that "reading is not a half-sleep but, in the highest sense, a gymnast's struggle. . . . Not the book so much needs to be the complete thing, but the reader of the book does." Reading with the high, earnest energy Whitman recommends will complete you, make you whole and strong, as much as anything can.

In the twenty-first century, there are more obstacles than ever before to practicing the kind of reading that I recommend in this book. Whether we like it or not, the Internet has caused a revolution in the way we read. Friends and foes of technology agree that our relationship to the written word has changed forever. Even devotees of the Internet often confess to being frustrated by what happens when they are online: they waste hours of time every day with distractions, and learn little beyond some handful of facts that are soon forgotten.

This book will teach any interested person how to be a good and careful reader, a slow reader, even in the age of the Internet. The Internet fosters light reading: we scan and graze, searching for tidbits. The World Wide Web encourages us to consume words in small, easy bites. But slow reading demands time and practice. *Slow Reading in a Hurried Age* will guide readers to the new habits they need to develop in order to get the most out of books. The rewards are great: the learning of the ages and the enjoyment that only attentive reading can offer.

This book is a how-to guide for the overburdened, hurried person who encounters "texts" all the time—e-mails, tweets, short online news pieces—but who wants something more rewarding, something that only slow reading can achieve. It's a *vade mecum* or handbook that I hope you will use in the most practical way possible. It offers guidance for seasoned readers who want to increase their skills, but also for those who have fallen out of practice. Perhaps you haven't read much since college, but you've been glancing yearningly toward the novels on your shelves that you remember from your favorite courses. As you become more ambitious, and travel to less-explored "realms of gold" (in Keats's phrase), you can rely on earlier reading as your home base, but also experience new delights. Open before you is an endless resource, always at the ready: the thrill that comes with truly substantial reading. Finally, my arguments are intended for concerned teachers and parents who recognize that constant use of digital technology has negatively affected our children's attention spans and their ability to work independently on challenging tasks. Slow reading can help improve concentration, both in the classroom and after school. This book offers practical advice about how to increase the curiosity and commitment of youthful readers.

In *Slow Reading in a Hurried Age* I quote and discuss a range of examples, mostly from literature, but some from history and social science. Many of them are canonical texts, though a few are not. My focus is on the celebrated works of Western tradition, from the Bible and Homer on. I have chosen these books because they shed light on the problems and opportunities of reading well, and because they offer so much sophisticated pleasure to the reader, even when they are hard to read. As a teacher of freshmen for many years in a Great Books program, I know the excitement that reading classic texts can give.

A word about the format of this book. I begin with a survey of the pressing dangers that the digital age presents to the serious reader. This opening discussion, "The Problem," may at first seem unrelated to the practical advice for reading that I present later on. In fact, nothing could be more important than recognizing the way that the Internet, which has transformed some things for the better, has also made it more difficult to read seriously, slowly, and well. In "The Problem" and the following chapter, "The Answer," I confront the true dimensions of the digital revolution, which has radically changed everything that has to do with reading. Unless we think soberly about how to control, and at times to counteract, the growing influence of digital technology on our lives, we will not be able to pursue the work of worthwhile reading.

After "The Problem" and "The Answer," I go on to my fourteen rules for reading. This chapter offers a concrete program for those who feel frustrated by literature's intricacies, especially when a literary work is noticeably difficult. How often have I heard, from well-read grown-ups, comments like "I just don't understand poetry!" If you enjoy books but feel that there must be more to see, and say, about what you've read, these rules will enable you to become a more able and careful reader, to know what to do better when you open a book. My fourteen rules can be read in any order; each reader will find some more helpful than others, depending on his or her prior reading experiences. The rules should be applied in the way that works best: take what you can use.

I don't want my stress on the rules to get in the way of the reader's excitement. Ralph Waldo Emerson charges us to "read for the lustres," for the glittering, momentary peaks that rise up within a book. I don't intend to level those heights with my programmatic advice. Instead, I wish to give you a method for finding them.

The rules are followed by five broader excursions into key genres, chapters on reading short stories, novels, poems, plays, and essays, and then by a conclusion. These chapters give you a chance to apply the fourteen rules of reading, which I refer to frequently as I discuss a variety of authors. Here I guide you through some of my favorite books, ones that cast a bright light on the reading experience and on other members of their genre. The books that illustrate each genre have a classifying power: they show something about what a novel is, what a poem is, and so on for the other genres. In an important sense, the essay is Montaigne; drama is Shakespeare. I hope that you will decide to read some of the books I describe if you haven't already: they span the literary cosmos, from the mournful and humane comedy of Chekhov to the acute, self-deluding clarities that Henry James trades in; from the dire nobilities of Shakespearean tragedy to the pure air breathed by Willa Cather; from Wallace Stevens, who can be lush and restrained at once, to Beckett with his spare agonies. Any such collection is bound to be personal, partial, and somewhat arbitrary, and I have had to omit many of my most cherished authors: discussing all the books I love would have meant writing ten volumes, not one. But I've made a start, and provided an example, I hope, of how to speak about the books you feel closest to.

The great English Romantic critic William Hazlitt advocated reading with gusto. To read well requires appetite. My primary advice to you, always, is to be hearty in your desire for the written word, and to keep your sense of fun. Reading should not be drudgery, and not mere escape either, but a form of life lived at a higher pitch. Properly done, it offers you, as Harold Bloom insists, more life: more people than you could ever meet, more intense visions of love and fate, bliss and woe than are likely to come your way otherwise. The universe that the great authors made vies with the created world for pungent variation, for beauty and darkness, for the novelty that makes us admire. Through the unbounded energy of words, it gives you surprise, the most valuable of gifts. And it's always open to you, every moment. The books are waiting.

The Problem

It's late, and God knows it's been a long day. The kids are in bed at last, the argument with the boss (or husband or wife) largely forgotten. Most of us, at the end of a trying day, know just where to turn: we pick up the laptop and cruise for easily digested morsels of entertainment or news; we glance at Facebook or e-mail. Eventually, tired of clicking from one Web site to another, we are ready for bed.

There's a better alternative, as you already know: reading books. A book will give you truer, more sustained companionship than the glimmers of the online world can provide. Even if you already read avidly and widely, knowing more about how to read will enable you to truly lose yourself in a book: to let it do its work on you, and allow it to reveal new prospects, new experiences. It's necessary to unplug the social, preoccupied self in order to be ready for this newness. Then, as Robert Frost puts it in his poem "Directive," you'll be "lost enough to find yourself / By now." The book you yield to may disorient or bewilder you, but such lostness will allow you in the end to recover a truer version of self.

Nearly every influence that surrounds us argues against the kind of reading I advocate in *Slow Reading in a Hurried Age*. The Age of Digital Distraction throws up unprecedented challenges in the face of readers. We are primed to scan and skim, to get the gist of an opinion and move on; we are obsessed with speed. We want fast downloads, moment-to-moment news, the latest tweet.

My intent is not to deliver a mere crotchety jeremiad, or to claim that the old days were always better. You may be wondering why I am preaching against electronic media rather than simply praising books and reading. The reason is simple. I am sounding the alarm about the hazards of the digital age because it's important to realize what we are up against as readers. The challenge must be met openly, with full acknowledgment of how much harder it is to read well than it was just a few years ago. (It's also true that the new technology has advanced research in the sciences and humanities and has led to scientific discoveries; but I am focusing on this technology's impact on the life of reading, a much gloomier picture.)

Engulfed by a never-ending flood of text, we barely have time to stop and reflect. Quick and sloppy messages cascade around us constantly. This tidal wave of bad writing, much of it demanding a rapid response, gets in the way of true reading, which takes time and concentration. *Slow Reading in a Hurried Age* will show you how to read in a strong and productive way, a way that increases your mind's creative power instead of sapping it. Even in the midst of today's relentlessly connected, hooked-in lifestyle, in-depth reading is possible. But if you want to read deeply and well, you will need some guidance: more now than ever before, given the new plague of byte-sized diversions.

The current digital hailstorm is truly unprecedented. Even twenty years ago, no one could have imagined it. During the twentieth century, academics wrote and published a barrelful of polemics on behalf of books and against newer media (movies, TV, comics). They trumpeted the need to "save reading" in the face of its cutting-edge enemies. But none of these tweed-jacketed scolds, some of whom were worthy campaigners indeed, pre-

dicted what in fact happened: the ever-present online environment of words that envelops us like the air we breathe. When
Mortimer Adler championed book reading in postwar America,
he was worried about a future in which people wouldn't read,
period. (Adler's *How to Read a Book,* which he wrote in 1940,
sold millions of copies in the following decades.) Adler was afraid
that, glued to the television (then a recent invention), we would
become couch potatoes able to absorb only images, not print.
He could not envision the future that actually occurred, one in
which everyone reads constantly, and badly. Writers like Adler
and Charles Van Doren (who revised *How to Read a Book* with
Adler in 1972), or Neil Postman in his 1985 anti-media polemic
Amusing Ourselves to Death, never foresaw the cloud of micro-
texts, the e-mails and tweets and instant messages, that dart and
float about us all day long.

The Internet has put everything in a new light: lightning-
quick, yet blurry. The casual, makeshift sentence is now prized
as more vital than the adept, finished one. Eloquence and careful elaboration seem mere time-wasters belonging to an older,
less wired generation. Could Proust, who cherished the rewards
and punishments that time affords the soul, have borne the Era
of the Tweet?

Not all tweets are created equal, of course. Epigrammatic
concision and wit are possible on Twitter. But they are rare:
Twitter militates against the polished statement; it favors words
that feel disposable. If something is retweeted around the globe,
that's usually because it appears to carry news, not because it
sums up a feeling or a thought with lasting accuracy. The most
popular tweets often resemble headlines, jokes, or insults: hard-
hitting, sardonic, a little crude. On Twitter, the swift punch is
preferred to wisdom. Celebrity tweets let us slurp from the
fountains of gossip or invective, sources which, in any modern
society, never run dry. But gossip is for the moment; it loses its

flavor over time. One would no more want an anthology of Kanye West's, or even Jay-Z's, tweets than one would want a collection of last year's newspaper headlines. Even if they were catchy at the time, they are old now.

Real reading of real books, reading designed to augment the reader's creative strength, never loses its power. It is not subject to time the way that e-mail, Twitter, and instant messaging are. Such reading demands time from you, in order to give you something that will last: knowing a book in a way that convinces you to come back to it over and over, so that you reap greater rewards the more time you spend with it. Time—the need for it, what it's good for—is the key to my idea about worthwhile reading. In the Age of Information we place a premium on getting what we need, or what we think we need, as rapidly as possible. The problem is that everything happens so quickly that our decision-making power is stolen from us. We sense, correctly, that we are no longer capable of deciding what deserves our attention and what doesn't. We have begun to suffer as a result. Children and teens have become addicted to the continuous activity of clicking, the herky-jerky rhythm that rules their young lives. A rally of ultra-Orthodox Jews against the Internet at New York's Citi Field in May 2012 raised the alarm aggressively (though, one must add, in somewhat reactionary style). We are on the way to becoming "click vegetables," argued Rabbi Ephraim Wachsman: "If you're bored with something, just click."

Two recent and well-publicized surveys of teachers conducted by the Pew Foundation and Common Sense Media confirm the growing perception among teachers that the constant use of digital technologies by students is affecting their ability to concentrate: nearly 90 percent of the teachers who participated in the surveys believe that digital technologies are creating "an easily distracted generation with short attention spans." "Boy, is this a clarion call for a healthy and balanced media diet," said Jim Steyer, the chief executive of Common Sense Media, commenting on the results of the survey: "What you have to understand as a parent is that what happens in the home with media consumption can affect academic achievement."

Cultural critic Mark Bauerlein cites a 2005 Kaiser Family Foundation survey that shows that reading books during one's free time is the most accurate predictor of whether kids between eight and eighteen will go on to, and succeed in, college—and the Internet steals time from serious leisure reading the way nothing else does. Most of us want our kids to go to college (even if, like me, we are old enough to have forgotten most of what happened there). Constant Internet use hampers a young person's readiness for the intense study habits that college requires.

We can't do away with the Net; and, really, we wouldn't want to. It has made our world much more convenient, more connected. We can find the information we need quickly and communicate with a far wider range of people than before. We've expanded our acquaintance with what's happening now, everywhere. But there is a substantial downside: the loss of private, thoughtful pleasures, like serious reading. The Internet, unlike a book, is a persistent nag. I periodically hear from friends who report an increasingly rare experience: their joy on being separated from the Internet for a weekend, usually in some remote vacation spot; they could actually relax and focus, they tell me, and escape their usual harried existence. The Internet is a reminder of all the things we have to do, at the office and, increasingly, at home too. When it's gone for a while, we feel free.

The Internet presents a seemingly infinite volume of choices. But when we plunge into this electronic ocean of possibilities, we often feel that choice has been taken away from us. In contrast to a supermarket, the Net doesn't usually ask you to pay for your choices; it proudly asserts that information is free.

But the online abundance of possibilities fails to liberate. The Net rules us by demanding that we choose as much as we can, as frequently as we can, so that we don't miss out on anything. This especially applies to the reading matter that makes its way onto the Internet. We have too many choices of things to read—or glance at. The result is Continuous Partial Attention (CPA), which occurs when we try to do too much at once. Linda Stone, who coined the term, explains that CPA is not the same as multitasking. When we multitask, she argues, we pair one activity that is fairly automatic with another that requires more attention. For example, we eat lunch while writing or making phone calls. The main activity—writing, talking on the phone—always remains our primary focus. Eating that sandwich won't steal attention from our main task.

CPA is different, Stone writes, because when it kicks in, we're "motivated by a desire not to miss anything." CPA instills in us

> a kind of vigilance that is not characteristic of multi-tasking. With CPA, we feel most alive when we're connected, plugged in and in the know. We constantly scan for opportunities— activities or people—in any given moment. . . . Continuous partial attention is an always on, anywhere, anytime, any place behavior that creates an artificial sense of crisis. We are always in high alert.

In small doses, such vigilance can come in handy. But current technology, which besieges us with opportunities to notice something new, imposes CPA on us. "More and more," Stone concludes, "many of us feel the 'shadow side' of CPA— over-stimulation and lack of fulfillment." Every minute, it seems, a new link snags us, an article or post teases us with a sexy head-line, promising us we can be in the know if we just click and spend a few seconds looking at it. The point is to get you to click: to entice you to "the jump," so that you'll arrive at the rest of the article (and, more important, a new advertising page).

Stress-related diseases, now more prevalent than ever before, go along with the Internet's ever-beckoning presence in our lives. The stress hormones norepinephrine and cortisol have been running rampant, stimulated by our new sense of distraction, frustration, and lost time. We look for answers, at least partial ones, for our frazzled nerves and fractured attention spans: anti-anxiety drugs, meditation, an afternoon of swimming or golfing away from the iPhone. These are all legitimate refuges from Internet-spawned agitation. But reading is the best response of them all, the one that offers the most precious rewards, as I explain in this book.

The problem of divided attention didn't begin with the digital age, of course. But only recently, only now that we carry instant electronic connectivity wherever we go, has it reached avalanche proportions. Walter Kirn, meditating in *The Atlantic* on "the nightmare of infinite connectivity," quotes Publilius Syrus, a Roman freed slave and aphorist from the first century BCE: "To do two things at once is to do neither." These days, we're constantly doing two (or three, or four) things at once.

In his article, Kirn recalls the early promise of the Internet:

> "Where do you want to go today?" asked Microsoft in a mid-1990s ad campaign. The suggestion was that there were endless destinations—some geographic, some social, some intellectual—that you could reach in milliseconds by loading the right devices with the right software. It was further insinuated that where you went was purely up to you, not your spouse, your boss, your kids, or your government.

As we now know all too well, Google and Amazon are watching our every move, and telling us just where to go: telling us so effectively that we don't even realize they're doing it. Jaron Lanier, a trailblazing computer scientist, says that the Internet seduced us into giving up our freedom. What "free" access to information turned out to mean was willingness to let corporations have free access to us. For writers, composers, and artists, it also meant letting millions of other Internet users take their creative work without paying for it. "Right now," Lanier writes, "we get certain free cloud services in exchange for not being paid and being spied on, while still paying too much for bandwidth." Freedom was the last thing on the Web masters' minds. What they wanted, it turned out, was to mold and shape the consumer—us—by figuring out our patterns: what we read and bought and watched and wrote online. "Where do you want to go today?" they asked. In order for them to amass enough information about us, we had to go places (or "places"), not just today, but every day (every hour? every minute?). Suddenly (by about 2005, let's say), this didn't feel like freedom any longer.

The unfree character of our interactions with the Net also shows up in the rigid rhythms it imposes on us, the constant toggling between competing sources of attention. Anyone trying to think long and hard about what he or she is doing can easily get tangled up in the Net's temptations. In Homer's *Odyssey*, the Sirens told Odysseus that they had the up-to-the-minute postings about his fame, those brave deeds that were rippling across the Mediterranean. Supervisors of his PR, they also claimed to have the last word on his psyche: they promised to tell the world-renowned hero who he really was. Like the Sirens, the Net's clickable links flatter you by telling you that you really ought to be on top of things: you should know what's happening in the world and therefore what's happening to your self (the "therefore" is obscure). Why not follow up some potentially relevant tidbit of knowledge? Or take a look at an article that could—who knows?—give you an important new idea? Or why not just take a break, a really quick one, for a little fun? Before you know it, you've frittered the day away on stupid kitty videos, and your eyes and soul are aching.

Kirn reports that "the constant switching and pivoting" that our hours on the Internet demand from us "energize regions of the brain that specialize in visual processing and physical coordination and simultaneously appear to shortchange some of the higher areas related to memory and learning." An experiment at UCLA asked subjects to sort index cards, first in silence and then while listening for particular sounds which they had to identify as they sorted. "The subjects managed to sort the cards just as well with the musical distraction," Kirn writes, "but they had a much harder time remembering what, exactly, they'd been sorting once the experiment was over." Their brains had shifted focus from the hippocampus, which handles memory, to the striatum, which manages rote action. They were able to perform the task, but they couldn't recall what they had done. The same is true for our children and teenagers, the majority of whom habitually do something else while reading: cruising the Internet, checking for and sending texts, watching videos, listening to music (sometimes all at once). The decline in young people's ability to focus on a single source of interest is palpable, as many teachers and parents have noted with alarm. Kids who grow up with digital technology are more susceptible to the disease of constantly divided attention than older generations who discovered the online world later in their lives. According to a study by Innerscope Research of Boston, "digital natives"—people who grew up with the new technologies—switch from one digital source to another an average of twenty-seven times per hour. (The rate for "digital immigrants," those who started to use mobile technology as adults, is seventeen times per hour.)

A majority of digital natives, 54 percent, say that they would rather text people than talk to them. (Only 28 percent of digital immigrants prefer texting to talking.)

Doing two or three things at once decreases efficiency, because of the stress induced by constant shifting of attention. Such CPA prevents you from devoting yourself sufficiently to any one thing. In the Internet era, we often feel that we've achieved complete freedom to look at or listen to whatever we want, anytime we want. Yet we don't know how to determine priorities: how to decide what's worth our attention. We feel lost, helpless. In our search for diversion, we always seem to have too much to do.

Kirn suggests that our habitual, frantic switching back and forth between iPhone, laptop, e-books, Twitter, Tumblr, and YouTube—with an occasional intermission for the person standing in front of us—will, in some better future, be revealed as the Sorcerer's Apprentice labor it is. "When we look back on it someday, at our juggling of electronic lives," Kirn remarks,

> the spectacle will appear as quaint and stylized as those scenes in old movies of stiff-backed lady operators, hair in bobby pins, rapidly swapping phone jacks from hole to hole as they connect Chicago to Miami, reporter to city desk, businessman to mistress. Such scenes were, for a time, cinematic shorthand for the frenzy of modern life, but then communications technology changed, and those operators lost their jobs.
>
> To us.

The escape from our current bewitchment, from the multiple media platforms that entrap us, is dedication to one task, and the determination to do that task well. Slowness and concentration are needed to learn to do anything well that is worth doing well, from fly-fishing to electrical engineering to playing the violin. The same is true of reading. Slow reading, as an increasing number of commentators have recognized, is the only way to truly experience a book.

Skimming and rapid, informational reading have always been with us. A good newspaper story, backed by a juicy headline, has always been designed so it can be read for a few key paragraphs, rather than all the way to the end. The classic tabloid style was adopted, and accentuated, by the Internet, which encourages us to graze the digital meadows instead of making us dive in and ponder a subject. But there is growing discontent with the prevailing model of news-for-skimming. Sites like Longform.org cater to readers who want to read substantial essays, and want to read them to the end. These readers are hungry refugees from the regime of endless, tasty-but-unsatisfying bits of information. They want something considered, something worth reading slowly and carefully. Max Linsky, one of the founders of Longform, reports that on the day Osama bin Laden was assassinated, his site received 800,000 hits from people searching for thorough, essayistic explorations of bin Laden. They were not looking for the sensational two-paragraph wrap-ups that were bobbing up all over the Internet, but for something deeper.

The Internet is the epitome of a postmodern age that prizes quickness and fast connections above all else. But this seeming efficiency turns out not to be efficient at all; our busyness and swiftness don't end up being productive. Reading on the Internet in three-minute slices is different from serious reading, just as flipping from one radio station to another is different from serious listening. When I was in high school and college, every new record album of significance got what seemed like an endless number of listenings. We thought we were wasting our time, but we were wrong. Our obsessive eighteen-year-old's reverence for the latest vinyl apparition of the Talking Heads or Elvis Costello was not mere aimless tuning-out, but loving devotion to the details that only appear when you hear something over and over. Reading requires the same kind of devotion: the test of any good bout of reading is whether you're tempted to go back to the book and read it again.

In the brave new digital world, we are intent on speed rather than repetition and slow study. As a result, we have lost sight of the fact that reading well requires time and patience. This point can't be repeated often enough. Book-length arguments and works of imaginative literature reveal themselves only over time. We must work hard to get more out of the books we read—and good books always reward slow-moving, careful attention. The point is a pedagogically necessary one as well. We are not doing our children any favors by encouraging the idea that everything they do should be easy, effortless, and quick. Too often these days, "research" for a high schooler, and often even a college student, means glancing at Wikipedia, doing a fast Google search, and cutting and pasting some quotations together. In the best-case scenario, the student will put quotation marks around the pasted passages: because of the Internet's constant offers of ready-for-use text, plagiarism is an ever-increasing plague. Bad writing, the mere assembling of sentences from the Net with some alterations or additions of one's own, goes along with bad reading.

What goes for writing goes equally for reading. Our constant production of slapped-together texts is allied to the new fashion for spontaneity masquerading as creativity: on the Internet, a poem (or "poem") may take only a minute or two to write, or to read. But the truly creative work—whether it's making something interesting or interpreting something in an interesting way—requires you to acquire technique so you can accomplish your goal. There is no mastery of any skill or craft without time, dedication, and concentration. This is true for mastering the piano, excelling at a sport, drawing a picture—

and reading. "There is then creative reading as well as creative writing," Ralph Waldo Emerson proclaimed. "When the mind is braced by labor and invention, the page of whatever book we read becomes luminous with manifold allusion. Every sentence is doubly significant, and the sense of our author is as broad as the world." Emerson's great insight is that creativity requires a "labor" twinned with "invention"; it takes work.

The labor needed for truly rewarding reading stands in contrast to the lazy manner of surveying texts we have developed during the last few Internet-dominated decades. Researchers have discovered that people read online texts, whether blog posts or Facebook pages or news stories, in an F-pattern. They begin by reading the first line, or first few lines, of the piece, all the way across (the top line of the F). Then, further down, they read partway across, stopping before the right margin (the lower, shorter branch of the F). Sub-headlines or bullet points provide additional branches of the F: to conform with the F-pattern, such sub-headings tend to be shorter than the main headline at the top. Eventually, about halfway through the piece, the reader's eye starts to make a beeline down the left margin of the page, following the vertical stem of the F and "finishing" the text without actually reading most of it. Pressed for time, the reader races downward, plummeting ever more quickly to the end of the article.

David Risley, a "blog marketing strategist," remarks on the ruling importance of the F-pattern: "most blog readers are riddled with ADD [attention deficit disorder] . . . so your content has to be structured to accommodate." Advertisers are well aware of the F pattern: the most expensive ad is generally at the top left-hand side of a Web page, in the fattest, most attention-worthy corner of the F. (This inverts the traditional design of newspapers, in which the top right-hand side usually contains the lead story.)

We can resist the F-pattern that the Net uses to structure our reading, and adopt a more fitting pace, one that lets us encounter a text more thoroughly. Each of us has the choice to read as he or she wants to; the new technology may stand in the way, but we still have the ability to take control of our own reading experience.

While the ever-increasing dominance of the Internet in our lives is cause for deep concern, it should not be reason for despair. The notion that the Internet has changed the structure of our brains for the worse is clearly wrong. That can't happen in the span of a few decades; evolution takes time. But heavy Internet use from a very early age, when a child's brain is still developing, can have an effect on that brain, just as drugs have an effect. (You wouldn't give your toddler caffeine or speed, would you?) And even in adults, constant recourse to the Internet shapes our responses in a way that, as I've been describing, many now find imprisoning rather than liberating. It will probably take some time before researchers establish just how much Internet use at exactly what age can lead to ADD. But the evidence suggests an explosive increase in ADD among our kids, coinciding with the ever-greater Internet use of the past decade. The sheer volume of prescriptions doctors have written for Adderall and Ritalin is staggering, and frightening.

The young are most vulnerable to the dangers of the digital age. The average teenager sends about three thousand texts a month—an astonishing, and dismaying, figure. Mark Bauerlein has described the pressures exerted by this ever-present peer-to-peer contact: teens swap words and images all day long, and much of the night too. The teenage bedroom has become a "command center," Bauerlein writes. Texts and tweets and pictures "pour in every evening, and if kids don't respond, they fall behind." Bauerlein argues that "kids need a reprieve and a retreat"; they need to be protected from the minute-to-minute demands of the peer group. Reading is a world that a young adult can enter alone and at will, taking as much time as she wants. She can free herself from the hassle-filled job that the smartphone inflicts on her: formulating a knowing rejoinder or responding with a wisecrack to every sentence she reads. Bauerlein, a college teacher, writes that his own students feel compelled to tune in, to open the phone the moment that class is over. They might miss something, they fear—and "is anything worse than exclusion?" Bauerlein asks. But the students' faces are tense, not joyous, as they busily consult their hand-held screens. Under the new regime of relentless checking and responding, pleasure has been lost. Bauerlein cites a number of critics of the Internet, including Lee Siegel, Nicholas Carr, and Maggie Jackson, who concur with his estimate of the damage inflicted on our souls by the digital age.

The good news is that the effects of online addiction are reversible. You haven't suddenly become an idiot because you're an Angry Birds junkie, any more than a gambling addict loses the ability to think after a long stint at the slot machines. The way the Internet prompts and primes you for "action" (note my skeptical quotation marks) resembles gambling: there's an aura of the compulsive about it that casts a grim shadow even when you're having a good time. Web surfing can't deliver the gambler's exhilaration; neither can it, except in rare cases, take away your home and family (unless those are gambling sites you're clicking on). But the two phenomena, gambling and surfing the Web, share a common element: they proceed at an artificial, rapid-fire pace that remains utterly different from the rhythm we adopt when taking a walk, talking to a friend—or seriously reading a book.

The difference between the tempo of the online environment and that of the other activities I've just mentioned is not merely that the Web prizes speed. It's also that the Web's rhythm feels rigidly imposed rather than expressive, even when the links turn over quickly. The fastest computer in the world will still make you a slave of its reaction time; it will still present you with an array of options for clicking. It simply can't respond to you the way a human being, a landscape, a painting, or a book does. Music, too, presents a seamless environment in a way that the Net never can. In this artificial, arm's-length aspect of the Internet, Jaron Lanier sees its lack of expressive capacity. Literature, music and art express; computers, by contrast, lead you in a step-by-step way. You're not immersed in a reality, you're staring at a screen that asks you questions and demands responses.

You can never become lost in the Web the way you can be lost in a book; you are never really free while waiting for a screen to change. That's why the best e-readers simulate the feel of books as closely as they can. The basic appeal of the e-reader is that it relieves us from carrying around bulky tomes. (Though it also subjects us to yet another screen; if we've been staring at one in a cubicle all day long, we may desire the printed page as an escape.) We want the e-reader to supply the intimacy of a book: we want to browse, flip pages, write a note in a margin. To put it another way: e-readers are wonderfully convenient, but is there anything they can do that print books cannot? E-readers can link to music, art, and video in ways that books can't. But books ask for our full attention, so that such electronic extras usually just get in the way. Do you really want to listen to Beethoven while reading Anthony Burgess's *A Clockwork Orange,* whose thuggish characters constantly have "Ludwig Van" on the stereo? The answer is no; remembering what Beethoven sounds like is more than enough. If you listen at the same time that you read, the music will win out over the words.

Though a well-performed audiobook often adds to our understanding of a written text, books exist first of all on the page. They are writing, not speech. And there's a difference between the two. We don't often record our conversations for later listening: they don't have the refined shape of memorable pieces of writing. Talk happens in the moment; writing is something you go back to. With the advent of instant messaging and Twitter, though, the distinction between speech and writing is eroding fast.

The linguist John McWhorter, who is fascinated by Twitter, says that it is writing in the technical sense only: Twitter is really talk in written form. There's nothing wrong with that, except that we get acclimated to it. When confronted with real writing, writing that demands focus, we find ourselves defeated and frustrated. We feel bored before we even know what it is we are being bored by. Glancing at a tweet takes a few seconds; understanding a novel takes days, sometimes weeks. There's no reason an avid reader can't also be a skillful tweeter, any more than an opera fan can't also love the three-minute pop song. But keep in mind that a tweet is more like the chorus of a pop song, rather than the whole thing. Even three-minute songs have an architecture, and often enough a high artistry, to which tweets just can't, don't want to, aspire. A tweet is a blip, a break, a momentary sensation. You can't live on that diet. Eventually, you'll become frustrated by such tiny portions at such frequent intervals.

We need continuity, the steadiness of working on the same object, moment after moment, page after page. The point applies to reading as it does to listening to music or watching movies. There's a reason that toggling among different sources of interest is frustrating, while doing one thing is satisfying. Even in childhood, we sense the all-important distinction between being distracted and being happily absorbed; knowing this difference is part of our evolutionary inheritance. One of the signal achievements of toddlers, usually occurring around the three-year mark, is their new ability to focus on a single activity for an extended period, instead of darting from one toy to another every few minutes (the characteristic mode of the two-year-old). This early maturity comes as a relief to parents, who feel proud that their child has learned how to concentrate on one thing and explore it more fully. The capacity for lengthy absorption in a plaything (or video, or book) continues to grow as a child develops, along with the thirst for repeated experience: the desire to hear a story again or listen to the same song over and over. The wish to be absorbed by an object is one thing that defines what it means to be a grown-up human. Our capacity for rapt and long-lasting attention has also led to enormous cultural milestones: we would not be the mathematicians and physicists and chefs and computer programmers and writers and artists that we are if we didn't have an appetite for silent, fascinated absorption. We give ourselves the space and, above all, the time to figure out a problem, or to create something carefully and slowly. When Freud said that humans need work and love to survive, he was pointing to a basic element that these two activities share: the best work elicits our love, and love is worth little if we don't work at it. Love means sustained, cherishing attention; and when we work (instead of just being wage slaves), we devote ourselves to a process that becomes ours. Such work may look like mere obsession with details, but it's not.

True work, by which I mean any worthwhile craft or practice, often seems individual or solitary, even when someone else is working right beside you. Reading, as a form of work, needs solitude. Social chatter, of the kind that seeps through every corner of the Internet, hampers our ability to do work. When the chatter is good, it entertains, at least for a moment; when it's bad (as in the often nasty talkbacks to blog posts and news articles) it can be disturbingly malicious. Arguing in a way inspired by deep reading differs from just voicing ardent opinions—the usual practice in Blogland, where we bristle and denounce so freely, proud of our thin skins. Cass Sunstein has noted that opinions tend to reinforce themselves on the Internet, instead of becoming part of a dialogue. Most of us have noticed that the Net, perhaps because of its anonymity, encourages users to hit the warpath. When you don't know who you're talking to—when you're talking, potentially, to everybody—you tend to become defensive about your opinion, and, as a result, needlessly aggressive. Flaming disparagement and hectic banner-raising are not true conversation.

Readers' comments about books on the Internet are usually more inclined to the weakly complimentary than the rabidly insulting; and the capsule comments on Amazon, accompanied by their inevitable stars, are usually more akin to blurbs than to considered responses. There is an important place for conversation about the books we read; but this conversation must be nurtured by a wish to engage responsibly with other readers, rather than scoring points with shoot-from-the-hip opinions, or simply patting the author on the back. The difference between a thoughtful comment and a blurted-out reaction is something to keep in mind not only when you talk to other readers, but to the authors of the books you read—since reading really is a conversation with an author. (I will say more on the subject of reading as conversation later on.)

Some argue that the digital age is not just a blizzard of distractions, but that it has given us something new and important, innovative forms of mental exercise and creativity. What about video games, for example? In 2012 a story appeared in the British newspaper the *Telegraph* under the headline "Video games 'more creative than reading.'" The subheadline was just as inflammatory: "Middle-class parents should not be afraid of letting their children play computer games because the experience is more creative than reading, one of the country's leading playwrights claimed yesterday." The playwright, Lucy Prebble (author of the satirical drama *Enron*), confessed to being a video-game addict as a teenager, back when video games were much less slick and multidimensional than they are now. In her original article on the subject for the *Guardian,* Prebble wrote that gaming "is creative, in comparison to the passivity of watching a film or reading a book. You are making choices and, often, are even designing the world yourself."

It's too early to tell whether video games will become an art form to rival novels or theater or movies. But Prebble is clearly wrong to say that playing a video game is creative, whereas reading a book is merely passive. If you read intelligently—that is, if you learn how to read in the best way—you are making choices every moment. You are thinking about what matters in the sentence in front of you, about how the book hangs together, about how the author has done her or his work. Noticing as many aspects as you can of an author's art makes you the partner of the author, not a passive receiver of text. You work with the words of the book as you figure out what strikes a chord with you and why. There's a technique to your choices about how to respond to a book, just as there's technique required in any activity that you need to learn, from ballroom dancing to playing music to drawing.

I will say more about how the techniques of reading can unlock your creativity in my chapter "The Rules," but for now the essential point is that reading, though it differs from playing a game, also shares something with games (it has rules, for example). To a casual observer, playing a game, whether on a screen or off it, may seem more active than reading because it requires physical motion. The player of a game must click or swipe, or throw a ball or move a piece. The player's decisions are visible in a way that a reader's can never be. When you read, you follow the trail of words; at times you may be aware of making decisions (for example: is the writer being ironic or straight-faced? Is the plot heading toward tragedy or a happy ending?). Mostly, though, you sense the tone of a piece of writing without needing to consider such alternatives so explicitly. The work you put into reading takes the form of learning the depth of what is there on the page: getting used to seeing a book as fully as possible, in all its dimensions. The proper analogy is to a pianist who gets a better and better feel for a piece as she practices it, learns it by heart, then works at truly knowing it for a few weeks or months or years. When you read well, you don't figure out how to manipulate rules of play to your advantage, how to make a dull situation more interesting, or how to compete against an opponent (all of which are basic video-game skills). Reading is more like a recognition of what is already there in a text; it requires understanding who an author is and what she or he is trying to do. Such understanding is creative, just as playing Mozart or Beethoven with insight and feeling is creative. Like the musician's, the reader's personality colors her understanding. Nothing could be more active.

There have always been plenty of distractions. The subject comes up in the Bible's book of Proverbs ("Let thine eyes look right on. . . . Ponder the path of thy feet" [4:25–26]). Bewigged eighteenth-century pundits warned against newspaper-reading with much the same degree of fervor I am mustering against the online world. But this time really is different, I'm convinced. The Internet makes available, at the touch of your finger, information about everything under the sun. The instant, crushing volume of options intimidates us into sampling a little of anything we see, and as a result we go home with nothing. Kant called such an endless array of possibilities the "mathematical sublime": a dizzying infinity of choices that makes us feel helpless rather than powerful.

The man-made universe of the Internet resembles the Tower of Babel in Genesis. Babel's builders tried to reach the heavens.

Instead, they were scattered over the earth, and condemned to speak different, mutually incomprehensible languages. The builders of Babel had collaboration, but not vision; they built for the sake of building. Connecting as many people as possible, extending a network as far as possible, is a Babel-like project. But incoherence—a scattering of people over the earth, despite their digital connections—looms as the likely result, because there is no vision to go along with the drive for extension, for the vista of site after site ad infinitum.

Jorge Luis Borges, in his short story "The Library of Babel," imagined, long before the Internet age, a library containing all the books of the world. Each book in the library of Babel is exactly 410 pages long, and full of letters that are "exact, delicate, intensely black, inimitably symmetric." There are enormous regions of Borges's library where every book is a chaos, strings of letters that make no sense. But the library also contains, somewhere in its endless shelves, everything that has been or could be expressed, in all the printed languages of the world. When its inhabitants discovered the library's infinite capacity, Borges writes, "the universe suddenly expanded to the limitless dimensions of hope." Various seekers set off in quest of the book that would foretell their own future, but they all failed. Borges remarks that in an infinite library "the calculable possibility of a man finding his own book, or some perfidious variation of his book, is close to zero." When this realization hits home, the people in the library begin to despair. They leaf idly through nearby volumes, expecting to find nothing important, only cheap diversions to lighten their gloom. They become hopeless Web surfers *avant la lettre*.

Google would kill for a collection like the one Borges describes, consisting of all texts that have ever existed or might exist. Google is not quite there yet; there are quite a few books that have not yet been scanned, millions of them, in fact. The Internet does not actually contain all recorded utterances in human history: it only seems to. But our feeling that absolutely everything exists somewhere in cyberspace is important, even if it's not strictly accurate. Our minds are boggled by the sheer scale of what's out there. How do we get from such a vast universe of facts and ideas and opinions and rumors to something that could really reach us and answer our need?

Confronted with the near-infinite options that the Internet offers, you stand a slim chance of arriving at what you are looking for: words that would speak to you, renew the strength of imagination within you, or even change your life. Just as it's hard to encounter memorable individuals during rush hour in a big city, it's difficult to locate that one crucial book while you are being buffeted by the Internet's wild and whirling words. Paradoxically, when there are fewer choices courting us, we are more likely to find what we need. It's far more satisfying to wander through a cozy, idiosyncratic small-town library than to scale the towering stacks of a major university's collection. We must prevent ourselves from being dazzled by the huge scope of reading matter that the Internet presents, which is far more vertigo-inducing than even the largest library.

Once we have defended ourselves against the Net's constant distractions, we can settle down—and slow down, ready to get delightfully lost in a book. Slowness, and the patience that goes with it, is the key to good reading. This is the thread that runs through all my remarks about the kind of reading we should be doing, for pleasure and understanding. If you think of reading as just uploading information, then it will *always* seem too slow. Reading for true enjoyment and understanding is an altogether different proposition than reading for information. Discovering how an argument unfolds or how a narrative works requires time and concentration.

In a famous aperçu, Marilyn Monroe said, "I read poetry to save time." She was right: it does, in fact, take only ten or twenty minutes to read a short lyric by Yeats, while a novel by Dickens can consume whole weeks. But in another way Monroe missed the point. Reading even a page-long work of real literature requires serious time, time for pondering. It means removing ourselves from what John Ruskin, that sublimely persuasive enthusiast of reading, called "shallow, blotching, blundering, infectious 'information.'"

The Answer

As I write this book, I've been using the Freedom app. For a few hours—you decide how long—Freedom lets you write on your computer while blocking access to the Internet. The Freedom app is to the Internet what celibacy is to an orgy. Why do I, along with a few other writers I know, find it such a useful tool? Because we need to shield ourselves from the omnipresent distractions of the Net; we need to strategize. It's a war, and the stakes are our creativity, our ability to work.

Reading, like writing, is a creative act, as Emerson resoundingly stated. And you can't create in a hailstorm of flashy possibilities all trying to get your attention. You need control, quiet, seclusion. You must shut out the digital hurricane outside in order to focus. Freedom from excess environmental stimuli makes possible a proper appreciation of the object in front of us, the series of words on a page. When we are released from the pressure to respond every moment to something outside our book, we become capable of reading slowly and carefully.

The Internet quickly molds itself to our likes and dislikes, offering instant options to suit our taste. It gives us the power of the consumer, broad but superficial: We grab and go. Slow reading, by contrast, means that we subject ourselves step by step to an author. Slowness means discovery. A good book dawns on us, and within us, with gradual sweetness and strength. As Ruskin emphasized in his polemic *Sesame and Lilies* (a classic argument for reading to which I will return in my "Rules" chapter), what we get from even a single good book, slowly and carefully read, is an education. Moving at a deliberate pace, we discover what writers really think, and as a result we develop our own minds. Such education is something that the Internet can't provide.

There is a new movement championing slowness: slow food, slow travel, slow friendship (as opposed to the manic friending of thousands of near strangers on Facebook). Slow work, too. One of the trend's advocates, Carl Honoré, notes that IBM has told its employees to check e-mail less often, and that a number of companies have built chill-out spaces for their workers and added mandatory pauses for relaxation to the work day. Slow reading is a part of the new idea of slowness, the answer to the frazzled nerves and sometimes witless frenzy of the linked-up world we live in. Slow reading is not an organized campaign, and it has no party platform. Like the allied term deep reading, slow reading became a cause in the 1990s (though, as I am about to explain, it has a long and distinguished lineage). Slow reading was championed by the critic Sven Birkerts, and John Miedema, Thomas Newkirk, and others have since written books about it.

Reading of this careful sort has a tradition. Sixty years ago, Reuben Brower of Harvard University instituted a course in what he called, for the first time, slow reading; the term properly belongs to him, though he is better known as a founder of "close reading," a very similar idea. Close reading became a widespread technique for teaching literature in the 1950s, in part through an influential textbook (still well worth reading), *Understanding Poetry* by Cleanth Brooks and Robert Penn Warren. As it came to dominate the literature classroom, close reading sometimes became narrow, even sterile; it tended to value a particular kind of work above all others, one that prided itself on carefully controlled ambiguities. John Donne was more welcome than D. H. Lawrence in the close reader's canon. But this development has less to do with techniques of reading than with the values and taste of professors in the postwar era. In Brower's original course, the view of literature was much more generous. Slow, or close, reading meant dedication to a book, whatever that book happened to be.

At Harvard, Brower and his colleagues taught students to weigh the word choices of an author and to see that small points of style make a big difference. He insisted that readers must take the time to get to know a book, to understand its rhythm and atmosphere, to figure out how it works. The first step in learning to read better, Brower emphasized, is to slow down. The term "deep reading," which I've mentioned a few times already, was developed decades later, in 1994, by Sven Birkerts. Birkerts means much the same thing that Brower meant, and that I mean: slowing down so that you can let a book take possession of you, and so that you can get to know it better. Brower was flying against the breezy swarm of verbiage on the radio and television, and in newspapers; Birkerts, against the ever-burgeoning Internet, with its tendency to maim attention spans and reduce us to Google-addled distraction.

Slow reading didn't begin at Harvard, but in ancient Israel, where, from about the year 200 CE on, rabbis and commentators argued about the Bible's characters and stories. Often, the rabbis' debates revolved around small turns of phrase or particular words: no feature was too minute for their often contentious consideration. The rabbis' works, Talmud and Midrash (derived from the Hebrew word *darash,* "to seek") are often fanciful, and profoundly imaginative, in their interpretations of the Bible. But these early readers also attended to details in a careful way that still speaks to us today. For example, the rabbis wondered why, in the six days of creation described at the beginning of Genesis, only the second day is not said to be good. (Their answer: because the second day separates the heavens from the newly formed ocean, and by implication, God from the rest of the world, it is not good.) Another puzzle: Only at the end of the first chapter of Genesis, after the first humans have been created, does God deem the creation "very good" rather than "good"; ancient commentators were determined to explain this detail as well. Is it only after the addition of human beings that the world becomes very good, rather than just good? (What do you think?) The rabbis who wrote midrash, and who debated one another in the pages of the Talmud, invited the participation of their readers. These readers had to decide for themselves what the nuances of the sacred text might mean. Often, in the Talmud, rival interpretations battle each other, and we are expected to join the argument.

Reuben Brower and his colleagues at Harvard were probably unaware of the early Jewish commentaries on the Bible. If they had known them, they would have been put off by the rabbis' frequent departures from the sense of the text. The Jewish sages are often brilliant, precise, and loyal to the words on the page; but when they are not, they fly off into a region where, instead of merely interpreting, they invent a whole new book in place of the Bible that we know. There is an admixture of wild speculation in Jewish, as in later Christian, interpretations of the Bible: a determination to make the text mean what one wills it to mean. Midrash abounds in invented backstories for the characters of the Bible, and devotes itself to filling in the gaps in the laconic biblical text with sheer, provocative fictions. The famous story of Abraham smashing the idols of his father Terah occurs nowhere in Genesis, but most Jewish school kids know it well: it's midrash.

Brower and his fellow teachers of slow reading avoided the impulse to make up stories about the books we read, and in this respect we must follow them rather than the old rabbis. Slow readers don't make up a plot for a short story or a poem, or imagine what might have happened before or after the events that the writer describes for us. Instead, they keep to the script that they've been given, and try to remain as faithful as possible to the words on the page.

In a landmark essay, "Reading in Slow Motion," Brower condemned "the old-time appreciation course in which the teacher mounted the platform and sang a rhapsody which he alone was capable of understanding and which the student memorized, with the usual inaccuracies, for the coming examination." Instead, he wanted students to figure out what it was like to read a particular story, poem, or novel. They had to take an active role, to see how the text worked. "Let's see what we can do with it" was his classroom's battle cry. The teacher worked alongside the student; they were partners—not in crime, but in the pleasures of reading and understanding. Brower wrote that "literature of the first order calls for lively reading; we must almost act it out as if we were taking parts in a play." We must make an effort to inhabit the voices that speak through a book, to live, for a few hours, in its world.

Brower claimed that literature is special "in its mysterious wholeness, in the number of elements embraced and in the variety and closeness of their relationship." He was right. Literature repays our attention because it is finely worked, because we can take it inside ourselves, sustain ourselves on the aptness and strength of its words. A worthy piece of literature is never the illustration of an ideology or a moral idea or a historical event. Instead, it is a living thing, complex and ambivalent like a human being. We have to live with a book, at least for a while, in order to see it truly. That's why Brower's discipline of reading in slow motion is necessary. Rather than gulping down our books, we must digest them with deliberation.

The meticulous yet passionate discipline that Brower championed lives on in some academic courses. But all too often colleges and universities neglect reading, instead telling students to get the gist of a book: don't worry about the details—about how something is written—just grasp the main points and be prepared to discuss them on an exam. The ascendency of cultural studies is part of the problem. Madonna has now yielded to Lady Gaga as a key subject of academic attention, and the devotion to literary nuance continues to suffer. English departments eagerly submit to current trends, not always to the benefit of students. The desire to read books subtly and with love, to get lost in the world an author has created, has increasingly given way to commentary on social fashions and media images, whether of the Victorian age or the present day. Instead of literature, the history of social life has become the true subject in some English departments.

Like the Internet, the academy sometimes stands in the way of deep (slow, close) reading. If you want to experience the responses of a true reader in print, you're often better off reading an essay in the *New Yorker,* the *New Republic,* or the *New York Review of Books* (or similar magazines) than an article in an academic journal. Some academic articles are well written; but when they are not, their theories about writers become hard to trust. You should pay attention only to essays and reviews that try to give you the feeling of what it's like to read a particular author, and while they do so make an argument for that author's value. Sweeping, abstract ideas about modernity, capitalism, or evolution rarely result in useful insights about books.

Lindsay Waters, in "Time for Reading," a provocative article he wrote for the *Chronicle of Higher Education* in 2007, espoused slow reading as an antidote to professors who mine books for statements about history and society, and use literature as a mere source of information. "The problem with reducing books to themes and morals is that it slights the experience of reading," Waters wrote: we need to make time and space for truly experiencing, and enjoying, what we read.

Reading for enjoyment rather than for a distilled lesson takes time—and willingness to reread. Waters pointed out that, often, we only really get to know a book when we reread it because "we learn that the first time we read too fast." Nietzsche, Waters added, defined the job of the philologist as slow reading: "to go aside, to take time, to become still, to become slow." Nothing could be more antithetical to our culture of rapid results and hasty decisions.

Reading out loud and memorizing, like rereading, are effective ways of making yourself slow down and absorb as fully as possible the rhythms and meaning of what you read. You can seek out an anthology like *Committed to Memory,* edited by John Hollander, or *Essential Pleasures,* edited by Robert Pinsky, or just pause as you read to speak a favorite passage. If it's a passage of dialogue, give in to your theatrical inclinations when you read a few lines aloud.

The traditional practice of a family reading a book together out loud has faded, but it need not: it requires time and effort, but it's an exciting and absorbing pastime, one that brings everyone together over a shared text. Reading together occurs in other circumstances too. Religious Jews study the Talmud with a partner or a group, and they always read a passage aloud before discussing it with respect for every detail, every nuance. (It can take days, even weeks, to make your way through a few pages of Talmud.) When you read with a lover, you are subject to the age-old temptation of Paolo and Francesca in Dante's *Inferno:* after immersing themselves in a tale of chivalric love, Dante pithily tells us, "that day they read no more."

Memorizing may seem like a daunting task, but the key is to approach it step by step. In 2009, Jim Holt described in a *New*

York Times editorial how he had memorized a generous hand-ful of great poems: every day he would add a line or two to what he already knew, hooking each new segment on to the previous, already memorized one. Before he knew it, he had a whole poem by heart. He found himself reciting Keats or Shakespeare in idle moments. While walking down the street or waiting on line, he grew to rely on the poet's words in his "deep heart's core" (as Yeats writes in "The Lake Isle of Innisfree").

Holt concluded his editorial by remarking that he had dis-pelled three myths about memorizing poems:

> *Myth No. 1: Poetry is painful to memorize.* It is not at all painful.
>   Just do a line or two a day.
> *Myth No. 2: There isn't enough room in your memory to store a lot*
>   *of poetry.* Bad analogy. Memory is a muscle, not a quart jar.
> *Myth No. 3: Everyone needs an iPod.* You do not need an iPod.
>   Memorize poetry instead.

As children, we effortlessly memorized nursery rhymes, songs, and beloved stories, and later the Pledge of Allegiance and the Gettysburg Address (at least in my day) . . . maybe even a Shake-speare soliloquy or two. Most American adults have dozens, even hundreds, of popular songs by heart. Why not poems?

We often think of reading as a solitary act. But talking about books, like talking about movies, enhances our experience be-yond measure. Other readers can help: you're not alone. We can talk to the other members of a book group, classmates, friends—even remote online acquaintances, now made reachable by new technology (which has benefited us in this, at least).

In our lifelong conversation about books, we are bound to encounter disagreement. Tastes differ. Theodore Roosevelt called Henry James "a little emasculated mass of inanity," while oth-ers consider him our greatest American novelist. (Roosevelt, incidentally, was a heroic reader of novels, able to concentrate on a book even in the toughest circumstances. During a harsh winter in the Dakota territory, he read all of *Anna Karenina* while walking forty miles through the snow; he was leading a pair of thieves whom he had caught after they stole his rowboat. Carrying his Winchester rifle, he kept one eye on the crooks the whole time, and one eye on the page. Few of us could resist Continuous Partial Attention in such a setting; but Roosevelt read Tolstoy's novel with undaunted devotion.)

Not all books are for all readers. You won't like everything, and you shouldn't try—not even if the book in question is certifiably "great." I seem to have an allergy to Faulkner (and I realize I may have just lost some of my readers by saying that), but I recognize that almost everyone regards him as an author of masterpieces. For whatever reason, I just can't seem to fall in love with his work as so many others have. But I realize this is my own limitation, since so many people whose literary judgment I respect love his novels. I do love some Faulkner, like the beautiful, sparse *Wild Palms,* which intertwines two striking novella-length narratives. But Faulkner will never be one of my favorites.

There have been a memorable series of "battles of the books" over the centuries (Jonathan Swift's extraordinary eighteenth-century satire *The Battle of the Books* will give you a taste of such combat). Arguments over how to judge the worth of books are perpetual and unavoidable; they are also deeply useful. Such arguments can be invigorating and helpful no matter what side we're on. They can save us from a dull insistence on our personal taste. We ought to stretch that taste, to see where it might lead. Be hard on yourself; think about why you liked or disliked something in a book, and how someone else might respond to your judgment.

Try to see the whole of a literary work, and appreciate the author's aims; when you do so, you will be able to avoid the instinctive, unbaked opinion. "I *hated* that character!" might be countered, as you ponder the matter further, by "But didn't you think she was a great contrast with the hero—really made me think about how they balanced each other."

Readers should understand an author's values. Good books are ways of seeing the world; if we are bothered by what we think is an author's bias or prejudice, odds are we have not delved deep enough into that author's project. First, the reader needs to achieve sympathy with a book's idea of itself. If she ends up rejecting the book, that decision should come as a discovery rather than a reflex. Much depends on our evaluation of an author's personality, from the very first page on. Even when we instinctively dislike a book, we must understand why. An author's values are implied by her personality; our own values might differ. But we can still learn something about ourselves through our encounter with any book—and when we discuss the book with others, we learn something about them, too.

Harold Bloom writes that reading augments the self, and (echoing the Jewish sage Hillel) "until you become yourself, what benefit can you be to others?" Bloom points to the truest reward of reading: becoming ourselves. We can reach this goal by facing honestly our own reactions to books, and trying to know why we react as we do. In other words, we must do some deep, slow reading.

In order to deep or slow read a book (whether a print book or an e-book), the reader must shut down the Internet browser, avoid Twitter and text messages, turn off the television: cut through the increasingly loud and distracting buzz of electronic gadgets. Reading should be a refuge, an island in the sea of technology that engulfs us all day long. Technology, a central part of our lives, cannot simply be wished away: next day, at work, the computer screen beckons. But for the hours when we are reading, we must push away the devices that force us to stay "in touch." Long before the digital age, Henry David Thoreau noted, "We are in great haste to construct a magnetic telegraph from Maine to Texas, but Maine and Texas, it may be, have nothing important to communicate." We must look deeper than the constant updates that the Web gives us, so that we can achieve a real connection to history and to the world in which we live. The world of the past survives largely in books, and we get to know other people and other cultures best by reading about them. (Few of us, even if we possessed time or money enough, would be inclined to travel to every country and province in the world, given all of life's other demands.)

When we read, we are alone. Reading calls us to our sole self, and away from the world of distractions; but it also furnishes us with far-reaching connections to other people. The enforced leisure of a desert island is not a bad image to have in your head as you prepare to read. No earthly storms can reach you here; you are safe. The desert island image reinforces the idea that reading is a fundamentally solitary experience. Reading has also always had a social dimension, however, as it does in our early lives: our first acts of reading are performed with parents and teachers standing by and guiding us. These mentors left their stamp on how we approach a text; they gave us the tools we use to get closer to the words on the page. And there is, of course, another social connection in reading: we always converse, by implication, with the book's author.

The teachers and parents who stood by our elbow and taught us how to read disclosed for us not just a universe of wonder, but also a system of rules. Rules may seem to get in the way of an activity, like reading, that is done for the love of it. But the notion that rules are mere shackles for the reader is far from the truth. Reading well requires a skill born of technique, just as playing music or painting does, and the technical is always rule-bound. Technique, and the rules that go with it, will free you, not imprison you. The sociologist Richard Sennett argues that "there is nothing mindlessly mechanical about technique": good technique is also good thinking.

Sennett champions what he calls "repetitive, instructive, hands-on learning." In this respect he swims against the current. He notes that "modern education fears repetitive learning as mind-numbing. Afraid of boring children, avid to present ever-different stimulation, the enlightened teacher may avoid routine—but thus deprives children of the experience of studying their own ingrained practice and modulating it from within." The cult of spontaneity, of free, offhanded improvisation, flees from boredom. But steady repetition is in fact how we master a process, and how we discover what is truly interesting, the new facets that appear when we go over the same ground many times. Sennett cites the Isaac Stern rule: the virtuoso violinist declared that (as Sennett reports) "the better your technique, the longer you can rehearse without becoming bored." The musician, playing a sequence of notes again and again, puzzles over the peculiar character of a moment in the piece she is playing. Her practice leads to a work of exploration. Similarly, someone making a drawing will correct his work: retracing lines, testing possibilities. Writers change nearly every sentence they produce, sometimes many times over, in the course of their painstaking work. The tactile and palpable sense of a material object being worked on—a sentence, a canvas, a piece of wood or metal, a musical instrument—this is crucial to the craftsmanship of the artist, the writer, the musician. All technique is expressive.

It may seem strange to think of our reading experience in terms of technique. But reading requires technique just as writing does; you read in a style and with a perspective that is all your own, yet informed by generations of readers before you. Seen in this way, technique has moral implications, as Ruskin asserted; it asks for an honest assessment of faults and a wish to do better. Technical practice requires revising one's work, and each revision tells you something. Going over the same ground (for example, returning to an especially fascinating passage of a book) makes something happen: it provides a deeper insight into what the passage means. In this way, the repetitive rhythm of practice looks ahead and offers discovery.

We are used to thinking that expression and rule-bound practice are opposed, but practice and rules are in fact needed so that we can express ourselves in a satisfying way. You can't talk or write without a firm sense of grammar and idiom. Similarly, you can't read without knowledge of the tools required for unlocking the depths of a text, for discovering how words mean on the page.

Sennett argues that "the belief in and search for correctness," for truth in practice, "breeds expression." A curiosity about the object we are working on—in our case, the book we are reading—develops into an effort to get to its truth, to see what it really is. We gradually prune away errors as we figure out which interpretations work and which don't. We learn to deal with ambiguities, not by wishing them away or prematurely solving them, but by pursuing them in order to get a clearer sense of the work.

Every book is unique; to enjoy it, you must savor its special character. Rules cannot be applied in an automatic, thoughtless way; doing so will ruin the book's specialness. Painting by numbers doesn't work: you can't successfully cram a literary creation into a preconceived set of categories. We all remember classes in which the teacher approached literature as an object for taxonomy. In such a class we might be told, for example, that the play we have just read is an example of theater of the absurd, meaning that it meets the following three criteria: it depicts a meaningless universe, it shows that action is futile, and it recommends suicide. The sterile perfection of such easy classifications is profoundly unconvincing. You learn nothing about a work by being able to fit it into a precut pattern, just as you learn nothing by "writing" a paper cobbled together from Wikipedia entries. If reading (or writing) doesn't stimulate you, then you're not doing it energetically or originally enough; you're relying on ready-made categories and definitions instead of figuring things out on your own. When you work in this lazy and inaccurate fashion, you're missing out on the fun. Each of us can do good work; we just need to get organized. Not everyone can become a professional book reviewer or critic, but we can all learn to read well. Reading slowly and carefully requires no special talent; instead, it demands that you stay engaged with, and find yourself taken up by, a practice.

The book you're reading, if it's a good one, is capable of exerting an influence on you, and so you need to decide what you think about it. The classics, especially, resemble an earlier generation, one that wields substantial authority over your world, though you may not always be aware of it. We often use the adjectives Machiavellian or Kafkaesque: Machiavelli and Kafka were there before you, shaping your sense of things. As much as any figures in scripture, they can be counted among your spiritual parents, even though their lessons are frequently dark ones. Parents provoke unease and ambivalence; they don't always comfort. Who are they to you, and what are you to them? There's a difference between aping (or rejecting) the mannerisms of your parents and actually growing up: figuring out how you're related to them and what you think about that relation. Like growing up, reading requires thought. It means evaluating yourself, too, along with the book you're reading.

A new book is a whole new world. You must get to know it gradually: be open to it; see what it feels like to live there for a while. When you read, try to enter the world that the author has created, and to stay in that world for a few hours or days. A new book is a kind of foreign country, with its own distinctive customs and traditions. You, the reader, are first a tourist, then a potential resident; you will have a much better, more rewarding time if you decide to be an involved and willing traveler. Getting all you can from your voyage to this new land means surrendering to the sights and sounds of the place, remaining alert to all its surprises. Later on, you can evaluate what you have seen. If you love what you read, you may even decide to live there for a while: to return again and again to Austen, or Milton, or Chekhov.

When you take a trip to another country, you need a map, a guidebook, and (ideally) some knowledge of the native language. These are the tools that make your journey worthwhile. Although we may think that we travel spontaneously, purely for pleasure, in fact we seek out the rules that govern our destination, the facts of weather and culture and landscape. Mexico is not Norway, and we had best know that in advance.

Traveling may seem casual, but it requires preparation. The same is true of reading. We usually do not realize that reading is a practice or craft, that it requires certain tools. *Slow Reading in a Hurried Age* offers strategies for becoming more active as a reader: learning how to focus and what to focus on, how to develop the patience and discernment necessary to truly experience a book. The skills required are very different from the reading comprehension, summarizing, and paraphrasing taught in secondary school. Background information found on Wikipedia or Google will not, by itself, enable a reader to genuinely understand and enjoy a book. Finding information is often a necessary preliminary for reading, but it differs from reading itself. And when we have finished reading, we take away not a set of facts or a sense of the book's "message," but the memory of an experienced place, a country we have traveled to. The ardent, rewarding commitment to a book we have learned to love: this is the real point. Not every book will become close to your heart, of course. But I guarantee that, if you read slowly, carefully, and with pleasure, you will find plenty of books to love.

The traditional book, whether in electronic or bound paper form, remains the best format for reading. I prefer the printed book, since I love the shape and feel of it, and the sense that, as I turn pages, I am being touched by the presence of the words, the testimony of an author who has made the thing I hold in my hands. Others say they get the same feeling from a Kindle, an iPad, or a Nook. (You can use this new technology to your advantage, by scribbling notes in e-book margins and by keeping a reader's diary in electronic form.)

To many readers, the e-book has been an exciting advance: now you can take a trip without lugging a bag of books with you. Yet e-books have a disadvantage: they promote forward motion rather than slow, considered reading. It's harder to flip back and forth in an e-book than it is in an old-fashioned printed volume. A print book is designed to aid slow reading, by making it easy for you to look back at what you've already read. By contrast, when you read an e-book, the earlier pages seem to vanish. It's not surprising, then, that even those experienced readers who are most enthusiastic about e-books often still retain a love for print. To their surprise, publishers have discovered that the same people who buy e-books also buy print books—but that they finish the print books far more often than they finish the e-books. Often, an e-book is an impulse buy: it doesn't take up space in a cluttered apartment, it's there on your iPad or Kindle if you ever want it, but it remains pretty much invisible. A print book reminds you that it's there, ready for your attention; it has the presence than an e-book lacks.

Whether in electronic or paper form, a book still differs enormously from a Web site. The amorphous Internet prevents deep reading; books promote it. A book imposes a fixed structure on readers. It pushes back as the web cannot. A reader becomes more capable and confident only by grappling with the demanding structure of a full-length book.

The intimacy with a book and its author does not come without effort. In setting out a program for readers to increase their interpretive strength, and, as a result, their enjoyment, I offer a set of rules for reading. These rules are my own, based upon years of reading and teaching works of literature. My emphasis is on reading not just the classics but any good book, that is, any book that is worth your while. Although most of my examples come from well-known authors (spanning, from Homer to Alice Munro, a good 2,700 years) the lessons are applicable to any worthy novel, short story, poem, or piece of non-fiction. Our lives are not endless, and so we want to read what will repay our time and energy. It makes sense to investigate the classics, the books where so many have found unmatched treasures.

Whatever you decide to read, remember to challenge yourself. To return to my foreign travel analogy: seek out literary places that are strange and instructive, rather than those too close to home. You'll have a much better time. Instead of picking up another thriller, get a foothold in a new genre. "The benefit of books promiscuously read," as John Milton put it in *Areopagitica,* is that we may encounter works that challenge us and overturn our preconceptions like nothing we've known before. You can only have such encounters if you explore widely—and if you pay some attention to the recommendations of readers who have journeyed before you, who have found the classics that still astonish and provoke, often after hundreds, even thousands, of years. One friend, a well-known writer, tells me that he only reads the works of authors who were born before he was. I don't go that far, but I admit that I prefer the older authors, because they are more distant and therefore have more to tell me. Their strangeness wakes me up: they remind me that my world is not the only one, that I have much to learn about other realms.

Reread as often as you can. Often I have returned, sometimes after many years, to books I loved earlier. In a few cases I was disappointed; in many others, I discovered new dimensions in the book, and realized why I had felt such a deep connection to it. I knew for the first time something about myself, as well as the book. In *On Rereading,* Patricia Spacks comments, "Rereading, we relate also to one or more version of our past selves." The novelist Robertson Davies remarks that "A truly great book should be read in youth, again in maturity and once more in old age, as a fine building should be seen by morning light, at noon and by moonlight." Davies's words are excellent advice, but remember that the contours of the building may shift radically over time.

"Curiously enough, one cannot read a book: one can only reread it," wrote Vladimir Nabokov. "A good reader, a major reader, an active and creative reader is a rereader." Nabokov added, "When we read a book for the first time the very process of laboriously moving our eyes from left to right, line after line, page after page, this complicated physical work upon the book, the very process of learning in terms of space and time what the book is about, this stands between us and artistic appreciation." Upon rereading, we see a book as a whole for the first time: our preliminary work done, we are able to take it in all at once.

When I tell you to reread your favorite books, I am recommending that you do what groups of readers in religious communities have done for many centuries. Canonical religious texts have become familiar through constant rereading, and, as a result, they bind communities together. But any book, not just the Bible or Koran or other sacred volume, can become an individual scripture and offer sustenance: a source of trust to the individual who feels impelled to reread it. If you want it to, any book can become part of your personal canon. Such a book nourishes the reader's selfhood, even if he or she rereads only a few pages of it. (Willard Spiegelman suggests that the definition of a personal canonical text is something you can pick up anywhere and read for as long as you like.) I urge readers to develop a "short shelf" of favorite books, ones to be opened often and reread (at least in part).

Rereading—not necessarily the entire book, but parts of it—is an essential way to avoid judging the author too quickly, and not thinking that one understands a book too soon. If the reader wants to grasp the richness of a book, she must measure her response: she must see how her first impression differs from her second, and try to figure out why. Comparing earlier and later responses to a book in order to understand it better is a way of developing your friendship with the book: we usually need to see someone more than once before becoming friends. After finishing study of a tractate of the Talmud, each reader recites the pledge, "We will return to you," followed by the name of the tractate, and then, "You will return to us." (This formula echoes the words addressed to God at the end of the Torah service: God and Israel will return to each other.) The essential promise is that a book we have cared about will be a continued presence in our lives. The book lives not just for us, the readers who value it, but with us.

Elizabeth Bowen, a remarkable novelist and short story writer, remembers "the over-lapping and haunting of life by fiction," which happens to "everyone . . . who reads deeply, ravenously, unthinkingly, sensuously, as a child." In her memorable essay on reading, Bowen describes the spell that reading casts on the life of the bookish child, a spell that makes life infinitely more alluring, and more obscure:

> Books introduced me to, and magnified, desire and danger. They represented life, with a conclusiveness I had no reason to challenge, as an affair of mysteries and attractions, in which each object or place or face was in itself a volume of promises and deceptions, and in which nothing was impossible. Books made me see everything that I saw either as a symbol or as having its place in a mythology—in fact, reading gave bias to my observations of everything in the between-times when I was not reading.

Reading, Bowen adds, gave her a feeling for characters, and especially "the incalculable ones": "It appeared that nobody who mattered was capable of being explained. Thus was inculcated a feeling for the dark horse."

At the end of her essay, Bowen invokes the way a book makes its potent impression, mixing itself with life:

> I may see, for instance, a road running uphill, a skyline, a figure coming slowly over the hill—the approach of the figure is momentous, accompanied by fear or rapture or fear of rapture or a rapture of fear. But who and how is this? Am I sure this is not a figure out of a book?

The world of a book, read intensely enough, becomes our world too; so Bowen insists. The more time we spend in it the more it takes us over, and not just in childhood.

Why do we read? We want to break away from our lives, to lose, and find, ourselves in a foreign and intriguing realm. Enchanted by a good book, we abandon all sense of time. With our book in hand, we find that whole days can be happily swallowed up, in what Joseph Epstein describes as "that lovely, antisocial, splendidly selfish habit known as reading." Bowen, though, reminds us that we read not just to escape, but to remake our lives, to feel our landscape marvelously transformed. The more slowly and carefully we read, and the more we combine the child's absorption with the knowing skills of the adult, the more marvels we encounter.

Getting Started

First, some basic advice. Shut off the laptop, the TV, and even, if possible, the phone. (Or, at least, ignore the phone when it rings.) Find a comfortable chair and some good reading light. Don't read too late at night when you're dead tired and can't focus. Stolen bits of time are sweetest: a snow day, an airplane trip. (Northrop Frye, the great Canadian literary critic, always read Walter Scott on planes; he felt that a stagecoach style suitably counteracted the fast jets of modern life.)

When to read? The French novelist Marguerite Duras only read at night, never during daylight hours. Wallace Stevens said that the early morning was best for poetry, as it was for prayer. The poet Allen Grossman imagines his boyhood reading as always taking place at eleven o'clock in the morning. Reading well gives us, in Harold Bloom's phrase, a perpetual earliness; it may be the middle of the night, but if our reading is as strong and full of life as it should be, it will seem like dawn.

Every reader has a best place to read. Whatever else it is, the place will be your own, distinctive. Some read on park benches; others prefer coffee shops or libraries; some, like the late novelist Stanley Elkin, are comfortable reading nowhere but in bed. The prone position has its advantages; in fact, it's my own favorite reading posture. You can stretch out as you can't at the office: a concrete symbol of how reading is the necessary antidote to the dull realm of getting and spending. Elkin mentions his vague but persistent sense that the sealed, secure world of the reader suggests preparation for death; perhaps this explains, he says, his inclination to read lying down: "It has something to do with being alone, shutting the world out, doing books like beads, a mantra, the flu," he writes. But we also dream and make love lying down, for the most part, and the strong element of fantasy and freedom in these activities marks their affinity with reading. At any rate, few read standing up. Walking is a different matter. I remember as a child walking home while reading, after checking out some particularly thrilling new book from the library, something I just couldn't wait to get to; and every so often I see on the street a boy or girl doing the same thing, accompanied by a parent who has been enlisted to watch out for red lights.

Wherever and however you read, remember to enjoy yourself. Enjoyment requires focus. If reading feels like drudgery, this means you are too far away from your book: too distracted, and therefore reluctant to commit yourself to its pages. Remember that it's just you and the book; while you are reading, nothing else matters. The page is an illuminated place, literally and figuratively. You need to build a fence around it, so that you can enter into its light. When you have done this, you are ready for the following rules for reading.

The Rules

My rules are not prohibitions, but guidelines. They are intended not to curb your imagination, but to help it take wing, so that you can discover yourself as you discover the book you read. When you step inside the light that words cast, you will see yourself, too, in new ways.

In these rules, I have tried to strike a balance between intelligent cheerleading for some of my favorite authors and nuts-and-bolts advice about how to read them. I raise colorful banners for books that I love, but I also emphasize method. My approach is informed by the general principles of slow reading; but the rules are my own. Most of them are rather brief, but two central rules, Three ("Identify the Voice") and Six ("Identify Signposts"), are divided into subsections, and give additional examples of the reading practices I recommend.

In the course of my rules, I discuss a wide range of authors who represent a spectrum of tones and approaches. Most of the writers I consider are novelists, poets, essayists, or playwrights, but I have included a few historians and social scientists as well. All of them will repay your careful attention.

Rule One: Be Patient

Cultivating patience is the most important of the rules, the one from which all the others follow. Let Kafka be your guide.

In his *Zürau Reflections,* Kafka writes,

> There are two cardinal human sins from which all others derive:
> impatience and carelessness. Impatience got people driven out
> of Paradise; carelessness keeps them from getting back there. Or
> perhaps there is only one cardinal sin: impatience. Impatience
> got people driven out, and impatience keeps them from getting
> back there.

Kafka's paragraph shrewdly dramatizes its own theme. He
rather hastily asserts that there are two cardinal vices, and then
takes it back. In other words, he has the patience to correct himself. Kafka even hints, tantalizingly, that with enough patience
we might have found our way back to Eden. No doubt this is a
lost hope like the many other lost hopes in Kafka; when his
heroes cling to patience, as they often do, one knows that they
are practicing not the art of salvation, but rather an exalted species of frustration.

Unlike Kafka's doomed characters, we readers can save ourselves by exercising patience. What I mean by this requires some
explanation.

Patience means a lot of things. We must be patient not to be
overwhelmed by a book's difficulties. We must be patient to let
ourselves be perplexed; to figure out, by trial and error, how to
ask the right questions of a book. We must be patient to put in
the time and effort needed to read well.

Every worthwhile project begins in perplexity, and reading
is no exception. Every reader has a humble beginning: struggling with the alphabet in childhood. But eventually the child's
struggle becomes a joyous possession: the ability to recognize
written words, and to play with them for the stakes of meaning.
Along the way, the child learns an important lesson—refusing
to get bogged down in a book's hard places. Knowing what to

trouble over and what to let go of is a lesson we keep teaching ourselves as grown-up readers too; we must acquire the right kind of patience.

Reading patiently also means bringing out in oneself a happy, and somewhat obsessive, desire for details. ("In reading, one should notice and fondle details," remarked Vladimir Nabokov.) The strength of our reading increases enormously if we anchor our sense of a book's characters and its argument in small, significant moments. These moments are islands in the ongoing stream of prose or poetry: they anchor our perception.

We must not rush to meaning, or demand that an author deliver the point in an easy, palatable way. If we feel frustrated with an author's elusive style, with the refusal to simply hand over a clear message, we have to remember that struggling with a book's meanings is the whole point of reading, if reading is going to be worthwhile.

Your patient struggle with a book should be fun, not tedious. Force-reading is as bad as force-feeding; if you're simply cramming down a book because you think it will be good for you, find something you'll like better instead. There's a difference between learning to stick with a book, even if you don't immediately love it—this is a very valuable lesson, and leads to some of the best reading experiences—and making yourself read something that, after repeated attempts, you just find utterly antipathetic. (But be sure you understand the how and why of the antipathy. Don't be mastered by your dislike; make something useful out of it.)

Patience is needed to develop our reading skills, which are also, more broadly, our cognitive and imaginative powers. Part of patience is working steadily at the techniques we need to read well. We must exercise our mind's muscles in order to reap the benefits of a book, just as we need to stay in shape in order to enjoy playing a sport. Keep working at your reading responses, and you'll be surprised at how much you're getting out of books.

Many times, I've found that a fumbling first, second, or even third encounter with an author led later on to a deep and abiding love. Patiently, we return to the book we laid aside. Sometimes our initial aversion to a book is just the rocky beginning of a beautiful friendship. And sometimes we need a teacher, or an experienced lover of an author, to show us the way. Other times, we just dive in, and fall for what we don't fully understand. I remember reading Joyce's *Ulysses* in high school, at my own instigation. I was on my own with this encyclopedic, bristling, beautiful planet of a novel: my parents, who never went to college, weren't readers, though they had a deeply-felt respect for learning. They certainly wouldn't have known who Joyce was, or Baudelaire or Nabokov or any of the other writers I was so eagerly imbibing. I'm not sure what I thought I was doing by reading *Ulysses,* nor how much of the book I "got." But I am certain that I adored every page of it, even the pages that mystified me. I had surrendered to Joyce's magic; without even knowing it, I was spurring within myself a patience with his wild cosmos of words. (It helped, too, that I had discovered in the public library Anthony Burgess's lively *ReJoyce,* still an excellent guide to Joyce for the common reader.)

Never rush through a book just so you can have a feeling of achievement at the end—just so you can say, "I'm finished." Patient, slow readers don't work that way. They brood over the twists and turns of a passage, and squeeze as much significance as they can out of them, even if they have to wait for a second reading to do so. In the course of these rules, I give you a number of examples to show you how much can be gleaned from just a few lines of a book. The more you understand an author's intriguing use of language and the way he or she brings characters to life, the more you'll profit from your reading. Instead of just reading for the plot, you'll be mulling over the shades of meaning that make the experience of any good author valuable. The more you can see when you look at a page, the better time you'll have.

There are a few key questions you should ask yourself during your first reading of a passage: Who is speaking? How does each speaker reveal himself, or herself? And finally, how does the passage work—what images and turns of phrase are most striking, and why? Think about how the characters show themselves, how they give evidence of who they are. What can we tell about them from their words? Stay active in your reading, and keep a mental file of topics that you can return to as you explore the book further.

I don't want to imply that you have to instantly become a grand master at slow reading in order to get more out of books. But I do want to demonstrate how far you can go, what treasures you can unearth, once you've started to read deeply. Go step by step, and don't try to grasp everything at once. To approach a complicated, rich text with confidence, you must proceed patiently. This is my first piece of advice, one that I will return to frequently as I explain the rest of my rules for reading.

You won't notice all aspects of a book on a first reading. Part of being patient is being willing to miss something the first time around, to save some delights for a second, more detailed journey through the text. Any difficult book needs to be reread, and this advice goes double for poetry and philosophy. The patient ability to return to a book will allow you to find what are you are seeking in it, and so will make reading worthwhile.

Listen to Henry David Thoreau in *Walden* on the reader's experience of searching, receptively and patiently, for an author's meaning:

> There are probably words addressed to our condition exactly,
> which, if we could really hear and understand, would be more
> salutary than the morning or the spring to our lives, and possi-
> bly put a new aspect on the face of things for us. How many a
> man has dated a new era in his life from the reading of a book.
> The book exists for us perchance which will explain our mira-
> cles and reveal new ones.

Thoreau's care is palpable as he waits for the discovery of the
miracle that reading gives us, a miracle that seems more precarious as goes on: notice the way he inches backward from "probably" to "possibly" to, finally, "perchance." He has patience
(*Walden* is a supremely patient book), but he has passion, too.
We cherish the details of Thoreau's prose, which is both excited
and exact, when he tells us that meaning can dawn on us like
the morning, awaken us like the spring.

The first crucial piece of advice, then, the one that prepares
the way for all the other rules I will give you, is to be patient.
Patience means being open to the new presence in front of you,
the book you have chosen to read. We may find we disagree
with a book's argument in the end, but first we need to enter its
world, and learn what it means to live in the distinctive cosmos
that the author has made for us. By yielding to an author's vision for hundreds of pages, and engaging in informed debate
with that vision, we become more capable, more discerning,
and more interesting people. We gain in intellectual skills by
learning to talk back to books in a productive way. The universe
of books is full of radically different voices, each one demanding that we listen and answer. Our sense of life broadens immensely when we start paying attention to them.

John Ruskin, whose thoughts on reading I recur to often in
this book, wrote, "There is a society continually open to us of
people who will talk to us as long as we like, whatever our rank

or occupation—talk to us in the best words they can choose, and of the things nearest their hearts." They "can be kept waiting round us all day long," ready for us to open the books through which they speak to us. When they begin to speak, we must hear them out—patiently.

Knowing how to read is, just as Ruskin suggests, rather like knowing how to talk to people. You're a good conversationalist when you can discover, in the course of conversation, a little bit of both yourself and the person you're talking to. You want to learn something about that person and, at the same time, give him or her a glimpse of you. Similarly, reading is a two-way process, a relationship between you and a book. You must expose some of yourself in order to get an interesting response. You have to give something to books in order to receive their rewards.

Sometimes others join in the conversation between reader and author: a teacher, a friend, the other members of a book group. Whether you read alone or with others, your goal must be to make your conversation with the book's author as intimate and challenging as possible. You must be alive to a book's provocations, and must learn to accept them, rather than turning away. You can fight with your book, but don't make it your enemy. Even if you disagree with an author's arguments, or find yourself alienated by a book's style, give yourself to the experience.

The novelist Robert Louis Stevenson, best known for his hair-raising *Dr. Jekyll and Mr. Hyde,* prized disreputable books. He wrote,

> It is men who hold another truth, or, as it seems to us, perhaps, a dangerous lie, who can extend our restricted field of knowledge, and rouse our drowsy consciences. Something that seems quite new, or that seems insolently false or very dangerous, is the test of a reader. If he tries to see what it means, what truth excuses it, he has the gift, and let him read. If he is merely hurt,

or offended, or exclaims upon his author's folly, he had better
take to the daily papers; he will never be a reader.

Once, when I was teaching Nietzsche to a freshman class, a
student told me that if she continued to read Nietzsche's *Toward the Genealogy of Morals* she would have to question everything she had ever believed. She said this with trepidation, but
with a thrill, too. Even if you're no longer in college, you
should cultivate the same aliveness when you read books like
Nietzsche's, which call on you to rethink your life and the
whole world you live in.

To really enjoy a conversation, you must be patient: ready to
listen, to realize that you have something to learn from your
conversational partner (even if, like Nietzsche, he is saying
something that might turn your world upside down). When
you let your sense of an author develop, slowly and patiently,
you will be tempted to turn to that author repeatedly. There
are certain people you prefer to talk to: your close friends. In
the same way, the more you devote yourself to reading, the more
you will be inclined to return to the same books. Those books
are like your close friends. They don't just make you feel better;
like true friends, they are willing to argue with you and make
you reimagine who you are.

There's a difference, though, between a book and a friend.
Years ago, I taught a course with an older colleague, someone
from whom I learned an enormous amount about teaching, and
about reading. We were beginning to study Plato's *Republic,* all
six hundred dense pages of it. My colleague began his lecture
with a single sentence: "Plato is smarter than you." We are not
necessarily convinced that our friends are much smarter than
we are; if we were so convinced, we might be too intimidated to
talk to them. But books, if they are truly worthwhile, are
smarter. We must be willing to learn from their authors, who

know much more than we do. We must patiently try to understand an author's argument before we state our own opinion, before we start talking back. In some cases, like that of Plato, it may seem nearly impossible to grasp the author's real point. Scholars still argue about whether Plato was an authoritarian or a free thinker, an idealist or a practical, worldly philosopher. The ambiguity of Plato's work, the difficulty of settling on what he means, is part of that work's riches. The more many-faceted a book is, the more inviting it becomes to the reader. If it is hard to decide what the author really means, this indicates that the book is offering you an opportunity to join in conversation with it. You are being invited to respond, to contend with the author in an exhilarating way. First, though, you must listen.

Books take up the reader who takes them up. They address the person "holding me now in hand" (so Whitman describes the reader who, joined with him, inquires into a new mystery, his poem). Books are trying to tell you something. The better the book, the more urgent its message, and the more patiently you are called on to listen.

My primary aim is to teach you how to listen to books. After you learn to listen, you may want to argue back, to raise the dialogue you have with a book to a new and more contentious level. But first, you must acquire the tools you need so that you can start to read well—to hold up your end of the conversation. Listening with patience is the first step.

Rule Two: Ask the Right Questions

When you read a book, think of yourself as a detective looking for clues. Any good detective needs to know what's relevant and what's not, which leads should be followed up and which ones go nowhere. Detectives are masters at figuring out which questions will move an investigation forward and which ones won't.

Asking questions is how you get from perplexity to engagement. As a longtime teacher, I've sometimes had the sense—not often, but it's happened—that a class can't figure out a good question to ask about a text. That's when the class needs more guidance from me: I have to give them an example of the kind of question that could aid them in their grappling with the book.

Useful questions connect elements of a book together: What does the beginning have to do with the ending? How do the characters balance or argue against one another? What does a particularly striking passage sum up about the book as a whole?

Let's begin at the beginning, with the title of the book (or story, essay, or poem) that you're reading. If you ask the right question of it, a title can tell you something crucial about the rest of the text. The proper thing to ask is this: How does the title comment on the work it introduces?

Flannery O'Connor called one of her most ferocious short stories "A Good Man Is Hard to Find." O'Connor's story is a violent and thrilling account of a serial killer named the Misfit who terrorizes a Southern family, dominated by a supremely annoying nudnik of a grandmother, during their vacation. The first thing to notice about the story's title is its dissonance: it doesn't fit the story, just as the Misfit doesn't fit the complacent, easily moralizing society in which he lives. "A Good Man Is Hard to Find" is an empty statement: the kind of vapid, platitudinous observation to which the grandmother in the story is addicted. But O'Connor's title is a wolf in sheep's clothing. It sounds bland, but it carries a hidden punch. The Misfit is obsessed with Jesus, and his murderous rampage turns out to be his perverse way of trying to decide whether Jesus was a good man or not. The Misfit is a bad man rather than a good one—he kills people instead of saving them—but his strategies are just as deadly earnest and just as extremist as those of the figure that Christians call the son of God.

Some famous titles have a principled and central relation to their books: Jane Austen's *Pride and Prejudice, Sense and Sensibility,* and *Persuasion* are in this category. This kind of title makes us reflect on the characters in the book, and tempts us toward making judgments about them. Does Elizabeth Bennet represent prejudice in her contest, and courtship, with the "damnably proud" Darcy? Are the two healed of their respective temperamental afflictions, prejudice and pride, in the course of the book? Is there a kind of pride that is free of prejudice? All these are questions that will get us somewhere significant, once we have continued our journey past Austen's title and into the exciting, insightful pages of *Pride and Prejudice.*

Wordsworth's "Resolution and Independence" is another title that we can profitably question, since it gives us insight into the text that follows it. To be resolved (that is, steadfast) and to find a resolution (to a problem) are two very different things; but the poem suggests that these two meanings are importantly linked. Wordsworth hopes that an independence stemming from resolution will turn out to be more secure than the independence that is not resolved because it is only instinctive or youthfully impulsive.

In "Resolution and Independence," Wordsworth evokes three doomed figures of independence: Burns, the ploughman poet with his carefree energy; the enraptured teenage bard Chatterton; and Wordsworth's friend Coleridge, who, gripped by the hypnotic strength of imagination, takes no thought for himself. None of these three men, inspired poets though they were, had the resolution necessary to survive. (Coleridge was still alive when Wordsworth wrote his poem, but he had been wrecked by opium addiction.) The leech gatherer whom the poet meets on the lonely moor in the poem's central scene is, by contrast with these vulnerable men of imagination, resolved: a steady, implacable, and reassuring figure. But he is far from

poetic. Wordsworth needs to anchor himself in the stolid leech
gatherer, but he desires something else: he wants to capture the
spark that inhabited the daredevil spirits, Burns, Chatterton,
and Coleridge. He is attracted to bold, even reckless vision, and
this frightens him; such vision might lead to early death (the
fate of Burns and Chatterton) or a ruined life (Coleridge). And
so Wordsworth wishes for a kind of independence that would
rely for inspiration on someone like the humble, antipoetic leech
gatherer, rather than his fellow poets, who are inspired but far
too vulnerable. Wordsworth's staging of the debate between
contrasting models of how to live one's life repays careful study.
I will return to "Resolution and Independence," one of the
most sublime and most central poems in English, in Rule Five,
"Notice Beginnings and Endings."

Some titles offer a commentary on the action. Shakespeare's
Twelfth Night, or What You Will (which I discuss further in
my chapter "Reading Drama") evokes the final evening of the
Christmas feast: it hints at a revelry that is about to end. In
Shakespeare's play, the taunting of Malvolio, which begins in
hilarious excitement, goes sour, and a sobering morning after
looms. (Shakespeare's subtitle, *What You Will,* is a Renaissance
catchphrase meaning something like "do your worst" or "come
and get it": both a bristling challenge and a seductive dare.)
Measure for Measure, an equally multivalent title, alludes to the
Sermon on the Mount in the Gospel of Matthew, in which Jesus says (in the King James Version): "For with what judgment
ye judge, ye shall be judged: and with what measure ye mete, it
shall be measured to you again." Shakespeare's play is all about
payback; those characters who mete out punishment (above all,
the deeply unpleasant hypocrite Angelo) find themselves pun-
ished in turn, with aptness and precision, by the dramatist who
pulls the strings. Yet the play has a happy ending, one that lets

off the hook even the corrupt Angelo: here Shakespeare seems to be emulating the grace promised by Matthew's Jesus, as he gives his characters much more than they deserve.

The pioneering sociologist Erving Goffman entitled a book *Stigma: Notes on the Management of Spoiled Identity*. Goffman's subtitle is a pure piece of poetry. It reimagines a social issue by means of a metaphor from food (spoilage) while at the same time giving us a crucial clue to his point of view. Goffman's perspective is cool and, at the same time, compassionate. He will embrace the attitude of the stigmatized ones: his word "management" gives them credit for handling their own cases, even in the harsh glare of society's unfair judgment. Goffman wields his title the way O'Connor, Austen, and Shakespeare do theirs: as a tool of meaning, an important way into the book it announces. When you read, be on the alert for titles like these that boldly proclaim their significance.

Now let's go beyond titles and explore a few of the other questions one should entertain about a book—and others that one shouldn't. There are some questions that can be asked and answered on a first reading, others that might be addressed later on, and, finally, questions that the book can't answer. I call this last kind of question a false lead (to return to the idea of detective work). You won't get very far inventing a prequel to *Hamlet* depicting the prince's relationship with his father. Shakespeare has deliberately withheld this story, for a reason: he wants the connection between Hamlet and his father to remain uncertain, fraught, and challenging. Hamlet admires his dead father beyond all reason; when the father appears as a ghost, he is an elusive, troubled figure, moaning bitterly over the sins he has committed. Hamlet's imagination of his father is the thing that is heroic and godlike, not the father himself. To pin the father down by showing him as he was in life would be to confine what can't be confined: Hamlet's wild, immeasurably brilliant mind.

There are a few cases in which it does pay to speculate about what a book deliberately omits. In *Othello*, Shakespeare gives us Othello's moving account of how he seduced Desdemona into marriage, but he leaves out an account of their first episode of lovemaking—if indeed such lovemaking occurred! Some critics argue that, if we look closely at the play's time scheme, we discover that Othello and Desdemona would not have had time to consummate their marriage. *Othello* presents a rare instance: we might want to decide whether or not something happens that the play doesn't describe for us (sex between Othello and Desdemona), because the question is so important to the story that Shakespeare tells us. Even in this instance, however, we won't get anywhere by making assertions about what that sexual encounter was like (assuming it happened). "I think Othello was disappointed, not thrilled, when he made love with Desdemona": this is to develop a midrash, to add to the play a scene of your own design instead of patiently figuring out what's there. You could just as easily have said that Othello was thrilled— why not? If nothing Shakespeare actually says could count as evidence for or against your idea, then you've launched into a play of your own. You've left Shakespeare behind—to your loss.

What are the right questions to ask, the good leads? The rest of my rules, and the chapters on genre that follow them, will give you some good examples. You need to ask about the important images in a work; about its key terms; about its mood and tone of voice; about the connections between its beginning and its ending. In some cases, you will need to find out about the historical background of a work: not to reduce it to history, but to make sense of it. Eventually you will want to ask questions about the work's relation to others, by the same author and by that author's precursors.

When you read a Greek or Roman classic, you will need to look into the myths and stories that these works allude to. A good edition with footnotes will give you such information. The tragedy of the House of Atreus depicted in Aeschylus's *Oresteia* cannot be understood without knowing something about the bloody and ruthless conflict between two brothers, Atreus and Thyestes, that took place a generation before the events Aeschylus describes.

Asking questions about historical background will give you a way of making sense of the story you are reading, if that story alludes to what really happened in history. But make sure that you are not using the facts of history to simplify the meaning of a work, to reduce it to the author's expression of a political opinion. Writers of literary works rarely take up positions about the events of their time, even when they discuss these events closely; literature can't be translated into political position-taking. Even in books of political theory, the author's aim is, almost always, not simply to voice an opinion, but to present an argument and model a way of thinking.

The details of history and politics are often important to the world of a literary work. We need some basic facts about the French Revolution, its aftermath, and its effect on French society in order to appreciate the strivings of Balzac's and Stendhal's heroes. If we have no knowledge of the brutal suppression of African Americans in the post–Civil War South, we won't understand James Weldon Johnson's *Autobiography of an Ex-Colored Man.* (Johnson's unnamed protagonist decides to pass as white after seeing a gruesome, pitiless lynching.) Without knowing about Charles Stewart Parnell and his fall, it's hard to grasp Joyce's *Dubliners* or his *Ulysses.* Joyce refers often to Parnell, the Irish nationalist hero who was ruined by the scandal of his affair with a married woman, Kitty O'Shea, and the myth of Parnell becomes central to his work. Yet it is important to remember that Parnell is precisely this for Joyce: a myth. Though he often sees Parnell as a betrayed Christ figure, he is less interested in taking a political side than he is in testing the power of history as legend (as so much of Irish history has become legend). It would be wrong to limit Joyce to a political stance, even when some of his characters heatedly voice their opinions. His point of view reaches beyond political squabbles; it enfolds the monumental with the trivial, the small and dirty with the dignified.

Though he admired Ibsen, Joyce did not share Ibsen's topical bent, his impulse to take a stand on social issues. Ibsen is one of the rare authors who does espouse causes, but even here, we do the great force of his work a disservice if we reduce him to an advocate of positions. Ibsen doesn't derive his authority from the rightness or wrongness of his feelings about issues like women's rights or public health, but from his imagining what it means to want power over others, or to feel imprisoned by one's fate, or to be caught in an erotic trap with someone who you suddenly realize is your utter opposite. (I will say more about Ibsen in my chapter "Reading Drama.")

You're asking the right questions about a literary work if your questions always lead you back to the book you have in hand, rather than taking you away from it into the realms of politics or history. And in the case of books that are about politics or history—Machiavelli's *The Prince,* for example—you need to focus on the dynamics of the work, the way it uses its concepts and stages its pivotal scenes, rather than abandoning the book and its artistry for a simple dose of information about Machiavelli's time and place. Every historian, every biographer, and every political thinker has an idea of character to impart, and a peculiar vision of how the world works. Try to identify that vision, and to sympathize with it, instead of just accumulating facts about the events that the author describes.

In this rule, I've tried to guide you toward asking the right questions. Whatever those questions are—about character, about structure, about mood and voice—they should all point you toward the essence of the book you're reading.

The essence of a book is often hidden in plain sight. An example from journalism will help here. Journalists have a venerable trade secret known as the "nut graf." Graf is journalist-speak for paragraph; the nut is the real core of the matter. Every newspaper or magazine story has a nut graf. Almost never the first paragraph, the nut graf tells you what the story is *really* about. Journalists like to hide the nut graf to make things more interesting for the reader, to keep the reader's attention. Authors of full-length books do the same thing. In a book, the nut is rarely a single key paragraph; often, it's subtly distributed throughout the book. Adam Phillips's *Houdini's Box* seems at first to be an account of the great escape artist's career along with a collection of anecdotes from Phillips's own practice as a psychoanalyst. Only gradually does the real point, the nut, emerge: Phillips wonders about the situations in which we make traps for ourselves; he asks whether devising enigmatic forms of bondage, and then escaping from them, is a way of asserting the powers of the self to maintain its mystery (no one can hold me, not even myself; I'm permanently elusive). Phillips uses Houdini as a means to investigate a persistent feature of human nature: being captive to, but also potentially master of, illusions. If you read through *Houdini's Box* without grasping this argument, you have missed the nut.

Your challenge is to find the nut in the book you read: the central thoughts, the pivotal images and characters, the essence of the world it creates. (In Rule Nine, "Find the Author's Basic Thought," I will give further advice about discovering the nut within the book you're reading.)

Rule Three: Identify the Voice

"It is a truth universally acknowledged that a young man in possession of a good fortune must be in want of a wife." I have just quoted the renowned first line of Jane Austen's *Pride and Prejudice*. Who speaks this line; what does this voice sound like? We are tempted to say that it is the voice of the novel's heroine, Elizabeth Bennet. In *Pride and Prejudice*, Austen likes to ventriloquize: even though the novel is narrated in the third person, Elizabeth's way of speaking comes through clearly. In other words, when Austen describes Elizabeth's feelings, often enough you could replace "she" with "I" and credit Elizabeth herself with authorship of the passage. This kind of narration, in which the third person masks the point of view of one of the characters, is called "free indirect style": Gustave Flaubert made it his specialty in *Madame Bovary*.

There is indeed something of Elizabeth in the opening sentence of *Pride and Prejudice*. The forward tone of such statements prompts the sympathetic but wary feeling we have about Austen's heroine in the first half of the novel, before Elizabeth decides she has been wrong about Darcy, and that she had better change the way she sees the world: that she had better become more generous, less quickly condemning. Figuring out what we are meant to think of the sentence's confident assessment—its pride—is as tricky as evaluating Elizabeth herself. As we go on in our reading of *Pride and Prejudice*, we start to suspect that confident assertions may lack discernment; often, the more confident Elizabeth sounds, the less discerning she is. After a few chapters, we go back to that first sentence with raised eyebrows.

Austen's first sentence turns out to be untrue: Darcy, the young man of good fortune, is *not* in want of a wife. The sentence, with its exalted trumpeting of a "truth universally acknowledged," actually represents conventional expectation, not the rock-solid wisdom it claims. It's a prejudice, not a philosophical insight. Part of Austen's job in *Pride and Prejudice* is to tease such merely customary assertions: sometimes the teasing is gentle, sometimes severe. She shows that playing with conventions, and making fun of the pretensions of those for whom they are a solemn article of faith, doesn't mean dynamiting them into oblivion. Austen's voice—wise, mocking, balanced—remains starkly distinct from the hidebound conventional credo with which she begins *Pride and Prejudice,* which seems to want to arm-twist us into agreement. Austen makes us ponder both the rewards and the costs of being conventional. Elizabeth, though she upholds convention, separates herself from its stupider, stricter adherents by attacking them with vivid satire. Austen is an energetic, if careful, satirist; daring yet respectable, she cultivates these same qualities in her heroine, Elizabeth, who proves bold enough to enlighten herself.

Let's turn from Austen to examine another grand master of voice, Flaubert. Flaubert's adroit use of free indirect style in *Madame Bovary* balances the author's voice with the character's. Consider this description of Flaubert's Emma, who is newly afflicted by boredom in her marriage to Charles Bovary, a country apothecary. Already, Emma is dreaming of other men. She fantasizes about what a different husband would be like:

> He might have been handsome, witty, distinguished, attractive, as, doubtless, were all the men her old friends from the convent had married. What were they doing now? In the city, with the street noises, the hum of the theatres, and the lights of the ballroom, they were living lives in which the heart expands, in which the senses blossom. But her life was as cold as an attic with

northern exposure, and boredom, that silent spider, was spinning
its web in all the dark corners of her heart. She remembered the
days on which prizes were distributed, when she climbed to the
platform to receive her small wreaths. With her braided hair,
white dress, and openwork shoes, she had a gentle manner, and
when she was back in her seat the gentlemen leaned over to compliment her. The courtyard was filled with carriages; the people
said good-bye to her through the windows; the music master
greeted her as he passed by with his violin case. How far it all
was! How far!

(translated by Mildred Marmur)

The opening sentence of this paragraph shows us Emma's voice
in all its frustrated, empty yearning. Emma's futile image of the
husband who might have been is dully stereotypical: the unreal
man of her dreams is "handsome, witty, distinguished, attractive." Flaubert uses the list of adjectives to convey Emma's
cliché-bound view of happiness. There is something depressingly predictable about her thoughts, expressed in such drearily
standard terms. When she pictures the existence of her school
friends, she thinks they must be "living lives in which the heart
expands, in which the senses blossom." Flaubert wants us to
feel the almost excruciating blandness of Emma's dreams, the
dead metaphors she relies on (blossoming senses, an expanding
heart). She fantasizes in vague and conventional terms because
she, too, is a creature of convention.

But now comes something more interesting, something that
Emma could not have thought of herself: "Her life was as cold
as an attic with northern exposure, and boredom, that silent
spider, was spinning its web in all the dark corners of her heart."
These are two striking and foreboding images: the chilly, prison-
like attic, and boredom as a silent spider, determined to entrap

Emma in its web. We suddenly picture Emma as the victim of her own baffled desire. This is Flaubert's idea, not Emma's. He virtually pounces on her from on high; he intrudes on her inner life.

Just one sentence later, though, Flaubert returns to Emma's thoughts when he describes her pathetic longing for the admiration she received as a schoolgirl, when she graciously accepted prizes in front of an audience of impressed grown-ups. We sense that Emma really wants to be back in the world of her girlhood. She inclines to nostalgia because she cannot think of a way out of the tedious existence to which she has been sentenced by her husband, her society, and her own weakness.

Flaubert, then, stages himself both inside and outside Emma. The voice of *Madame Bovary* is that of its title character, but also that of its author. The two voices interrupt each other, and even comment on each other. Emma's memory of girlhood answers the spiderweb image: it's as if she is determined to counteract her author's grim perspective with something softer and more comforting.

The voice of *Madame Bovary* is double, partly Emma's, partly Flaubert's; but there are also books that employ a single voice, and do so effectively. We can turn to a work of sociology for an example. Social scientists, if they are good writers, cultivate voice; this they have in common with novelists and poets. David Maurer's remarkable *The Big Con: The Story of the Confidence Man* was first published in 1940. Maurer, a linguist by profession, was also a sly, deft scholar of a gritty milieu, and a beautiful writer. His book deals with the confidence men who, thieving and deceiving, wended their way through American culture in the early twentieth century. Maurer begins his first chapter, which bears the confidential-sounding title "A Word about Confidence Men," this way:

> The *grift* has a gentle touch. It takes its toll from the verdant
> sucker by means of the skilled hand or the sharp wit. In this, it
> differs from all other forms of crime, and especially from the
> *heavy-rackets*. It never employs violence to separate the mark
> from his money. Of all the *grifters*, the confidence man is the
> aristocrat.

You can sense already that Maurer will bring the reader close to
the con men he describes, that he wants us to admire their
shrewd, predatory ways. As it turns out, there's a sly irony about
this: as Maurer later reveals, one of the con man's most reliable
tools is getting his victim, the mark, to think that he is the con
man's partner in crime; this is invariably the prelude to the con
man fleecing the mark. But that insight comes later. For now,
there is the delectable caress of a choice adjective, the erudite
"verdant," in "verdant sucker": you can almost see the con man
salivate with anticipation. Notice that "it," not "he," does the
work of deception; the grift seems to have a mind of its own.
"To separate the mark from his money" is the sort of playful
euphemism that the con man loves. Maurer deploys his terms of
art—grift, sucker, mark, heavy racket—with a finesse that we
readers are meant to share. This first paragraph of *The Big Con*
honors expertise with its praise of the "gentle touch," the "skilled
hand," the "sharp wit." The fact that the expert in question is a
criminal spices the sauce, and gives us an illicit-feeling thrill.

In *The Big Con,* Maurer recounts many high tales of deception. These stories, of feats pulled off in bars and on trains and
at horse races, are calculated to leave the reader open-mouthed
with astonishment: they are dinosaur cons, masterworks of the
old school. Maurer reveres the con man's monumental achievements the way art lovers revere the old masters. The author's
voice is like the voice of the con man he studies: aristocratic,
knowing, both wised-up and refined.

Voice and Sense of Place

Another aspect of voice is description of place. When you read, you should attend to an author's way of portraying places, with all the implications for voice that such description carries. Charles Dickens is a master at the art of expressing a mood and an argument by depicting a particular place. The settings he portrays in his novels give a mighty sense of character; his people often seem to arise out of their locations. In his work, place itself seems to have a voice.

My example of slow reading for sense of place comes from Dickens's *Great Expectations,* a book so tense with excitement that it can be dreadfully hard to put down—prepare to stay up late if you're reading Dickens. (I remember a long-ago interview with the rambunctious critic Leslie Fiedler in which Fiedler announced that Dickens was his favorite bathtub reading; get ready for some long baths.) If you've never read *Great Expectations,* or if you read it in early youth and haven't picked it up since, now is the time to open, or re-open, Dickens's gripping marvel of a novel. This is what you'll see on the first page (the third paragraph, to be exact):

Ours was the marsh country, down by the river, within, as the river wound, twenty miles of the sea. My first most vivid and broad impression of the identity of things, seems to me to have been gained on a memorable raw afternoon towards evening. At such a time I found out for certain, that this bleak place overgrown with nettles was the churchyard; and that Philip Pirrip, late of this parish, and also Georgiana wife of the above, were dead and buried; and that Alexander, Bartholomew, Abraham, Tobias, and Roger, infant children of the aforesaid, were also dead and buried; and that the dark flat wilderness beyond the churchyard, intersected with dykes and mounds and gates, with scattered cattle feeding on it, was the marshes; and that the low leaden line beyond, was the river; and that the distant savage lair from which the wind was rushing, was the sea; and that the small bundle of shivers growing afraid of it all and beginning to cry, was Pip.

"Hold your noise!" cried a terrible voice, as a man started up from among the graves at the side of the church porch. "Keep still, you little devil, or I'll cut your throat!"

Dickens's passage presents a fearful and harrowing scene of origins: the narrator and hero of *Great Expectations,* Pip, tells us when and where he received his "first most vivid and broad impression of the identity of things." Pip finds himself in a churchyard, where his mother and father and infant siblings are all buried. The country Dickens shows us becomes more gloomy and threatening as he goes on: the "dark flat wilderness" of the marshes of Kent, where little orphaned Pip lives with his sister and her husband, the amiable blacksmith Joe Gargery; the "low leaden line" of the river Thames; and finally the "distant savage lair" of the sea. Most remarkably, Dickens caps his bleak description with Pip's mention of himself in the third person. Pip's first identity in the novel is a "small bundle of shivers growing afraid of it all and beginning to cry": hardly a person at all. He is fright and cold bundled together. His name appears at the paragraph's end as a helpless squeak—and is instantly followed by the terrifying apparition of Magwitch the escaped convict, who means, he says, to cut Pip's throat. The scared voice of Pip is at one with the raw, dark place that gave birth to him.

Place is important in *Great Expectations:* not just the dank, foreboding marshes, with the prison ships, the Hulks, moored on the nearby river; but also the abrupt, bustling labyrinth of the London streets to which Pip is transplanted midway through the novel. In Miss Havisham's morbid, cobwebbed house, Pip sits with his beloved Estella. He recalls, "In the heavy air of the room, and the heavy darkness that brooded in its remoter corners, I even had an alarming fancy that Estella and I might presently begin to decay." The reader must pause over Dickens's place descriptions to get a feel for these tableaux; character often grows from physical place in Dickens. Instead of rushing past description to get on with the plot, practice slow reading: linger for a few minutes with Dickens's voice, the way he depicts his often bleak and chilly settings. On this first page of *Great Expectations,* Pip learns to stand outside himself, an ability that he will carry with him. In the marshy graveyard that Dickens gives us at the novel's beginning, Pip discovers himself, a small shivering thing. Later, he becomes an expert at getting ahead in life; but he always retains his original sense of being the tiny presence at the edge of a forbidding landscape, menaced by the ragged, murderous cry of an unknown man.

Competing Voices

Some books set several voices against one another; they stage a competition among these voices. Competing voices feature in two of the most memorable works of Western literature: Balzac's *Père Goriot* (also known as *Old Goriot*), and Shakespeare's *Henry IV, Part 1.* Both Balzac's novel and Shakespeare's play are propulsive, filled with the energy of a central character, a young man who wants to conquer the world. And so he does: Balzac's Eugène Rastignac and Shakespeare's Prince Hal both preside in triumph over the endings of their respective works. Along the way, though, they have been challenged by characters who speak with notably different voices: Balzac's Vautrin and Goriot, Shakespeare's Falstaff and Hotspur. Each of these two works features a trio of contenders for dominance over a powerfully drawn fictive world; in both Balzac and Shakespeare, only one man wins out.

Père Goriot is the story of an old man, Goriot, who lives in a rooming house, having sacrificed all his wealth for his beloved daughters' aristocratic lifestyles. To the very end of his life, Goriot cares only for his daughters' happiness, not his own. Another character in the rooming house, Vautrin, is an arch-villain, a famous criminal living under an alias. He tries to corrupt Eugène, the young man who befriends Goriot and who courts both of Goriot's daughters in turn. (The daughters are married, but Balzac makes clear that the world he describes, the Paris of the 1830s, is a happily adulterous milieu.)

Balzac, then, draws a triangle: Goriot, Eugène, and Vautrin. The willfully disreputable Vautrin indoctrinates Eugène in the way of the world when he tells the ambitious young man that

> "The problem of quick success is the problem that fifty thousand young men in your position are trying to solve, at this very moment. You are a single one in that battle. Imagine the efforts you have to make; imagine the slaughter! You'll have to eat each other like spiders in a teapot; for we all know there aren't fifty thousand places. Do you know how people get on here? Either by dazzling genius or by skillful corruption. You must either cut through this mass of men like a cannon ball, or creep into it like a plague. Honesty is no use at all."
>
> (translated by Henry Reed)

Vautrin produces a loose barrage of metaphors: the most extravagant and gruesome is that of the spiders eating one another in a teapot, but his advice to Eugène to turn himself into either a plague or a cannonball is almost as flamboyantly memorable. Vautrin burns his way through the text of *Père Goriot,* vile yet dynamic, a straight-talking force of nature. As *Père Goriot* goes on, the rabid Vautrin finds himself exposed as a scoundrel with an infamous criminal past; and so his violent cynicism is discredited. His voice won't be allowed to rule Balzac's novel, even though something of his steely, ice-cold sensibility is present in Balzac as well.

The two remaining major characters vying for control of *Père Goriot* are Goriot himself and Eugène. As the novel concludes, Goriot declines into a profoundly pathetic, utterly broken man, who mixes adoration for his daughters with revulsion at their betrayals of him. Goriot's self-deluding sentimentalism prevents us from esteeming him; he simply cannot see clearly, even in the face of disaster. Eugène, who has been deeply sympathetic to Goriot, veers away from him at the end. He caps the action of Balzac's novel with a declaration of cold ambition. Walking alone after old Goriot's funeral, Eugène surveys Paris and, with it, his own prospects:

> Eugène, now alone, walked a few steps to the topmost part of the graveyard. He saw Paris, spread windingly along the two banks of the Seine. Lights were beginning to twinkle. His gaze fixed itself almost avidly on the space between the column in the Place Vendôme and the cupola of Les Invalides. There lived the world into which he had wished to penetrate. He fastened on the murmurous hive a look that seemed already to be sucking the honey from it, and uttered these words:
>
> "Now I'm ready for you!"
>
> And, as the first move in the challenge he was flinging at society, he went back to dine with Madame de Nucingen.

So ends *Père Goriot:* the dead old man is swept away as Eugène determines to conquer Goriot's daughter Madame de Nucingen, the first step in the triumphant future he sees for himself. Balzac takes a sudden turn in these last few lines of the novel: he gives himself wholly to the voice of Eugène, who is already aching for victory. The pathos of Goriot is not the final significance of the book, despite its title, and despite Goriot's agonizing death scene. On the last page of *Père Goriot,* the dead Goriot is upstaged by Eugène, whose confidence now seems titanic. The column in Place Vendôme was raised by Napoleon to honor his victory at Austerlitz; and the French emperor is buried in Les Invalides. Like Stendhal's Julien Sorel in *The Red and the Black,* Balzac's Eugène can't resist comparing himself to Napoleon. As Balzac's novel draws to a close, the voice of the old and defeated Goriot yields to that of the young firebrand; strangely, Goriot's death has catapulted Eugène into a knowledge of his own heroic worth.

The youthful firebrand in Shakespeare's *Henry IV, Part 1* is the appropriately named Hotspur, who leads the Percies's rebellion against the shuffling, anxious king of Shakespeare's title. Hotspur is perhaps the most bravely self-propelled of all Shakespeare's characters; he is sheer energy, so much so that he can hardly keep up with himself. Here is Hotspur at one of his many fervent moments. In Act 2, Scene 3 of Shakespeare's play, Hotspur reads from a letter sent to him by a nobleman reluctant to join the conspiracy against the king. Hotspur intersperses his quotations from the letter with his own hearty scorn for the "lord fool" who has declined to join the Percies's revolt:

> "The purpose you undertake is dangerous";—why, that's certain: 'tis dangerous to take a cold, to sleep, to drink; but I tell you, my lord fool, out of this nettle, danger, we pluck this flower, safety. "The purpose you undertake is dangerous; the friends you have named uncertain; the time itself unsorted; and your whole plot too light for the counterpoise of so great an opposition." Say you so, say you so? I say unto you again, you are a shallow cowardly hind, and you lie. What a lack-brain is this! By the Lord, our plot is a good plot as ever was laid; our friends

true and constant: a good plot, good friends, and full of expectation; an excellent plot, very good friends. What a frosty-spirited rogue is this! Why, my lord of York commends the plot and the general course of action. 'Zounds, an I were now by this rascal, I could brain him with his lady's fan. Is there not my father, my uncle and myself? lord Edmund Mortimer, my lord of York and Owen Glendower? is there not besides the Douglas? have I not all their letters to meet me in arms by the ninth of the next month? and are they not some of them set forward already? What a pagan rascal is this! an infidel! Ha! you shall see now in very sincerity of fear and cold heart, will he to the king and lay open all our proceedings. O, I could divide myself and go to buffets, for moving such a dish of skim milk with so honourable an action! Hang him! let him tell the king: we are prepared. I will set forward to-night.

Hotspur's eager repetitions show a vitality that stokes itself in an effort to ward off nervousness: "a good plot, good friends, and full of expectation; an excellent plot, very good friends." In this bravura speech, Hotspur does indeed "divide himself and go to buffets." He reads the letter and answers it in one breath, and so verbally battles against the lord he has invited to rebel with him. Hotspur buries any possibility of wavering under a tsunami of words. His self-assurance is as bold as it is illogical: "out of this nettle, danger, we pluck this flower, safety." When we read or see *Henry IV, Part 1,* we feel liable to be scorched by Hotspur's fiery tongue if we doubt his purpose; but we remain far from convinced of his strategic talents. It is no surprise to us that the rebellion fails, and that Hotspur finds himself vanquished by his mighty opposite, the cold-blooded and calculating Prince Hal (the future Henry V).

In *Henry IV, Part 1,* Hal's voice competes with Hotspur's. The prince is infinitely less attractive than the young Northern rebel, but his mastery impresses us nonetheless. In a deeply unsettling speech that comes early on in Shakespeare's play, Hal announces that he has merely been slumming with what we thought were his boon companions, including the incomparable Falstaff (whom Hal will decisively reject when he becomes king). Hal addresses the audience in soliloquy, and lets us in on his secret: he has staged his bad behavior in order to redeem himself spectacularly later on. In his profoundly chilling monologue, Hal describes his low-life Eastcheap friends ("you all," including the magnificent Falstaff) as mere useless idlers:

> I know you all, and will awhile uphold
> The unyoked humour of your idleness:
> Yet herein will I imitate the sun,
> Who doth permit the base contagious clouds
> To smother up his beauty from the world,
> That, when he please again to be himself,
> Being wanted, he may be more wonder'd at,
> By breaking through the foul and ugly mists
> Of vapours that did seem to strangle him.

The word "strangle" is unexpected in its brutality, but it is telling. In contrast to Hotspur's passionate, uncontrolled speech, Hal's words are methodical: he follows through his metaphor of the sun and the clouds with cold precision, while Hotspur rashly throws forth his careless image of the nettle and the flower. (All these images make us sit up and take notice: see my discussion in Rule Six, "Identify Signposts.") Hal is all too reasonable, even repellent in his cleverness. The apex of Hal's profoundly unlikeable career in *Henry IV, Part 1* comes when he reproaches his father, who has long thought Hal a ne'er-do-well, and whom Hal has just saved in battle: Hal reminds King Henry that he could have let him die, if he were really such a bad son as Henry deemed him.

There is a third dominant voice in *Henry IV, Part 1,* and it is the one that will finally win out: the voice belongs, of course, to the immortal Falstaff, who cheers us as no other Shakespeare hero does. Falstaff, by the calendar an old man, is truly and forever young. He has the innocent greed of a child, along with a child's capacity for love. And it is Hal whom he loves most of all; this is Falstaff's tragedy.

Falstaff is not a ruthless enthusiast like Hotspur or a schemer like Hal, but a lively improviser, ready to sacrifice any advantage for a good jest. As he boisterously reminds us, he embodies the never-resting engine of comedy, and it matters nothing to him whether he plays the joke or the joke is played on him:

> Men of all sorts take a pride to gird at me: the brain of this foolish-compounded clay, man, is not able to invent anything that tends to laughter, more than I invent or is invented on me: I am not only witty in myself, but the cause that wit is in other men.

Falstaff's exchange with the Lord Chief Justice, his feeble straight man, can stand for his credo. The Lord Chief Justice reminds Falstaff, who has just described himself as a young wag, that he is in fact rather old: "Every part about you blasted with antiquity . . . and will you yet call yourself young? Fie, fie, fie, Sir John!" Falstaff's reply, in which he insists that he ever has been and will always be the same, his authentic, irreplaceable—and, yes, youthful—self, more than suffices to establish him as the truly superior spirit in Shakespeare's play:

> My lord, I was born about three of the clock in the afternoon, with a white head and something a round belly. For my voice, I have lost it with halloing and singing of anthems. To approve my youth further, I will not: the truth is, I am only old in judgment and understanding.

Falstaff's voice has what Hal and Hotspur lack: he charms us, and adds to our power as he wins us over. Shakespeare, like Balzac, was too canny to ever ally himself completely with the voice of any character in his work; he balances one figure against another. But in *Henry IV, Part 1,* as in *Hamlet,* he comes as close as he ever does to letting a single character preside over a play. Just as Eugène Rastignac, a young man with a future, proves himself the ruling voice of *Père Goriot,* so Falstaff, the ageless, ever-wise clown, rules *Henry IV, Part 1.*

Rule Four: Get a Sense of Style

Writers sound very different from one another on the page. Style is their way of thinking and being; and in style, which is always an individualizing signature, a writer will confess the most intimate details of argument and personality. Style is related to voice (which I discussed in my previous rule, Rule Three), but while one can pick out different voices in a book, and even contrast the author's voice to the hero's, style is uniform and pervasive. The style of a book is singular, since through style alone the author announces his or her inmost self.

Consider the urbane and elaborate style of the eighteenth-century historian Edward Gibbon, who, in his magnum opus on the decline of Rome, gives an account of the newfangled sect of Christians. Gibbon here emphasizes the Christians' intransigent opposition to paganism. He begins with a contrast between the Christian abhorrence of idolatry and the more easygoing habits practiced by skeptical Roman philosophers:

> The philosopher, who considered the system of polytheism as a composition of human fraud and error, could disguise a smile of contempt under the mask of devotion, without apprehending that either the mockery, or the compliance, would expose him

to the resentment of any invisible, or, as he conceived them, imaginary powers. But the established religions of Paganism were seen by the primitive Christians in a much more odious and formidable light. It was the universal sentiment both of the church and of heretics, that the daemons were the authors, the patrons, and the objects of idolatry. Those rebellious spirits who had been degraded from the rank of angels, and cast down into the infernal pit, were still permitted to roam upon earth, to torment the bodies, and to seduce the minds, of sinful men. The daemons soon discovered and abused the natural propensity of the human heart towards devotion, and, artfully withdrawing the adoration of mankind from their Creator, they usurped the place and honours of the Supreme Deity. By the success of their malicious contrivances, they at once gratified their own vanity and revenge, and obtained the only comfort of which they were yet susceptible, the hope of involving the human species in the participation of their guilt and misery. It was confessed, or at least it was imagined, that they had distributed among themselves the most important characters of polytheism, one daemon assuming the name and attributes of Jupiter, another of Aesculapius, a third of Venus, and a fourth perhaps of Apollo; and that, by advantage of their long experience and aerial nature, they were enabled to execute, with sufficient skill and dignity, the parts which they had undertaken. They lurked in the temples, instituted festivals and sacrifices, invented fables, pronounced oracles, and were frequently allowed to perform miracles. The Christians, who, by the interposition of evil spirits, could so readily explain every praeternatural appearance, were disposed and even desirous to admit the most extravagant fictions of the Pagan mythology. But the belief of the Christian was accompanied with horror. The most trifling mark of respect to the national worship he considered as a direct homage yielded to the daemon, and as an act of rebellion against the majesty of God.

Exploiting his exalted taste for the comic, Gibbon produces a magnificent paragraph. Gibbon's style is a high-wire act: in perfectly poised, well-balanced sentences, he gives us a zinging tour de force. To see the stylistic drama in Gibbon, you must notice the sly, backhanded, heavily barbed commentary that insinuates itself into his seemingly staid pronouncements. A dignified narrator, Gibbon yet has a powerful satirical vein. He relishes his picture of what he clearly regards as the Christians' ludicrous, and duplicitous, feeling about demons, whom they insistently reject but still credit with all manner of spectacularly persuasive achievements, from oracular pronouncements to miracles. You can sense when Gibbon's starched formality yields to the merciless lancet of his wit, when he gives in to a crack that he cannot resist making: for example, when he remarks that the demons' "long experience and aerial nature" enabled them, according to the Christians, to play the roles of the classical gods "with sufficient skill and dignity."

Gibbon's paragraph sets the flagrant superstition of the early Christians, and their obsessive interest in the demons they despised, against the lofty, worldly-wise stance of the pagan philosopher. Gibbon clearly identifies himself with the ancient philosopher, rather than the gullible Christian believer. In his mammoth history, Gibbon pays the same lip service to Christianity that the philosopher paid to the ancient gods: he barely conceals his "smile of contempt under the mask of devotion." Gibbon's confidential, expansive style invites us to adopt along with him a superior view of all religions (as well as all societies and all political disputes). We get a sense of his personality, with its propensity for masterful and subtly stated judgments, as he makes his case about the drawbacks of a fervent, defensive (and therefore, he implies, easily hoodwinked) belief like that of the early Christians. The suave neutrality that Gibbon espouses when he discusses the battle between Christianity and pagan Rome is meant to appeal to us as a kind of freedom, the privilege of the knowing ones who have unshackled themselves from loyalty to conventional prejudice—specifically, the prejudice that prefers the Christian to the mere idolater.

As we see in the case of Gibbon, style involves the writer's partnership with the reader as they pursue an argument together. D. H. Lawrence, whose aggressive way of repeating words and phrases conveys his will to get to some blocked reality, urges us forward with him; unlike Henry James, with his acrobatically balanced clauses, his sentences that seem to recede from, and sometimes bewilderingly to tease, the reader. But both Lawrence and James dance with the reader. They give vivid voice to the frustration as well as the power they feel when they tell a tale; they want us to join in as they attempt to make sense of the lives they describe. Both are consummate stylists, and for both, style is a way of thinking. When you read Lawrence or James, you need to follow the author like a partner in a dance, rather than struggling against the rhythm.

Consider Lawrence's great poem "The Ship of Death" with its seemingly crude chant, repeated swayingly, "Oh build your ship of death, oh build it!" Lawrence swings his lines with the stubbornness of one of his fictional protagonists; his style suits the ways of his characters. He's like the Cornish wanderer in his story "Samson and Delilah," who strides back into the life of a woman he has abandoned sixteen years earlier and plants himself squarely before her: an insistent man, bearing a brute knowledge of desire and belongingness.

Now turn, for another pressing instance of style, to the beginning of James's short story "The Middle Years," which depicts an aging novelist not unlike James himself. Dencombe, a writer afflicted by ill health, is taking a holiday in Bournemouth, on the coast of England. He has just received the proofs of his latest book, also called *The Middle Years:* a book which he wants to see as a resting place for his pride and ambition, the capstone of his career. As the story opens, Dencombe is looking out over the landscape, measuring his own thoughts, and estimating the point of his convalescence:

> The April day was soft and bright, and poor Dencombe, happy in the conceit of reasserted strength, stood in the garden of the hotel, comparing, with a deliberation in which, however, there was still something of languor, the attractions of easy strolls. He liked the feeling of the south, so far as you could have it in the north, he liked the sandy cliffs and the clustered pines, he liked even the colourless sea. . . . he was better, of course, but better, after all, than what? He should never again, as at one or two great moments of the past, be better than himself. The infinite of life had gone, and what was left of the dose was a small glass engraved like a thermometer by the apothecary.

James's style is full of qualifications, and it matches his protagonist (who, tellingly, likes "the feeling of the south" only when he can have it in the North). Dencombe is a specialist in hesitant definition: he is "better, of course, but better, after all, than what?" In Dencombe's mind, the state of his health melds with the state of his artistic success. His sense of himself proves so fluctuating that it threatens to slip from his grasp. Yet when he does grasp his life's meaning, which resides firmly in the books he has written, he surveys that meaning strictly: so James gives us the apt and elaborate metaphor of the small glass engraved like a thermometer.

James casts shocking interruptions in the path of his calm-paced prose. In a few pages we will be told of Dencombe's feeling "that practically his career was over—it was as violent as a rough hand at his throat." When Dencombe experiences the opposite feeling, the exhilaration of success, James writes, "What he saw so intensely to-day, what he felt as a nail driven in, was that only now, at the very last, had he come into possession." The hand at the throat, the crucifixion nail: these are signs of the piercing element of reality that the circumlocutory poise of Jamesian style, which mimics the thoughts of his protagonists, is designed to ward off. But James wants to violate poise too; he wants to get to achingly real feeling, iron-hard fact.

In the course of "The Middle Years," Dencombe meets a fanatical admirer of his work: a young physician, Doctor Hugh, employed by a wealthy old lady who has promised to remember the young man in her will. Doctor Hugh is the perfect audience, or at least the perfect echo chamber, for Dencombe's musing on his own career. Dencombe's young admirer stays by his side, even after he realizes that his benefactress will cut him out of her will for abandoning her in favor of Dencombe.

At the end of "The Middle Years," Dencombe is on his deathbed, and Doctor Hugh sits attentively beside him. Now, at the climax of the story, Dencombe pronounces his credo, a summing up of his life and career: so much of his life has been spent to produce, so laboriously, his quiet final satisfaction with his work, and the satisfaction is mixed, now as always, with self-doubt. Dencombe murmurs, "We work in the dark—we do what we can—we give what we have. Our doubt is our passion and our passion is our task. The rest is the madness of art." We are aware, when Dencombe speaks these telegraphically memorable sentences to Doctor Hugh, that James has allowed his novelist hero to rise to a concision, streamlined and monosyllabic, that fits his debate-riven, embattled pride. The last of Dencombe's three epigrams even lets James's cautious burrower praise a reckless "madness." The sudden shift in James's style here, away from its usual spiraling gentility and toward a firm, chiseled summation, pays tribute to Dencombe's last moments, and to Dencombe's drive to find a drastic formula for his life (also for "our" lives, the lives of all creators, including devoted, self-sacrificing readers like Doctor Hugh). Style suits substance, as time grows short and the deathbed pronouncement does its work. Whether Dencombe's eloquence is self-delusion or not, whether he too high-handedly turns doubt into satisfaction, every reader must decide for herself: the final paragraphs of James's story offer ammunition for both sides.

As a contrast to James's studied, carefully alert style, look at the beginning of *The Big Sleep* by Raymond Chandler, the master of hardboiled American noir:

It was about eleven o'clock in the morning, mid October, with the sun not shining and a look of hard wet rain in the clearness of the foothills. I was wearing my powder-blue suit, with dark blue shirt, tie and display handkerchief, black brogues, black wool socks with dark blue clocks on them. I was neat, clean, shaved and sober, and I didn't care who knew it. I was everything the well-dressed private detective ought to be. I was calling on four million dollars.

The main hallway of the Sternwood place was two stories high. Over the entrance doors, which would have let in a troop of Indian elephants, there was a broad stained-glass panel showing a knight in dark armor rescuing a lady who was tied to a tree and didn't have any clothes on but some very long and convenient hair. The knight had pushed the vizor of his helmet back to be sociable, and he was fiddling with the knots on the ropes that tied the lady to the tree and not getting anywhere. I stood there and thought that if I lived in the house, I would sooner or later have to climb up there and help him. He didn't seem to be really trying.

Chandler's narrator is also his hero, Philip Marlowe, a "private dick on a case" (as he describes himself later on). Chandler's, or Marlowe's, voice is insouciant, stylishly insolent: notice the reference to the stained-glass lady tied to a tree, with her "very long and convenient hair," and to the overly majestic entryway that "would have let in a troop of Indian elephants." By implication, Marlowe has come to assist the knight who is "fiddling with the knots that tied the lady to the tree" (like the knight in "dark armor," he wears mostly dark colors). Within a few pages Marlowe will encounter his own damsel in distress, the gloriously distracting Carmen Sternwood, the heiress who lives and amuses herself in this ornate, oversized mansion. Meticulous and sarcastic, Marlowe has seen everything; he habitually plays it cool. Yet he has, though reluctant to admit it, some principled ideas about the detective's job, and labors devotedly in his vocation.

My last example of style comes from an author who combines the plain and the exalted, and who is utterly self-assured. John Ruskin, the great Victorian prose prophet and critic of culture and the arts, is, unlike Chandler's Marlowe, devoid of self-deprecation; he speaks straightforwardly the gospel of responsibility. Ruskin expresses not a professional code like Philip Marlowe's, but a high-moral argument incumbent on all of us, and his stylistic thrust is accordingly lofty and direct.

Ruskin's *The Queen of the Air* is a set of lectures dedicated to the powers of the goddess Athena, who, he says, "does not make men learned, but prudent and subtle: she does not teach them to make their work beautiful, but to make it right." Rightness is Ruskin's dominant value; it carries beauty, and all other virtues, in its wake. Late in *The Queen of the Air,* Ruskin finds himself contemplating a drawing of Lake Geneva and the hills around it made by J. M. W. Turner, the artist whom Ruskin celebrated as the greatest mind of the nineteenth century.

Turner's moral strength, at one with the great painter's artistic strength, infuses Ruskin's soul, and he writes,

> As I myself look at it, there is no fault nor folly of my life,—and both have been many and great,—that does not rise up against me, and take away my joy, and shorten my power of possession, of sight, of understanding. And every past effort of my life, every gleam of rightness or good in it, is with me now, to help me in my grasp of this art, and its vision. So far as I can rejoice in, or interpret either, my power is owing to what of right there is in me. I dare to say it, that, because through all my life I have desired good, and not evil; because I have been kind to many; have wished to be kind to all; have willfully injured none; and because I have loved much, and not selfishly;—therefore, the morning light is yet visible to me on those hills, and you, who read, may trust my thought and word in such work as I have to do for you; and you will be glad afterwards that you have trusted them.

In these words you have Ruskin, complete and plain, willing to give you his thought, his perception, his virtue. The sincere open address to the reader is palpable and untheatrical, voiced in Ruskin's simple, ascending sentences. Moral and artistic sight support each other, in his view; so we trust this prose as we trust his vision. "Language best showeth a man," the Renaissance poet and playwright Ben Jonson remarked: "Speak that I may see thee." Ruskin's style makes us see him. When he evokes the morning light on the hills in Turner's drawing, the piously raised Ruskin may be thinking of the most direct and affecting psalm in the Bible, Psalm 121 (which begins, in the King James Version, "I will lift up mine eyes unto the hills, / From whence cometh my help").

The Queen of the Air is at times an extravagant book, but in the passage I have quoted, Ruskin stays firmly on earth. His style here is workmanlike in the best sense, as he tells us the work he can do for us. I think of another biblical passage, this one from Ecclesiastes (9:10), rendered in the King James Version as follows: "Whatsoever thy hand findeth to do, do it with thy might; for there is no work, nor device, nor knowledge, nor wisdom, in the grave, whither thou goest." Ruskin knows that he, like all of us, is going to the grave; with all he can muster, he celebrates and uses the light he still has here above. In Ruskin, as in Chandler, Lawrence, James, Gibbon, and so many others, style is moral; it displays the self of the author.

Rule Five: Notice Beginnings and Endings

You're probably thinking of this rule as pretty obvious advice. We can hardly help but notice the basic scene-setting that a book provides us on its first page. And, if the book is a good one, the ending supplies us with what we wanted, a satisfying conclusion.

But beginnings and endings are worth a closer inspection. How often do you look back to the beginning of a book (or poem, or short story, or essay) after finishing it? Not very often, right? Well, you ought to. The connections between a book's beginning and its ending are strong and tight; you will always be surprised and enlightened by putting a first and a last page together. When you do so, you'll also learn much about how a work's middle navigates the passage between beginning and end.

Let's take a look at the first stanza of Wordsworth's "Resolution and Independence," a poem I've already mentioned in Rule Two, "Ask the Right Questions":

There was a roaring in the wind all night;
The rain came heavily and fell in floods;

But now the sun is rising calm and bright;
The birds are singing in the distant woods;
Over his own sweet voice the Stock-dove broods;
The Jay makes answer as the Magpie chatters;
And all the air is filled with pleasant noise of waters.

It's a sunny morning, and the poet (we soon learn) is walking on a moor. The night's rough weather has been dissipated by the sun, which is "rising calm and bright." Wordsworth's sun is a visual emblem, but for the most part his opening stanza collects images of sound: first the wind's remembered roaring, then the singing birds, and finally the "pleasant noise of waters." Wordsworth divides his birds into two instances: the dove that broods "over his own sweet voice," and the jay that answers the chattering magpie.

The opening stanza of "Resolution and Independence" has a sharply defined beginning, middle, and ending. It begins with a memory of disruption (the night's roaring wind and heavy rains) and proceeds through the pictures of the sun and the birds. The stanza finally arrives at a soothing aural impression that answers the rough nighttime weather: the morning's "pleasant noise of waters." We go from dark and chaotic to tranquil, bright, sweetly harmonious.

Wordsworth's first stanza, then, dramatizes the dispelling of confusion. In this respect, it forecasts the plot of "Resolution and Independence," which moves from a disturbed memory of the sad fates of Wordsworth's fellow poets Burns, Chatterton, and Coleridge to, in its ending, a calm and steadfast resolution. But there is also a way in which Wordsworth's first stanza presents itself as the opposite of his last one (which I will quote in a moment). When he sees the morning after the storm, Wordsworth draws forth all the energy of new beginning, the refreshing, life-giving power of creation. If we know *Paradise*

Lost, by Wordsworth's great precursor John Milton, we will recognize in the phrase "Over his own sweet voice the Stock-dove broods" a reminiscence of Milton's description of the creation. The spirit of God, Milton writes, "dove-like satst brooding on the vast abyss / And madst it pregnant." (In the Hebrew of Genesis, the divine breath or *ruah* flutters over the universe during creation like a mother bird; here Milton finds, and is nourished by, his godly source.) Wordsworth's dove, unlike Milton's, nurtures his own voice. This sweet self-centeredness is echoed in the lives of the youthful poets that Wordsworth remembers in "Resolution and Independence."

The final stanza of "Resolution and Independence" offers a drastic contrast to the poem's beginning. The poet has been listening to an aged leech gatherer he has met on the moor. The leech gatherer describes his "hazardous and wearisome" existence: he spends his time searching for leeches in the moor's marshy ponds; propped on his staff, he seems barely alive. In place of the bounding, rejuvenating cheer of Wordsworth's opening, we end with a solemn gray tableau. The leech gatherer "the same discourse renewed," Wordsworth writes,

> And soon with this he other matter blended,
> Cheerfully uttered, with demeanour kind,
> But stately in the main; and, when he ended,
> I could have laughed myself to scorn to find
> In that decrepit Man so firm a mind.
> "God," said I, "be my help and stay secure;
> I'll think of the Leech-gatherer on the lonely moor!"

The leech gatherer is "kind" but, more important, "stately." He epitomizes firmness, rock-hard tenacity. The poem's speaker relies on this old man for an anchor, a secure source of strength. We couldn't be further away from the youthfully impetuous opening of "Resolution and Independence," from the spirit that bounds like the hare "running races in her mirth" (in Wordsworth's second stanza). There is no rejoicing at the end of Wordsworth's poem; instead, "Resolution and Independence" has matured into a rather grim but impressive realism. The birds and the hare yield to the withered leech gatherer, who is "bent double" by the pains of old age. Wordsworth compares the leech gatherer to a "sea-beast crawled forth" on a rock: the opposite of the innocent, tuneful birds and the racing hare of stanzas one and two.

How has Wordsworth gotten from his beginning, with its passionate sympathy for the springing energies of nature, to his ending, with its almost inhuman patience? Wordsworth has been scarred by the thought of tragedy: the deaths of Burns and Chatterton, the mad distraction of Coleridge. The leech gatherer signifies a persistence beyond tragedy: a vision of experience that refuses to be wounded, even by the harshest burdens (pain, sorrow, the physical wreckage of old age).

The poem's conclusion, with its battered yet even strength, asserts its superiority to Wordsworth's innocent beginning, but something has been lost. The beginning of "Resolution and Independence" is immensely more attractive than its ending, and the poet knows this. The gap between the two ends of the poem bears witness to Wordsworth's conscious inability to unite the worlds of innocence and experience. When we place the beginning and the ending of "Resolution and Independence" next to each other, we gain a palpable insight into the distance between the two, a distance that Wordsworth refuses to bridge.

Elizabeth Bishop's "At the Fishhouses" is a notably Wordsworthian poem. It even bears a specific resemblance to "Resolution and Independence," with an aged Nova Scotia fisherman taking the place of Wordsworth's leech gatherer. Like Wordsworth, Bishop carefully orchestrates her beginning and her conclusion, so that we benefit from placing the two ends of her poem side by side.

Bishop structures "At the Fishhouses" around a reminiscence: the speaker of the poem encounters an old fisherman by the docks. She gives him a cigarette (a Lucky Strike); they "talk of the decline of the population / and of codfish and herring." Then, as the poet descends to the brink of the water, the old man is replaced by a seal she has seen repeatedly at just this spot. The seal regards her curiously, "steadily, moving his head a little."

Here is how "At the Fishhouses" begins:

> Although it is a cold evening,
> down by one of the fishhouses
> an old man sits netting,
> his net, in the gloaming almost invisible,
> a dark purple-brown,
> and his shuttle worn and polished.

We see the fisherman performing a traditional, age-old activity, repairing a net. The old man and his humble craftsmanship stand out against the cold evening: a calm human presence is at the center of the scene.

At the end of "At the Fishhouses," oceanic cold wins out over the human. Bishop invokes an empty seascape, visionary and repellent:

> I have seen it over and over, the same sea, the same,
> slightly, indifferently swinging above the stones,
> icily free above the stones,
> above the stones and then the world.
> If you should dip your hand in,
> your wrist would ache immediately,
> your bones would begin to ache and
>   your hand would burn

as if the water were a transmutation of fire
that feeds on stones and burns with a dark gray flame.
If you tasted it, it would first taste bitter,
then briny, then surely burn your tongue.
It is like what we imagine knowledge to be:
dark, salt, clear, moving, utterly free,
drawn from the cold hard mouth
of the world, derived from the rocky breasts
forever, flowing and drawn, and since
our knowledge is historical, flowing, and flown.

In this chastened and prophetic conclusion, Bishop remembers a biblical passage, from Revelation 10:9–10, in which the narrator eats a book offered by an angel. The book tastes "sweet as honey," but, the narrator says, "as soon as I had eaten it, my belly was bitter." The knowledge that Bishop compares to the dark, salt sea is not sweet at all, but bitter; its stinging, impersonal pain conveys a freedom that has nothing to do with humanity. These "rocky breasts" do not nurture (unlike the soft "white breast of the dim sea" that W. B. Yeats imagined in an early poem, "Who Goes with Fergus?").

In the course of "At the Fishhouses," Bishop leaves behind first a human presence (the fisherman), then an animal one (the seal); she concludes with the one inanimate thing that is both ever-changing and ever the same: the sea. She hymns the crucifying cold baptism of the water, the trackless and blank intensity of it.

Bishop's poem begins with slow, detailed, realist depiction of the fishhouses; she ends with the driving, unforgettable chant "cold dark deep and absolutely clear," which occurs twice in her final verse paragraph. The chant hymns the burning lucidity of the ocean, which stands for the transience of everything, all personal acquaintance, all worldly knowledge. Bishop looks toward an inhuman strength, the "cold hard mouth / of the world"; not to espouse it, exactly, but to ponder it from a safer distance. The worn and familiar person of her opening lines, the old fisherman, is displaced in her ending by a much harder element, something that rebukes the human. Bishop has gone from the easy, knowing ways of the social world ("he was a friend of my grandfather," she says of the fisherman—Bishop was raised partly in Nova Scotia) to the ruthlessness of time, which she names "historical." Historical knowledge, since it is "flowing, and flown," immerses us in a destructive element, and then erases us and our intimacies; it silences all life stories.

Like Wordsworth and Bishop, James Joyce in his short story "The Dead" confronts his beginning with his ending; he puts the first and last page of "The Dead" at opposing poles. And like Bishop in "At the Fishhouses," Joyce moves from the social to the impersonal. The first sentence of "The Dead," as Hugh Kenner pointed out in his book *Joyce's Voices,* presents an example of free indirect style, in which the author gives you the feel of a character without actually quoting his or her words. (Flaubert, the master of this technique, uses free indirect style in the passage from *Madame Bovary* that I discussed in Rule Three, "Identify the Voice.")

"The Dead" begins, "Lily, the caretaker's daughter, was literally run off her feet." The phrase "literally run off my feet" is something that Lily herself might say, though she is not quoted directly. The pleasurable wrongness of the expression (you can't be literally run off your feet, only figuratively) marks it as the usage of a speaker who attacks the English language with gusto, and who enjoys exaggerating for a good cause (Joyce, or his Lily, is describing the bustle that attends the preparation of the annual dance given by the Morkan sisters).

The opening of Joyce's story deceives us a little; the author leads us in a wrong direction. "The Dead" will turn out to be a poised and ceremonious story, not at all a frantic one. The opening note of haste yields eventually to a slow grief: the separation of two characters, Gabriel Conroy and his wife Gretta, across a distance of time and desire. Joyce's first sentence, whose liveliness cuts against the title "The Dead," is a feint; Lily's girlish quiver will fade away as the tale proceeds toward its somber ending. That ending, like Joyce's beginning, uses free indirect style. In the story's final pages, Gretta confesses to Gabriel that she is thinking of Michael Furey, a boy who loved her and who died at seventeen. Gabriel looks out the window: "A few light taps upon the pane made him turn to the window. It had begun to snow again. He watched sleepily the flakes, silver and dark, falling obliquely against the lamplight. The time had come for him to set out on his journey westward."

We hear Gabriel's voice here, forlorn and yet strangely comforted. Gretta's dead admirer Michael was from Galway, in the west of Ireland; in country Irish parlance, to "go west" is to die. Identifying with Michael and sympathetically answering his wife's grief for the lost youth, Gabriel imagines himself too journeying westward, toward the shadowy realm of the dead.

The final sentence of "The Dead" offers a deliberate, incantatory rhythm. Gabriel is still watching the snow and, Joyce writes, "His soul swooned slowly as he heard the snow falling faintly through the universe and faintly falling, like the descent of their last end, upon all the living and the dead." You can't get much farther away from that first sentence about Lily being run off her feet. Here "falling faintly," smooth and soft, matches "faintly falling"; there is something elegant and entranced, something ghostly, about Joyce's picture of slow, swooning descent. (Compare Bishop's "flowing, and flown.") He conjures up the end that awaits us all: death. When we put the beginning of "The Dead" next to its ending, we have a poignant contradiction: the happy, rushed preparation for a dance and the quiet peace of death. The extreme contrast speaks to the breadth of Joyce's art, its ability to move between the lively and the solemn. Yet the contrast is also a parallel. There are two ways of uniting people, the busy social interaction of the Morkan sisters' dance and the silent communion of the dead. In the conclusion of "The Dead," Gabriel and Gretta, both thinking of the lost Michael Furey, are joined with him in spirit. This final, shadow-haunted sympathy furnishes a defining and conclusive bond among Joyce's characters, of a kind that could not be supplied by the earlier to-and-fro of the Morkans' party: so the movement from the first to the last page of "The Dead" suggests.

Whenever you think of the beginning of a work together with its ending, you will receive an insight into the work's argument like the ones we've just received about "The Dead," "At the Fishhouses" and "Resolution and Independence." The structure of a piece of literature tells you something you need to know about the way it thinks; openings and conclusions are the irreplaceable backbone of structure. In Rule Eleven, "Find the Parts," I will talk more about the structure of literary works; in the next rule, "Identify Signposts," I will give some examples of how different sections of a work engage in dialogue with one another.

Rule Six: Identify Signposts

A book's signposts tell you what to pay attention to, where to direct yourself in your journey through its pages. Signposts can take the form of key words, key images, key sentences or passages. Think of reading as a kind of travel; signposts help you map out your itinerary. Writers use signposts in order to direct the reader: a striking anecdote, a short sentence that makes you sit up and pay attention, a summary declaration that asks for your assent.

The signposts in a book resemble, contrast, and argue with one another. They are like busy hubs in a network of air or train travel—or, to vary the metaphor, like islands in an archipelago: nearly continuous with one another, and exhibiting a family resemblance.

As you develop your skills at slow reading, you will want to stop at as many signposts as you can, to carefully absorb the details of your book. Going at a deliberate pace, you will be ready to consider the book's central images, the knots that tie together the various strands that run through its pages. The web woven by such threads can be a nightmarish one. Shakespeare's *Macbeth* returns again and again to a few ominous images—blood, a baby, a knife. These motifs are as much aural as they are visual: Shakespeare's insistent use of the words "do" and "deed" hammers out a dreadful music as *Macbeth* goes on. Or the web of signposts can give a serene and joyful effect, like the one produced by the repeated pictures of the child in Wordsworth's *Immortality Ode:* a poem that as it goes on rises to somber maturity, but still clings to the innocence of boyhood.

Signposts are not merely useful; they are vital. W. B. Yeats, in his essay on his sublime precursor poet Shelley, wrote that "there is for every man some one scene, some one adventure, some one picture that is the image of his secret life, for wisdom first speaks in images." An image in a book can be the key that unlocks you, that gives you to yourself. It finds you, as much as you find it.

My first instance of a signpost passage, a hub of meaning, comes from the Hebrew Bible. The Bible is full of such cynosures: busy, powerfully expressive textual centers. In Genesis, especially, nearly every chapter is a hub linked to other hubs, so strong are the ties that bind the parts of the narrative together. The whole of Genesis is a web that persuades the reader to match episodes with one another, to delve into the likenesses and the disagreements among the far-flung sections of the story.

Here's an example of how biblical literature benefits from deep reading of a key passage, one that makes intriguing connections with earlier and later episodes. In Chapter 29 of Genesis, Jacob, the archetypal struggler and wayfarer, has come to the land of his uncle Laban to seek a wife. He encounters a group of shepherds, who tell him that it is not yet time to give water to the sheep; a heavy stone still lies on the mouth of the well. Then, with stunning effect, Laban's daughter Rachel, Jacob's cousin, appears:

> And it came to pass, when Jacob saw Rachel the daughter of Laban his mother's brother, and the sheep of Laban his mother's brother, that Jacob went near, and rolled the stone from the well's mouth, and watered the flock of Laban his mother's brother. And Jacob kissed Rachel, and lifted up his voice, and wept. And Jacob told Rachel that he was her father's brother, and that he was Rebekah's son: and she ran and told her father. And it came to pass, when Laban heard the tidings of Jacob his sister's son, that he ran to meet him, and embraced him, and kissed him, and brought him to his house. And he told Laban all these things. And Laban said to him, Surely thou art my bone and my flesh.

This pungent, concentrated account, which I give in the King James Version, echoes an earlier event, when Abraham's servant discovers Rebekah, who will become Isaac's wife and Jacob's mother, at a shepherds' well. That earlier betrothal scene was far less impetuous, less radically impulsive, than this one; it was slow-paced and elaborately repetitive, unlike Jacob's striking feat of courtship. Chapter 29 tells us something about Jacob's ardent nature: not waiting for the shepherds to gather their flocks around the well, he rolls the stone away all by himself—a task that requires heroic strength. Jacob's burst of adrenaline clearly derives from the sight of Rachel, with whom he falls instantly in love.

The kiss that occurs between Jacob and Rachel is unique: this is the only instance in the Bible in which a man kisses a woman who is not his wife, a woman he has just met. (His rapture echoes his mother Rebekah's first view of his father Isaac. "When she saw Isaac, she lighted off the camel," the King James Version translates, though "fell off" is probably more accurate: the sight of Isaac knocks her off her camel.) Even more remarkable is how Jacob accompanies his kiss: he lifts up his voice and weeps. With Jacob's tears, a sign of an intense joy that blurs into grief, the story forecasts a tragedy: Rachel will die in childbirth.

In Chapter 29, the disaster of Rachel's death is still far in the future. As the action speeds on, Rachel runs to tell her father of Jacob's arrival, and then Laban runs to Jacob to embrace him. We are meant to compare Laban's kissing of Jacob with Jacob's earlier kissing of Rachel. The two kisses are signposts; they refer to each other, and provide a telling contrast. Laban will defraud Jacob. He promises him Rachel in marriage, but in fact, after Jacob has worked for Laban for seven years, he gives Jacob his other daughter, Leah. Jacob's kiss signifies wholehearted, dizzying passion; Laban's kiss signifies deceit.

Laban's comment, "Surely thou art bone of my bone and flesh of my flesh," is another signpost. Here Laban decisively echoes Adam's surprised, exultant cry when he beholds the woman created from him: "this one at last is bone of my bone and flesh of my flesh." We should notice the contrast: God has given the unsuspecting Adam the person who completes him, his other half, and he responds with astonished gratitude. Laban seizes a connection with his kinsman Jacob, whom he correctly implies is just as tricky a customer as he is.

When Jacob lifts up his voice and weeps, we see one more signpost. Jacob's tears remind us that his twin brother Esau cried bitterly when he discovered that Jacob, in a scene master-minded by the twins' incomparably shrewd mother Rebekah, had stolen the blessing that their dying father Isaac intended to give Esau. The parallel between Jacob's and Esau's weeping implies that these two twins will swap places: Jacob is not merely a winner; he too knows loss, when the love of his life, Rachel, dies. The Zohar, the wondrous compendium of Jewish mystical thought, states that the Messiah will not come until the tears of Esau have been exhausted: so ineradicable is the sorrow of Esau, the excluded one. Esau and Jacob will recon-cile, with an embrace and a kiss that recall those between Jacob and Laban, and Jacob and Rachel, in Chapter 29 of Genesis. But Esau, who will become the father of the Edomites, is still shut out of the covenant, exiled from the children of Israel. The delicate strength of the biblical narrative lies in the way it bal-ances concern for the chosen ones, like Jacob, and the ones left behind, like Esau; for rapturous success (Jacob's discovery of Rachel) and bitter loss (Rachel's death); for victorious deception and deception that fails. Jacob will eventually steal away from Laban in the night, taking with him Laban's two daughters; and so Jacob becomes the consummate trickster, as he savors his revenge on the deceitful Laban.

Through its signposts hinting at parallel episodes, Chapter 29 reaches backwards and forwards in the biblical story, from the creation of Eve to the death of Rachel, from Jacob's strug-gle with Esau (which begins in Rebekah's womb, as each twin fights the other for the privilege of coming out first) to his long-running contest with Laban. The more one thinks about a sin-gle chapter of Genesis, the more slowly and patiently one muses on its implications, the deeper its connections will seem with what comes before and after.

Written many centuries after the Hebrew Bible, Edith Wharton's *The House of Mirth* relies on the same techniques of signposting that the authors of the biblical text used: striking turns of phrase, similes and metaphors that leap out at the reader, dramatic events that echo one another. Wharton's novel, a runaway success when it was published in 1905, takes place at the dawn of the twentieth century. Wharton portrays the gossipy, backbiting milieu of the nouveau riche who spend weekends in the fashionable towns of the Hudson Valley: a brittle background for a tragic tale. *The House of Mirth* begins when Lily Bart, Wharton's troubled and troubling heroine, runs into a friend, Lawrence Selden, at Grand Central Station. The two take a stroll together, through the bustling, kaleidoscopic streets of midtown Manhattan. Selden steals a glance at Lily's exquisite face and artful hair, and reflects that "she must have cost a great deal to make . . . as though a fine glaze of beauty and fastidiousness had been applied to vulgar clay." Lily will indeed prove to be vulgar clay in the course of *The House of Mirth*. Her interests are material ones; she seeks an easy, money-cushioned life rather than an interesting one.

Selden's perception of Lily's true character, beneath her artificially beautiful appearance, is fleeting; a few pages later, when Lily visits him in his apartment, he indulges in a more romantic and mystified vision of her. As Lily studies herself in Selden's mirror and adjusts her veil, Wharton writes,

> The attitude revealed the long slope of her slender sides, which gave a kind of wild-wood grace to her outline—as though she were a captured dryad subdued to the conventions of the drawing room; and Selden reflected that it was the same streak of sylvan freedom in her nature that lent such savour to her artificiality.

Wharton is being rather wily here: she gives us the faulty point of view of her character Selden. Lily is in no sense dryad-like; intent on ease and security, she embodies no "sylvan free-dom." This is Selden fooling himself, inventing a Lily who doesn't exist. Wharton has here created a signpost, and a warn-ing one: she has sounded the alarm about Selden, letting us know that his sight has been falsified by the romantic gauze through which he sees Lily. We instinctively turn back a few pages to Selden's earlier sense of Lily as clay, mere base material with a fine finish, and we measure that more accurate assess-ment against his new infatuation. These two images, the vulgar clay and the captured dryad, are rival signposts, and the reader must decide which one is more accurate. Lily, at this early point in the novel, sparks ambivalence in us; by the time *The House of Mirth* draws to its grim conclusion, we are ready to think of her as the fool of the Ecclesiastes quotation that Whar-ton alludes to in her title ("the heart of fools is in the house of mirth"). The doomed Lily herself delivers the definitive judg-ment on her own character and fate, shortly before the end of Wharton's book. Here Lily is speaking, once again, to Selden, who has largely, but still not completely, overcome his love for her:

> "I have tried hard—but life is difficult, and I am a useless per-son. I can hardly be said to have an independent existence. I was just a screw or a cog in the great machine I called life, and when I dropped out of it I found I was of no use anywhere else. What can one do when one finds one only fits into one hole? One must get back to it or be thrown out into the rubbish heap—and you don't know what it's like in the rubbish heap!"

The blunt, brutally simple images in this speech—screw, cog, machine, hole, rubbish heap—mark it as the polar opposite of Selden's thoughts about Lily as a sylvan dryad, at the opening of *The House of Mirth*. Here at last is the bare truth, in Lily's own words. The signposts are there in the crude, matter-of-fact images that Lily uses to sum up her life. These are the two poles of Wharton's novel: aesthetic connoisseurship and grim naturalism. In expert, disturbing fashion, the author shifts gears between hardnosed reality and refined pretense.

Following Signposts Step-by-Step

It's time for a thorough, step-by-step example of how signposts work: for this exercise, slow, patient reading will be needed. Like Genesis and *The House of Mirth*, Shakespeare's *A Midsummer Night's Dream* portrays its leading characters by means of signposts: memorable images and turns of phrase. Let's see how a key signpost image, the moon, works in a wonderfully luxuriant passage, the opening lines of *A Midsummer Night's Dream*. This sparkling early comedy, with its bewildered young lovers and its troupes of fairies, including the irrepressible Puck, enchants nearly every reader or audience member. The many-sided strength of Shakespeare is inexhaustible; you can read Shakespeare year after year and still find new treasures on each rereading. And central images, like the moon in *Midsummer Night's Dream*, provide your sustaining signposts on your journey through the works of our Top Bard (as W. H. Auden called him), the greatest of all playwrights and poets.

A Midsummer Night's Dream begins with a conversation between Theseus, the legendary founder of Athens, and his Amazon bride Hippolyta, whom he has captured in battle. Philostrate, present here as well, is a minor character, one of Theseus's court officials. This much we learn by inspecting the dramatis personae, the list of characters that precedes the play.

Now for the opening lines of *Midsummer*. As we begin, Theseus and Hippolyta await their wedding:

Theseus

Now, fair Hippolyta, our nuptial hour
Draws on apace; four happy days bring in
Another moon: but, O, methinks, how slow
This old moon wanes! she lingers my desires,
Like to a step-dame or a dowager
Long withering out a young man's revenue.

Hippolyta

Four days will quickly steep themselves in night;
Four nights will quickly dream away the time;
And then the moon, like to a silver bow
New-bent in heaven, shall behold the night
Of our solemnities.

Theseus

Go, Philostrate,
Stir up the Athenian youth to merriments;
Awake the pert and nimble spirit of mirth;
Turn melancholy forth to funerals;
The pale companion is not for our pomp.

What should we notice about these first lines of the play? Let's take them slowly, and as we go along, look for the ruling signpost image. We can start with the fact that Shakespeare synchronizes the royal pair's "nuptial hour" with the coming of the new moon. That moon is already a prominent presence in these first lines; it will be important in the rest of the play, and we should be taking note of its prominence. Though Theseus, the Duke of Athens and conqueror of the Amazons, is a proud and powerful ruler, he must wait for the moon to change in order to marry Hippolyta. He is subject to something beyond his own will, and that something is not a political force, but a strange, shadowy goddess: the moon, which presides over the world of dreams. There's an age-old tendency to link the moon with witchcraft and with madness (lunacy); it seems to have a subtle, ghostly effect on us. Later in *A Midsummer Night's Dream*, Shakespeare will associate the moon with magical influence, and with the desires that sway his characters without their knowledge. Theseus's political authority faces off against what really governs this play, the lunar enchantments of Eros.

Though Theseus begins by announcing that the hour of marriage "draws on apace" (that is, at the appropriate speed), he reveals his impatience a few lines later: "But O, methinks, how slow / This old moon wanes!" The moon moves at its own languid pace, and Shakespeare expresses its soft and majestic rhythm by slowing down the progress of his poetry. The words "old moon wanes" give us three stressed syllables in a row; all three are monosyllables, as are the three words that precede them. Several stresses in a row slow down a line, as do monosyllabic words. (A later chapter of *Slow Reading in a Hurried Age*, "Reading Poetry," explains how to scan verse in order to determine which syllables are stressed and which are not.) Monosyllables—think Hamlet's "to be or not to be"—offer a more deliberate and steady feel than polysyllabic words, which are swift and dexterous.

We can turn to another play, *Macbeth*, to see an example of what Shakespeare can make polysyllables and monosyllables do when he evokes a signpost image: this time not the moon, but the ocean. At one of the many terrified and terrifying moments in his murderous career, Shakespeare's Macbeth wishes that the ocean could wash away the blood that stains his hands. He proclaims,

No; this my hand will rather
The multitudinous seas incarnadine,
Making the green one red.

That second line speeds forward with its two newfangled, many-syllabled words, "multitudinous" and "incarnadine" (to make red or pink). The third line loses the speed; it turns spellbound and lethal with its three single-syllable words. As with *Midsummer*'s "slow moon wanes," there are three deadly paced stresses in "green one red." In Macbeth's stricken vision the sea's green becomes one (all) red—a single, ineffably murderous color. The effect is chilling, hypnotic; it enshrines the baleful image of the ocean at the center of Macbeth's consciousness, and our own.

Back to *Midsummer,* and to that old moon. The moon is often seen as feminine, perhaps because women were thought to be more changeable than men, waxing and waning in their moods. Theseus says of the moon, "she lingers my desires": a striking phrase. Usually we use the word "linger" for something subtle, perhaps almost imperceptible: a scent, an impression, a doubt. Shakespeare relies on the unusual, and now long vanished, use of "linger" as a transitive verb, one with a direct object. Theseus could have said that the moon prevents or obstructs his desire for Hippolyta by refusing to change quickly enough—a tyrant's objection. Instead, he murmurs that the moon draws out his desires, somehow sharing control of them. He is speaking magically now, not politically. To linger is to remain; to linger something out means, in Renaissance English, to prolong it, as a trip to the *Oxford English Dictionary* (known as the OED) reveals (see Rule Seven, "Use the Dictionary").

The moon draws out Theseus's desires, then; but also frustrates them, like an old woman who, not yet dead, "wither[s] out" the money (revenue) of the young man who waits for her to die so he can inherit. The moon is a tease, both leading Theseus on and threatening to diminish ("wither out") his erotic impulse. Patient listeners to Shakespeare's text, we've learned so far that Theseus is an eager and anxious lover, and that he senses how the moon sways his desire.

On to Hippolyta. The captive Amazon answers her warrior prince Theseus in strange and sensual fashion: "Four days will quickly steep themselves in night;/ Four nights will quickly dream away the time . . ." She is casting a spell, weaving a web of words. Look at the metaphors she uses: steeping (a sensual soaking, gradual and pervasive); dreaming (a reminder of the play's title, and of the tone of gentle fantasy that enwraps Shakespeare's delicious comedy).

Hippolyta now shows the difference between her imagination and Theseus's. She matches her bridegroom's simile of the moon as step-dame or dowager with a much more high-flown, lyrical image. For her the moon is "like a silver bow / New-bent in heaven." Hippolyta evokes quite precisely the way the waning moon resembles a bent bow (fitting words for a woman warrior!). As she expresses it, the slivery remnant of moon is implicitly "new": it heralds the coming of marriage and the fulfilling of desire. Instead of being ready to shoot, though, the moon's tense, silver bow will "behold" the couple's "solemnities." An impression of rapturous stillness possesses the scene that Hippolyta paints with so few, so choice words. To behold is not just to see, but to witness: the word has an air of the momentous. "Solemnities" is a sophisticated term for a wedding or other important ceremony, and it is designed to convey the special gravity that Hippolyta attributes to the moon, its authority over time and event.

Finally, we get to see Theseus display his character in an imperious gesture. He tells his officer Philostrate to command mirth and "turn melancholy forth to funerals," as if he could change a mood by giving orders. Expel all sadness, strike up the band; so Theseus decrees. Intent on his nuptials, he wants a party. The "pale companion" he mentions is melancholy, which makes people wan and listless; but it also reminds us of the moon, which Theseus cannot change or banish. There are limits to his power as ruler. He can declare a celebration, but the true influence lurks behind the scenes: the moon and all she represents (love, magic, delusion). The truly "pert and nimble spirit" in the play belongs not to the sensible workaday world of Athens that Theseus governs, but to the fairies, who are allied to moon and night.

As you go further with *A Midsummer Night's Dream,* you will learn to contrast the rollicking, quarrelsome marriage of the fairy king and queen, Oberon and Titania, with the tense, reticent relationship between Theseus and Hippolyta; you will trace the abundant symbolism of moon, magic, and night, of vision and desire. You will notice a later passage in which "Cupid's fiery shaft" is "quenched in the chaste beams of the watery moon," and recall Hippolyta's simile of the moon as a bent bow. Shakespeare's great play is a whole, and any one of its scenes shines a light on some other scene, or character, or beautiful fragment of language. The play does this by relying on signpost images like that of the moon: central symbolic presences that tie the action together, making it unified the way that tonic and dominant keys unify a piece of music.

If you steep yourself *in A Midsummer Night's Dream,* you will see more and more of the signposts. More than any other English-language author, Shakespeare loads his work with moments that are not just gorgeous, but that make us think, and that make it worthwhile to pore over his text repeatedly. Each time we do so, we are more astounded by our best poet's power of invention. Keep your eye on Shakespeare's signposts, his core images and words, and you will get in tune with the way his plays work, how they create their effects in you.

Writers of lyric poetry depend on images as signposts: Keats's Grecian urn and his nightingale stand squarely in the middle of the odes to which they give their names, and Wallace Stevens recurs often to the sun, the sea, and, in his "The Auroras of

Autumn," the aurora borealis, which he depicts as a devouring snake, a heavenly theater, and then later as a "crown and diamond cabala." Images are especially important in poetry, but they play a crucial role in other genres too. Virginia Woolf's essay "The Death of the Moth" evokes its central image in its title. Joseph Conrad's short novel *Heart of Darkness* returns over and over to the picture suggested by its title: the corrupt heart of Kurtz, which Conrad's narrator Marlow encounters at the core of deepest, darkest Africa, and where a kernel of all-important truth might be found. Conrad counters this centripetal drive of his work with an opposing image early in *Heart of Darkness*. The meaning of his tale, Marlow suggests, will be brought out "as a glow brings out a haze"; it will signify as moonshine does on a misty night. Meaning turns out to be diffuse rather than conclusive. The degradation of Kurtz does not prove anything; there is no secret to Kurtz's evil, nothing that can explain him.

Conrad uses the image of the glow bringing out a haze to illustrate the distinctive atmosphere he creates in *Heart of Darkness:* fraught and thick, full of cloudy, deceptive implication. Shakespeare relies on the moon in *A Midsummer Night*'s dream to convey just the opposite atmosphere: pellucid, light-tripping, gracefully magical. But both Conrad and Shakespeare depend on the images they place at the center of their books. These images help to shape their works, and help to guide us through them. They are signposts that lead us to the crucial meanings of these authors' work.

Rule Seven: Use the Dictionary

"The dictionary is my Scheherazade. Plus it can spell Scheherazade," writes the novelist Maxine Hong Kingston. The dictionary is indeed a Scheherazade: an enchantress, a storyteller. The more you visit it, the more alluring it becomes. Take the time to look up words that strike you as important, even if you think you already know their meaning. You'll be surprised at what you will learn from a good dictionary: dimensions of meaning that you could never have figured out on your own. A crucial aspect of readerly patience is the willingness to rely on a dictionary: preferably the best dictionary of all, the OED, but at the very least a good unabridged one like the *American Heritage Dictionary*. (Make sure your dictionary is unabridged: it is well worth the investment, since you will return to this thick volume over and over in the course of your reading life.) The OED, which is also available as an e-book, is the product of a heroic effort to compile a dictionary that would give the meanings of English words as those meanings changed over time. Abundant and helpful quotations illustrate each definition. (Simon Winchester's lively book *The Meaning of Everything* tells the extraordinary story of the OED; his *The Professor and the Madman* presents a dark, scandalous tale about one of the dictionary's contributors, a certified lunatic and Civil War veteran named W. C. Minor.)

The OED began publication in 1888, and volumes of it kept coming for the next forty years, until Z was reached. Supplements to the OED continue to appear up to the present day, as the English treasure house of words becomes ever-larger and ever more extravagant. (Recent additions include "gaydar," "grrrl," and "cyberslacking.") To browse this greatest of all dictionaries is an extraordinary experience: one wanders through centuries of authors, and watches from close up as English changes from the language of Chaucer and Shakespeare to that of Woolf, Beckett, and beyond.

You will enrich your reading experience immeasurably by consulting a copy of the OED—not constantly, but as often as you can without breaking the flow of your reading. You might not want to do this more than every half hour or so, but each time you do, you will be rewarded with fascinating information that will deepen your experience of the book open before you. Let's see how the OED can help us with the opening paragraphs of a classic book, Edmund Burke's *Reflections on the Revolution in France*. The Anglo-Irish Burke, a superbly adept conservative thinker, is also a consummate prose stylist. He shows his sly and reflective manner from the very beginning of his *Reflections,* which responds to "a very young gentleman at Paris," Charles-Jean-François Depont. Depont's excited letter to Burke had celebrated the French Revolution, then in full swing. *Reflections on the Revolution in France,* Burke's judicious, eloquent answer to Depont, stretches over some three hundred pages. Writing in 1790 in the thick of the turmoil, Burke is at times passionate, even overheated: his *Reflections* reaches its climax in a traumatic glimpse of Marie Antoinette's imprisonment (she was later executed). "I thought ten thousand swords must have leapt from their scabbards to avenge even a look that threatened her with insult," Burke lamented. "But the age of chivalry is gone." Such show-stealing melodrama is part of Burke's personality: he hams it up with utter sincerity. But he is also calculating and careful, as the very first page of his book shows.

Here is the beginning of *Reflections on the Revolution in France.* After a prefatory note, Burke commences his answer to Depont:

Dear Sir,

You are pleased to call again, and with some earnestness, for my thoughts on the late proceedings in France. I will not give you reason to imagine that I think my sentiments of such value as to wish myself to be solicited about them. They are of too little consequence to be very anxiously either communicated or withheld. It was from attention to you, and to you only, that I hesitated at the time when you first desired to receive them. In the first letter I had the honor to write to you, and which at length I send, I wrote neither for, nor from, any description of men, nor shall I in this. My errors, if any, are my own. My reputation alone is to answer for them.

You see, Sir, by the long letter I have transmitted to you, that though I do most heartily wish that France may be animated by a spirit of rational liberty, and that I think you bound, in all honest policy, to provide a permanent body in which that spirit may reside, and an effectual organ by which it may act, it is my misfortune to entertain great doubts concerning several material points in your late transactions.

Try to get in tune with the quality that makes Burke's writing literature, his distinctive, rather arch way of talking. (If you're itching for him to get to the point, you've missed it.) Can you hear the dignity, the enormous tension, the elevated seriousness of these lines? If you can, then you are on your way to discovering what makes Burke one of the supreme prose stylists. These opening paragraphs are an elaborate ballet, in the course of which Burke performs his chosen role to perfection. First, he shows himself modest and reluctant to speak (his "sentiments" are not "of such value" that he wants to be asked for them), then fiercely proud (if he has made "errors," his "reputation alone is to answer for them"), then cunning and ironic ("it is my misfortune to entertain great doubts"). Burke the ironist says one thing but means another: he really thinks it is his good fortune, not his misfortune, to entertain doubts about the French Revolution.

Burke's polite, cutting paragraphs are laced with word choices that may be unfamiliar to us, cyberslackers of the twenty-first century that we are. "Sentiments" straddle the line between thoughts and feelings: the OED gives for "sentiment" (definition 6a) "What one feels with regard to something; mental attitude (of approval or disapproval, etc.); an opinion or view as to what is right or agreeable." Burke's *Reflections* express what he feels is right and, at the same time, what he thinks is right: his heart and his mind collaborate. Another key word is "solicit": "To entreat or petition (a person) for, or to do, something; to urge, importune; to ask earnestly or persistently" (OED definition 2a)—but also "To disturb, disquiet, trouble; to make anxious, fill with concern" (definition 1). The French gentleman has not just requested that Burke declare himself on the question of the revolution. He has also disquieted Burke, and the *Reflections* give the response of a restless soul. History has stirred Burke to a deeply personal crisis, and the crisis shows itself in his anxious, brilliant writing and thinking.

There are other words on Burke's first page that we might stumble over simply because we employ them differently. For Burke, "late" means *recent;* "material" means *consequential* or *significant.* Only the wise use of a dictionary can guide us to these meanings. If we really want to get the point of what Burke is saying, we may need to consult the dictionary three or four times on this first page alone.

The Victorian sage John Ruskin argued in *Sesame and Lilies,* his fervent polemic on education, that the dictionary is an essential tool for every serious, aspiring reader. Ruskin even insisted that the truly earnest reader purchase a Latin and a Greek dictionary as well as an English one. Even if you don't know any Latin or Greek, Ruskin wrote, you can still benefit from dictionaries in these languages, which allow you to trace key words that have passed into English. Consider words like philosophy (from Greek *philos,* friend or lover, and *sophia,* wisdom), ethics (from Greek *ethos,* character), and vanity (from Latin *vanus,* empty).

Ruskin was right: it is helpful to have Latin and Greek dictionaries, and even to study a little Latin or Greek; if you do, you will learn an immense amount about the meanings buried in English words. But if you don't go all the way with his advice, at least attune yourself to the presence of these languages in English by becoming aware of etymology. The *American Heritage Dictionary* has an intriguing appendix on etymology that lists the Greek, Latin, and Germanic roots of many English words.

Here's an instance of Ruskin's linguistic acumen, his flair for etymology as a tool of meaning. In *Sesame and Lilies,* Ruskin writes about the greatest elegy in English, John Milton's *Lycidas. Lycidas* honors a recently dead classmate of Milton's, Edward King, but it is also about the poet's own career and the ferocious worldly forces that threaten that career with extinction.

Perhaps the most formidable of the anti-poetic, anti-humanist threats that Milton contends with in *Lycidas* is the English church, which he sees as a hotbed of fraud and corruption. Milton interrupts the gentle pastoral fiction of the poem, in which he depicts himself and Edward King as shepherds, to denounce in high prophetic terms the bad eminences of the church:

> Blind mouths! That scarce themselves know how to hold
> A sheep-hook, or have learn'd aught else, the least
> That to the faithful herdman's art belongs!
> What recks it them? What need they? They are sped;
> And when they list, their lean and flashy songs
> Grate on their scrannel pipes of wretched straw;
> The hungry sheep look up, and are not fed . . .

We can hear the impatient, seething fury in Milton's language, his staccato, icily dismissive questions ("What recks it them? What need they?"). We listen to the harsh fingernail-scratch of "grate on their scrannel pipes of wretched straw" (and we look up "scrannel" in our dictionary). Feeble, well fed, and rotten within, these ecclesiastical wolves in shepherd's clothing know nothing of the "faithful herdman's art"; they let their hungry flock starve. The church authorities are bad shepherds—and, with their "lean and flashy songs," bad poets too, by extension.

But it is the opening two words of the passage from *Lycidas* that pose a problem for the reader, and it is these two words that Ruskin focuses on: "Blind mouths." "A 'Bishop' means 'a person who sees,'" Ruskin writes, and "a 'Pastor' means 'a person who feeds'": "The most unbishoply character a man can have is therefore to be Blind. / The most unpastoral is, instead of feeding, to want to be fed,—to be a Mouth."

By relying on his Latin and his Greek, Ruskin unlocks the logic of Milton's small, pointed phrase. The Greek *episkopos,* a watcher or overseer, and only later a church official, stands behind bishop; Latin *pastor,* shepherd (derived from the verb *pascere,* to graze) stands behind our English word pastor. Etymological truth, Milton shows, blasts the church's lies. The sheep look up, but the bishop cannot see them; the pastor ignores the obligation to nourish his flock.

Ruskin, in his reading of Milton, offers an inspiring example of the places that the dictionary can take you. Use your dictionary, not just for words you don't know the meaning of, but for words that interest you. Rely on the OED or the *American Heritage Dictionary* as a way of pursuing questions. The better your question—the more substantial your interest in a word—the better the dictionary will serve you.

Rule Eight: Track Key Words

This rule follows from my consideration of signposts in Rule Six and my injunction to use the dictionary in Rule Seven. Key words are the vital threads that allow you to trace the argument of a book: to follow the drama of meaning that unveils itself in stages, from first page to last.

With key words, as with all the rules, patience is required. Patient, slow, and careful reading will let you see the landscape of a book fully. When you open a book, if you are a patient reader, you will be ready to find the words that jut out, the ones that capture the imagination with a sudden, surprising twist of meaning. Patience is needed in your quest to trace the peaks of a book: to look out for its significant words, and to see how the author puts these words at the center of the book's landscape.

Some famous books, like Machiavelli's *The Prince,* nimbly alter the definitions of key terms as they progress. Such an author gives a reader notorious hardship, but also great excitement. Machiavelli makes readers alert themselves to the difficulty of defining words like power, glory, and fortune. We are forced to assume an active role, and through this exercise we understand far more than if Machiavelli had laid down firm, inflexible definitions for us. Plato's dialogues offer another instance of beautifully controlled planning. He designs an enticing labyrinth for the reader, in which particular words are both the tantalizing obstacles in our way and the goals of our seeking. Plato's reader has to remain constantly aware of how Socrates and his conversational partners shift the meanings of these key words.

I will examine Machiavelli and Plato in a few pages. First, let's go back to Burke for a moment in order to investigate one of his key terms in *Reflections on the Revolution in France* (which I quoted and discussed in Rule Seven, "Use the Dictionary"): "rational liberty."

An author usually doesn't unveil the meaning of a central term right away; you need to wait for, and work for, that meaning. We just don't yet know what Burke means in his second paragraph when he tells the young gentleman to whom he is writing, and us as well, that he "heartily wish[es] that France may be animated by a spirit of rational liberty." In the phrase "rational liberty," Burke's emphasis is clearly on "rational." What is the difference between rational and irrational liberty? What kind of freedom does Burke value, what kind does he despise, and why? In the course of his 300 pages, Burke will overflow with explanation. For now we can only pause, taking careful note of the author's phrase, and waiting to see how his central idea, rational liberty, develops. Similarly, we will in time learn what kind of "permanent body" and "effectual organ" Burke thinks a revolution needs: these are the legislative instruments he finds lacking in the jubilant, violent new France. A patient reader of Burke notes the beginning of these two discussions, on rational liberty and on the political institutions that a revolution ought to put in place, and waits for the author's answers. We can't expect the answers to come immediately; in fact, the answers may change in the course of the work.

Here slow, patient reading is especially necessary, since Burke's formulations will not be clear until we delve deeper into the *Reflections,* and experience Burke's dogged yet suave presentation of his argument. Burke, who was an astonishingly confident orator, relies on all the subtle tricks of the speechmaker's art to explain his stance against the French radicals. When he finally unfolds his notion of rational liberty, we will be ready for it, having prepared ourselves by following the twists and turns of his book.

Machiavelli, like Burke, organizes his text around key words. One of Machiavelli's central words in *The Prince* is hard to translate: *virtù,* which is not the English virtue, with its hint of the self-righteous milksop, but rather something close to courage or strong daring. Another central word is *fortuna,* fortune. These two words battle against each other as *The Prince* charts its bold course, making arguments so bluntly unconventional that Machiavelli became infamous. He was thought to be a kind of devil for his approval of violent, deceptive tactics, which he argued were necessary to the man who seeks to achieve and retain power.

Fortune appears on the very first page of *The Prince,* in its dedicatory letter to Lorenzo de' Medici (the book was first dedicated to another Medici, Giuliano; after Giuliano's death, Machiavelli decided to direct his advice about ruling a state to Lorenzo). Machiavelli had worked for the Florentine Republic, but lost his job when the Republic fell and the Medici returned to rule the city in 1512. A year later, in 1513, the Medici tortured Machiavelli when he fell under suspicion of plotting against them; that same year, forced into exile in the country, Machiavelli wrote *The Prince* as a gift for his Medici torturers. The book is his iron-willed attempt to prove his usefulness to the Medici, and by doing so to get back into the political game.

Machiavelli ends his dedicatory letter, on the first page of *The Prince,* with a self-description: he is one "who has suffer[ed] the bitter and sustained malignity of fortune." Fortune here, as Lorenzo must have recognized, is a euphemism for the cruel efficiency of Machiavelli's Medici persecutors. Fortune in a different and wider sense, the unpredictable turn of events, will, over the course of Machiavelli's book, become the most serious factor in the career of the prince. (The prince that Machiavelli describes is no particular person, but an amalgam of various rulers from the past and present.)

In the penultimate chapter of *The Prince,* Machiavelli offers two directly opposed descriptions of fortune's power. Near the chapter's beginning, in a signpost image, he compares fortune to

> one of those torrential streams which, when they overflow, flood the plains, rip up trees, and tear down buildings, wash the land away here and deposit it there; everyone flees before them . . . yet this does not mean that men cannot take countermeasures while the weather is still fine, shoring up dikes and dams, so that when the waters rise again, they are either carried off in a channel or confined where they do no harm.
>
> (translated by Robert M. Adams)

Machiavelli here implies that you can prepare for the hurricane-strength onslaught of fortune at its worst. Indeed, if you are a prince, you need to prepare with steely fortitude: you must dam up fortune's rude stream and ensure your safety.

But on the next page Machiavelli concludes that fortune will always defeat such preparations; the very point of fortune is that it inflicts unprecedented change on us. We cannot anticipate what will happen next, and so are in constant danger of being crushed, no matter what we do. "No man, however prudent, can adjust to such radical changes," Machiavelli writes. "Not only because we cannot go against the inclination of nature, but also because when one has always prospered by following a particular course, he cannot be persuaded to leave it." Machiavelli ends his chapter with a change of course of his own: after admitting that fortune defeats the brave, he changes his mind and, in a remarkable vision, advocates manhandling fortune. "But I do feel this," he writes,

> that it is better to be rash than timid, for Fortune is a woman, and the man who wants to hold her down must beat and bully her. We see that she yields more often to men of this stripe than

to those who come coldly toward her. Like a woman, too, she is always a friend of the young, because they are less timid, more brutal, and take charge of her more recklessly.

(translated by Robert M. Adams)

The strong man, the man of *virtù,* can win by beating up fortune, Machiavelli now suggests in his flamboyantly misogynistic simile. But he has just demonstrated to us that fortune is far too elusive and unpredictable to be bullied into submission in this way. Machiavelli contradicts himself so that he can play a sophisticated game, one in which he assumes a double role: the weary skeptic who knows that when fortune rages, men fall; and the enthusiast of power who recommends the most brutal and cunning tactics, since they have the best chance of winning out. Is fortune a woman, or a violent, rushing river—both of which can potentially be disciplined? Or is it a force so ineluctable that it can't even be pictured in metaphor? Fortune is Machiavelli's goddess as much as *virtù* is; he wields these terms with a shrewdness that makes them change their meaning moment by moment. The changes enlarge the meaning of both fortune and *virtù.* The spectrum of meaning Machiavelli creates lets him take control of his bristling and complex subject matter, the ways of power and the ways of chance in political life.

Plato's *Republic,* like Machiavelli's *Prince,* is a book about an ideal, a fiction of greatness. In both these texts, the author credits the object of his praise with a victory that he justifies by appealing to certain key terms: the true prince must exhibit the perfect triumph of *virtù* over fortune; the true republic must be perfectly just. But these key terms—Machiavelli's *virtù* and fortune, Plato's justice—prove slippery. In the tumultuous first book of the *Republic,* which is packed with argument and action, Plato brings into contention several different senses of the word justice. Does being just mean following what tradition teaches you to do, mouthing the familiar words of authority figures? Does it, instead, mean figuring out for yourself what a just action is? It is just for each person to have what he deserves; but who knows best what someone deserves? (Perhaps some people deserve to have injustice happen to them.) Plato's various and conflicting definitions of justice—being pious in matters of tradition, being fair, giving people what they are owed, giving people what's good for them—are all still very much around today.

Socrates and his young friends Glaucon and Adeimantus try to sort through these complications in the *Republic*'s Book 1, but they seem to be getting nowhere. When a climactic point of frustration has been reached, the hungry, wolf-like sophist Thrasymachus leaps into the conversational fray and pushes a shocking idea: what's called justice is only the advantage of the stronger. Strong people, the ones in control, do injustice, thoroughly and remorselessly; but they succeed because they are experts at *seeming* just. We're mere dumb suckers if we believe this trick, Thrasymachus howls. Moreover, he says, we should aim at becoming strong ourselves, at deceiving others into thinking that we are just, so we can hoodwink them. This is Thrasymachus's pitch: it's better to appear just than to be just, since being just means becoming a victim of the unjust people, the ones with power.

Thrasymachus's power-hungry reading of justice as a mere sham throws a wrench in the conversational works of the *Republic*. Socrates is noticeably flustered, and starts a counterattack. At the end of Book 1 of the *Republic*, Socrates begins a steep uphill climb: he argues that being just is good for you, even if the world punishes you for it by torturing or killing you. Socrates has become a strident absolutist on the question of justice, but, in spite of his efforts, we still don't know what justice is at the end of Book 1. Nor do we know, at least not for sure, at the end of the *Republic*. Plato's point in the *Republic* is not to provide an ironclad definition of justice but to show why, for all our struggling over this cherished concept, we still can't come up with a persuasive way of defining it, one that everyone will agree on. The only thing we do all agree on is that we want to find that definition.

There's frustration in Plato's wrestling with the word justice, but there is also high reward for the reader. Stay tuned in to what Plato is doing, and you will gradually begin to see the world with new eyes. Your sense of Plato's other key terms— truth, beauty, Eros—will, like justice, be hard to capture in a single sentence. Instead, Plato's way with these words will expand within you, coloring your thinking as you ponder him more closely.

Confronted with writers like Plato or Machiavelli or Burke, who rely on elusive yet frequently repeated terms, you must be, above all else, patient: you must track the key words that these writers use and watch their shifting appearances. You will be repaid by a newly vivid sense of what such important words can do, and of how writers use them to accomplish their most crucial work: opening new perspectives in the reader.

Rule Nine: Find the Author's Basic Thought

Press yourself to discover the fundamental question that animates an author. This is perhaps the most challenging of all the rules; usually, it requires long acquaintance with the author's work. You won't get there right away. But with time, you will come closer and closer to a sense of the living core of an author's project, the basic thought behind it.

Imagine someone asking you, "What is that book you're reading about?" Then try to find the deepest and most rewarding answer to the question. You'll need to think about the possibilities that lurk in the word "about." Chaucer's *Canterbury*

Tales is not, except in the most trivial sense, about a collection of pilgrims on their way to the shrine of St. Thomas à Becket. Instead, it's about how a sympathetic appreciation of personalities can coexist with a satirical consciousness of their all-too-human faults, so that sympathy and satire comment on each other. The sympathy belongs to Chaucer's compassionate pilgrim-narrator; the satire, to the author who stands at the shoulder of his narrator, quietly pointing out the Chaucerian narrator's shortsightedness.

There are usually several basic thoughts to be found in an author. When you try to define the basic thought, you're not looking for a single right answer, but for the most essential truth you can get to about the work and its writer. You might see Shakespeare's work as a subtle attack on heroic, warlike values; or as a long story of men who rebel against their dependence on women, until the rebellion yields, in Shakespeare's late romances, to reconciliation. Critics divide: the first reading has been advocated by Mark Edmundson; the second, by C. L. Barber and Richard Wheeler. Neither interpretation negates the other.

One of our greatest thinkers, Plato, zeroes in on the basic thought of Greek tragedy, a form toward which he shows utmost suspicion. Plato asks after the motive of tragedy: What its goal is; why it pleases; and what view of the world it persuades us of. This may seem a strange way of thinking about art—as a means to persuade us that some particular picture of the world is the correct one—but it is Plato's way.

Tragedy, according to Plato, is the democratic art par excellence because it subscribes to the most widely shared idea: that the most powerful life is the best life. "To have all things happen according to the commands of one's own soul": Stephen Salkever sees in this sentence, from the *Laws,* the key to Plato's notion of how tragedy works. The sacrifice of the hero in tragedy, paradoxically, fulfills this fantasy of personal power. Even when the hero is crushed, his fate increases our feeling of potent mastery, whenever we read a tragedy or see it on stage. We want Clytemnestra to butcher her husband Agamemnon, and make his blood pour down like rain; we want Oedipus to blind himself, shouting to the heavens, his face streaming with gore. We take dominion over these brutal scenes; we are satisfied.

Plato suggests that Homer and the tragic poets are demagogues: they teach that the greatest good is living as one likes, that power and mastery are happiness. The joy of verbally crushing your opponent in a sophistic argument is like killing him in battle, the triumphant climax in which Homer's epic heroes exult. When we watch or read tragedy, we experience a vindictive satisfaction whether the hero is destroyed (like Sophocles's Oedipus) or triumphant (like Aeschylus's Orestes, in the *Oresteia*). Sophocles's *Electra* celebrates its heroine's revenge on her evil mother Clytemnestra, and by doing so stokes the audience's vengeful souls. This is tragedy's stock in trade, the persuasive, passionate jolt that Plato finds so objectionable, so dangerous.

Sophocles himself seems to concede, at least in *Electra*, the point of Plato's critique. Sophocles's chorus overpraises Electra's victory, seeing it as an act of wisdom rather than just thrilled vengeance on an enemy. Sophocles reveals a gap between how we justify tragic catharsis and how we experience it. There is, he implies, a crucial distance between a tragedy's shatteringly intense catharsis and the justification it claims for the catharsis: the justification, which comes second, furnishes a less-than-plausible excuse for the tragic audience's indulgence in the cathartic feeling of power, which comes first. When Electra glories in the death of her mother (as her brother Orestes administers the bloody strokes), she is not wise, but rather taunting and ecstatic: full of the godlike satisfaction that comes from turning the tables, she crushes her persecutor Clytemnestra. This split between feeling and explanation occurs also in Sophocles's *Oedipus the King*. We enjoy the spectacle of Oedipus's suffering not because we find him to be at fault, but because we passionately respond to his weakness. Oedipus's weakness, the fact that he is destroyed by an inexplicably cruel fate, feeds our souls. This feeling can never be explained by the reason behind Oedipus's punishment at the hands of the gods, for there is no such reason. Sophocles knows the rift between emotional response and explanation—this is the basic thought behind *Oedipus* and *Electra*.

The difference between the passion of Jesus, seen as a literary narrative, and the pathos of the Greek tragic hero is that there is no split between emotion and judgment in the Christian story as there is in the tragic one. The pathos we feel when we read about Jesus's martyrdom is meant to coincide with our discovery of his all-dominating significance. In the Garden of Gethsemane episode, which presages the crucifixion, Luke says of Jesus, "And being in an agony he prayed more earnestly: and sweat was as it were great drops of blood falling down to the ground" (Luke 22.43–44, King James Version). Jesus's response to his impending tragedy is prayer, an address to God the father; and, the text implies, so should we too answer the hero's agony. We are to learn the true, divinely borne significance of the story; Jesus's passion reinforces that significance. There is no chasm between emotion and explanation as there is in Sophocles. This coherence of cataclysmic event and all-embracing meaning, the redemption of humanity through the god-man's death, is the basic thought of the Christian gospels.

The basic thought of Homer's *Iliad* is utterly different from that of the Gospels, or of Sophocles. Homer suggests that the art of the poem itself is needed to transform the merely natural fate of humans. We inescapably end our lives as dead bodies, but we have a chance at glory, a chance that Homer's artistry alone can give us. Yet Homer adds that art cannot deny the untamable fact of death; his poetry recognizes that nature, in its brute power, outstrips art.

Nature looms over the Homeric battlefield, and its lethal significance is obvious. We see it on the first page of the *Iliad*, when, with savage irony, Homer describes the bodies of his dead warriors as "spoils for dogs and birds." The word "spoils" (*helôria* in Greek) is here a cruel joke. Spoils in the *Iliad* are characteristically the armor of a dead hero, stripped from his body by his triumphant enemy: the dead warrior's armor gives honor to his conqueror. A vulture can't eat bronze, the *Iliad*'s first page reminds us. The dogs and birds go straight for the dead body, eager to devour it; they don't care about a cultural symbol like the gleaming armor of the vanquished, carried high and admired by the winning soldier's peers. If you are one of Homer's men, whether Greek or Trojan, the point of your career is to kill bravely in battle, to become famous for your prowess even if you die young. Nature will reduce you to a rotting corpse, exactly equivalent to every other rotting corpse. This is why Homer, the maestro of heroic fame, needs to transform death into poetic art. Yet there's a caveat: all the while Homer knows, and subtly tells us, that dying has nothing whatever to do with art; when taken on its own terms (which are, of course, final), death always wins.

Homer's *Iliad* relies on irony, which is the poet's way of knowing, and telling us, the unbridgeable distance between death and art. One example is the death of Hector's charioteer Cebriones at the hands of Patroclus, Achilles's devastating, war-like companion. When Patroclus dies, Achilles will mourn him with a radical, life-denying pathos. Showing his glory before he is killed, Patroclus stands in for the reluctant Achilles on

the battlefield, and, as Achilles's representative, he exudes the
unmatched violence of the Achillean style, the godlike taste for
a victory heightened by malice. Patroclus hits Cebriones with a
sharp stone, smashing his skull and popping out his eyeballs.
Cebriones "flip[s] backward / From the chariot like a diver,"
Homer reports; and now Patroclus mocks him:

> "What a spring the man has! Nice dive!
> Think of the oysters he could come up with
> If he were out at sea, jumping off the boat
> In all sorts of weather, to judge by the dive
> He just took from his chariot onto the plain."
>
> (translated by Stanley Lombardo)

This savage speech is not enough: the next moment, Homer
tells us, Patroclus rushes like a wounded, maddened lion at Cebriones's corpse.

Patroclus's irony in his brief speech is exultant. He announces
over Cebriones's dead body that, far from war, Cebriones would
have made a great diver for oysters: a humble, peaceful occupation, one that requires great skill. You were skillful in your
death, Patroclus tells the charioteer whom he has so swiftly,
implacably slain.

When he describes the supposed gracefulness of Cebriones's
death, Patroclus delivers a sublime joke. Cebriones does not
intend to impress his killer with an adroit swan dive: his plunge
is sheer accident. In the dreadful face of the death meted out by
Patroclus, artful action is the furthest thing from his mind.
Homer's brilliant handling of this scene displays his supreme
talent for irony, the instantly recognizable signature of the
greatest epic poet of all time. When Patroclus fights for Cebriones's armor, he is a lion, the most ruthless of all predators: wild
and furious, not artless at all—the very opposite of the oyster-
diver. Patroclus's triumph over Cebriones shows Homer's basic

thought: that artfulness, the poet's credo, can take only a fragile stand against the force of mortality. Death, the ravening
lion, is the real master; it outdoes the precious designs made by
art. There is a further tragic twist: a page or so later, Hector
will be compared to a lion when he kills the momentarily triumphant Patroclus, and Hector's act will then bring on the
fierce vengeance of Achilles.

Let's move on to a modern instance of an author's basic
thought. The writings of W. B. Yeats revolve around the twin
poles of love and heroism. Yeats works through at least two basic thoughts in his career, both of them sublime ironies. The
first thought is that the tragedy of sexual love is, as Yeats puts
it, "the perpetual virginity of the soul." We expect to be transformed by love, but we remain the sole self we were when we
started: inexperienced, virginal. Yeats's lifelong devotion to Maud
Gonne—when he met her at age twenty-three, he wrote, "the
troubling of my life began"—was ultimately hollow-hearted,
because neither Maud nor Yeats could break through an impasse,
the idealism that remains virginal. Yeats could not use his love
for Maud to rise to higher truths, in the way that Dante used his
love for Beatrice.

The second of Yeats's basic thoughts, related to the first,
touches the hero rather than the lover. A hero, Yeats believes, can
embody the truth but not know it. This is for Yeats an especially
crushing irony, because he yearns so fixedly after a self-knowledge
that in fact will never come. You must play a role, make a mask
or persona for yourself; there is always something heroic about
the mask you use to enter the fray, since the mask reveals you
through action. But because you, as the self-fashioned hero of
your own life, cannot know the final truth of that life—you can
only enact it—you remain subject to an irony that both magni-
fies and frustrates. For Yeats, heroic role-playing always, in an
exalted way, fools itself, and so action however noble is bound

to end in disappointment. But without such disappointment we would have only the recurrence of passion: an unreal, ceaseless dreaming. Disappointment purifies us; we need this private purgatory. Human desire, human passion, must do something other than merely dote on or cherish itself, Yeats insists: we must come up against the hard rocks of reality. Yet reality remains something we cannot know fully; we still play a role, and so are still wrapped in illusion. Making the dream solid, a thing of conviction, is Yeats's goal; but the ironies he crashes against in his vision turn us back into dreaming things after all.

William Blake, who was a pervasive influence on Yeats, is another writer whose work stages itself around a central thought. If you have children, it's tempting to believe that Blake, who had no children himself, is the central writer. Not that he has a childlike sense of humor, though he can be proudly silly at times. Instead, Blake perfects a brand of hard, glinting wit, and for that reason he can seem somewhat inhuman. He often exudes malice more than sympathy. But for all that, he speaks powerfully to our sense of childhood and its aftermath. Blake worries about our constant wish to divide innocence from experience; he sees how this distinction torments us, and recognizes in this fact the sign of its inadequacy. Blake's *Songs of Innocence and Experience* has frequently been misread. People assume that the poems enshrine a division between two states: the happy child and the grim, pessimistic adult. But Blake attacks this division, rather than upholding it. He does so by exploiting an ironic format: in *Songs of Innocence and Experience*, the author disagrees with the poems' speakers. Entrapped consciousnesses speak Blake's poems, personae caught in prisons of their own making. Some of the prisons are innocent ones, others are built on the grim terrain of experience; but they are all partial, and so Blake rejects them.

Blake commands us to move beyond what he calls a cloven fiction: the view that life is permanently divided between the naïve, fresh, and vulnerable world of the child and the relentlessly frustrated, fearful, guilty adult world. What if this divided way of thinking is itself a means to keep us in bondage, by telling us what Blake deems an entrapping, stony falsehood: that freedom and creativity belong only to a childhood that must yield in the end to the sad realm of fact, and that this realm, the gray, grown-up world, is the only imaginable reality. Blake proposes a higher creativity, one that exists beyond the innocence / experience distinction. He wants us to free ourselves, to be unhampered by the law-bound dichotomy we impose, through lack of imaginative power, on our lives. Such creativity, he argues, could redeem the world, "for every thing that lives is Holy."

Blake, like Yeats, and like Homer, focuses all of his energies on a basic thought or thoughts, a matter of imaginative life or death. When you know an author well enough, you will be increasingly drawn to his or her basic thought, the burning flame that illuminates and gives life to everything the author writes.

Rule Ten: Be Suspicious

You should cultivate a suspicion of your judgments about the characters in a book. All too often, before you get very far along, you've already decided which characters you like and which ones you don't, who's evil and who's good. Such easy judgments prevent you from reading sufficiently deeply; it's best to resist them, since every good author wants to frustrate your desire for simple meanings. Edgar in *King Lear* seems to be a noble innocent, and his brother Edmund a heartless villain: but Edgar bears a punishing guilt for his failure to reveal himself to his father Gloucester, and Edmund takes a turn for the good at the play's end that surprises both himself and us. Two of Lear's daughters, Goneril and Regan, are revealed as monsters in the play's second act; but Goneril's complaint about Lear's raucous knights looks reasonable enough in Act 1. Lear himself can be seen as either a near-holy victim of persecution or a tyrannical, utterly impossible father. No matter how we want to interpret *Lear*'s characters, the play makes us aware that there are other, contrary possibilities. We must suspect our inclination to pick favorites when we read Shakespeare's play.

My main instance of the need to develop suspicion as you read is Homer's *Odyssey*. Homer, along with the Bible, forms one of the two primal sources of Western literary tradition. Despite the open, sunlit clarity of his style, Homer sets a number of traps for the reader; he forces you to stay wary about your own interpretive desires. In this discussion, I will focus on Homer's most splendid creation: Odysseus, the epic wanderer and hard-bitten struggler at the heart of the *Odyssey*. Homer uses Odysseus's career to warn us about seeing things too simply. The *Odyssey* demands that we suspect our snap judgments: our natural leanings to praise and blame characters, to see them as more straightforward and monolithic than they are.

The *Odyssey* is one of the most fulfilling experiences you can have as a reader. It has everything: adventure, war, love and marriage, mind-spinning storytelling. Homer's Odysseus is at the heart of the action, but in my comments I will also consider the suitors for Penelope's hand, the squabbling, riotous crowd who dominate Odysseus's house while he spends his twenty years away at sea. In the case of the suitors, as in that of Odysseus, Homer keeps readers on their toes. He forces us to muse over, and to change, our judgments about the characters he creates. In other words, he makes us suspicious of our own desire to read in a way that is one-sided and facile, to divide characters into easy categories and give them what we think they deserve.

In this analysis of the *Odyssey*, I refer to a few Greek words. My intent is not to make the Greekless reader feel inferior— Homer's *Odyssey* is a wonderful experience in any language, and millions of people have enjoyed and understood it without knowing a word of Greek—but to offer some taste of how subtle and precise Homer's word choices really are.

The *Odyssey* argues with itself about Odysseus's character, and the argument centers on his governing trait, his cleverness. (The poem's opening invocation famously gives him the adjective *polutropos:* the man of many twists and turns.) Homer urges us to read against the grain: to counter the *Odyssey*'s frequent emphasis on Odysseus's unmatchable cleverness with a contrasting sense that cleverness might, at times, prove useless. The poet invites us to a dispute about his most intriguing hero, Odysseus, and about other figures in the poem too. The sophisticated moral dynamics of the *Odyssey* encourage us to refrain from black and white decisions about its characters. Being good or being bad, like being clever, is a complicated matter in Homer.

In the first few pages of the *Odyssey*, Athena pleads to Zeus on Odysseus's behalf, and Zeus readily agrees: Odysseus is surpassing in his cleverness; moreover, he always offers the best sacrifices. Most of the students to whom I've taught the *Odyssey* quickly agree with Zeus and Athena that Odysseus deserves special treatment: his brilliant trickiness makes him worthy. Odysseus is certainly more cunning than his men, who are called fools in the invocation to the *Odyssey*, when the poet condemns them for eating the Oxen of the Sun (one of the many disastrous mishaps that delay Odysseus's return from Troy). Odysseus also far outshines the doomed Aegisthus, famous from the story of Agamemnon. Aegisthus does not appear in the *Odyssey*, but is named a fool on the second page of the poem because he refused to heed the gods' warning not to steal Agamemnon's

wife and his kingdom. Being foolish and being smart are clearly
ruling concepts in the *Odyssey,* and Odysseus himself seems to
be the acme of smart. As I will explain, though, Homer is intent on making the opposition between smart and foolish a
complicated rather than a clear matter.

As it nears its end, with Odysseus finally come home to
Ithaka disguised as a beggar, the *Odyssey* is particularly insistent
on the contrast between Odysseus's deft manipulations and the
cloddishness of others. The biggest clods are, of course, Penelope's suitors. Odysseus has to win, we know, because he's sheer
mind; the suitors have to lose because (so it seems) they are
pure fools. Mental agility, combined with due reverence for the
gods (shown in those abundant sacrifices), means control of the
plot: Odysseus is a born victor. There is also a more ambiguous
case: in the *Odyssey,* cunning can be its own reward, worth the
game even if it leads to no practical profit beyond self-display. A
key instance occurs in Book 8 when the bandy-legged god of
the smithy, Hephaestus, snares his wife Aphrodite and her lover
Ares in an intricately made net. Hephaestus pulls off a wonderful stratagem when he exhibits Aphrodite and Ares squirming
and squalling in his exquisitely crafted trap; he awaits the approval of the gods, but they laugh at the smith god, not at the
trapped lovers. Since this is Odysseus's poem, and he is a shrewd
contriver like the divine metalworker Hephaestus, we are inclined to think that the smart god wins out over the dumb
ones—even though Hephaestus's divine colleagues make fun of
him as a hapless cuckold, rather than mocking the adulterous,
dull-witted gods of love and war, Aphrodite and Ares.

In the *Odyssey,* being smart means not only playing the game
extremely well, but also honoring its rules. If you're wise, you'll
follow moral convention: treating guests well, respecting the
gods. On the surface, then, it seems that Homer endorses cleverness, twins it with reverence, and applauds the effectiveness of

the combination. As a long-time teacher of Homer, I've found that the two most prevalent student papers on the *Odyssey* are (1) Odysseus triumphs because he is both shrewd and morally sound—unlike the suitors or the savage, man-eating Cyclops Polyphemus, who, in their ignorance and their derision for proper *xeinia* (the honoring of guests), are neither; and (2) Odysseus triumphs because he is shrewd, and his ethical shortcomings don't matter. (Sometimes the rules must be broken; immorality can be good strategy.) Paper 2 exploits a dissonance, but it's still not dissonant enough. I think there's more to the story. The *Odyssey*—this is *its* cleverness—prompts us to ask whether Odysseus is not also at times a fool, and the suitors at times rather astute. These deviations from character are not mere lapses; rather, they suggest that foolishness is sometimes inevitable, and that to survive you need far more than cleverness. Cleverness can, moreover, get you into trouble. Let's say you need to have dumb luck, aka the gods, on your side.

Homer, in other words, makes us wonder whether cleverness and foolishness really have the explanatory power we want them to have. Perhaps, instead, the gods will have things their way; there are situations in which our strategies, no matter how accomplished, simply don't work. All this may seem obvious, and it is; but it becomes interesting because it argues against Homer's loudest emphasis, the way he stacks the deck so heavily. The poet tells us over and over that the suitors are *so* stupid, and Odysseus *so* smart, that the latter just has to triumph. Yet Homer, as I've been saying, also inserts clues indicating that all is not so easy: he teaches us to be suspicious of his poem's most obvious, most visible claims.

I will return to the suitors, but first I want to look at an episode in the *Odyssey*'s Book 3: a great moment for class discussion, I've found, and for the solitary reader's mulling over, because we usually gloss over the problem it presents (there are many such moments in the *Odyssey*). In Book 3, Homer calls Odysseus's shrewdness into question, and with it the value of shrewdness in general. In Pylos in Book 3, wise old Nestor, Homer's hoariest, most long-winded character, speaks to Telemachus, who has gone in search of his father Odysseus. Nestor, who fills in for us and for Odysseus's son the details of the Greeks' departure from ruined Troy, tells Telemachus that he and Odysseus were always of one mind, with only one exception. Just after the sacking of Troy, Nestor reports, "Zeus planned a bitter journey home / For the Greeks—who were not all prudent or just." The Greeks' faults, which we may assume are prevalent in all wars, cause Athena to sow dissension between the leaders of the Greek expedition, the brothers Agamemnon and Menelaus, who then call an assembly. Here's where we get to the fascinating part of Nestor's account. He says that Menelaus wanted the troops to ship out immediately, but that Agamemnon

> wanted to delay their departure
> And offer formal sacrifice to appease
> The wrath of Athena—the fool,
> He had no idea she would never relent.
>   (translated by Stanley Lombardo)

Half the men depart with Menelaus, Nestor and Odysseus, all of whom Nestor thinks cleverer than the foolish Agamemnon. The departing fleet then pulls in to Tenedos to make sacrifices, but Zeus stirs up "still more dissension." Nestor continues:

>   Some now turned back
> Their curved ships, following Odysseus,
> A kingly man with a flexible mind
> [*Odusea anakta daiphrona poikilomêtên*],
> Out of respect for Lord Agamemnon.
> But I fled on with all my ships,

For I knew that the daimôn had evil in mind.
Diomedes also got his men out then,
And Menelaus brought up the rear.
                              (translated by Stanley Lombardo)

(I've modified Lombardo's translation here to include Homer's mention of the daimôn—the vaguely defined ruling spirit, or god, that guides the self.) All then goes well for Nestor and Diomedes who, aided by the gods, reach home quickly. Menelaus, blown off course, becomes fabulously wealthy, eventually arrives in Sparta, and lives to enjoy (if that's the right word) his interrupted marriage with Helen.

Let's try to get Nestor's story straight. Agamemnon, he says, was a fool when he tried to appease the angry gods with sacrifices; it was best to sail on. But the reader must object that the foolishness of Agamemnon's decision became clear only in retrospect, after Nestor and Diomedes were sailing successfully for home. As a rule in the *Odyssey,* it is prudent to offer sacrifices and foolish not to; this instance is the mysterious exception. Nestor's boast that he "knew that the daimôn had evil in mind" for Agamemnon and Odysseus is unconvincing: only hindsight gives such knowledge. And even with the aid of hindsight, what kind of knowledge is this? It makes little sense that the gods don't want sacrifices, but reward those who omit them and leave town as quickly as possible. Are they like angry parents who prefer that the offending children just get out of sight for a while, rather than offering the elaborate apology which may seem, to the parents, merely self-serving?

Nestor here paints Odysseus in a strange light. He is a man of flexible mind, *poikilomêtês:* but this flexibility causes him to make the wrong decision; he turns back rather than sailing on. Nestor is at pains to compliment Odysseus to his son at the same time that he criticizes him, and so his diplomatic nature creates a gap in logic. To be *poikilomêtês*—*mêtis* is intelligence, and *poikilos* means something like intricate, subtle, ever-changing, many-colored—is a good thing, except when it leads you to change your mind once too often (as Odysseus does here), to make the wrong move when there are no reliable signs to go on. Nestor doesn't call Odysseus a fool like Agamemnon (the old man could hardly do that, talking to Odysseus's son!), but he does, unwillingly, imply that intelligence can lead you wrong, and that whether you knew what you were doing, whether you were smart or foolish, can depend solely on what happened afterwards. And so smartness becomes a mere label attached to whatever preceded success, rather than a quality that can be defined and judged independently of its consequences, as Plato's Socrates, incensed by Homer's chance-ridden world and his fickle gods, insisted on doing.

Book 3 of the *Odyssey* presents one kind of doubt about smart and foolish: whether these characteristics in yourself might not be, at times, anything more than self-flattering or self-lacerating ways of trying to explain an outcome, without really accounting for it at all. It is tempting, if you are a Homeric Greek (because game-playing is so central to you), to say "I was so shrewd" or, less often, "I was such a fool"—but perhaps you were neither. Homer knows this.

There's another kind of doubt about smart and foolish that Homer clues us in on: whether these two traits might not be more mixed together in a particular person than we realize. If you can be smart one moment and a fool the next, then these words are less informative, less reliable, than we think they are. Homer exploits this possibility in the conclusion of the *Odyssey,* and he does so with great subtlety. Once again, he instructs us in the art of suspicion.

So, to see how this works: back to the suitors, those roisterers we love to hate (in this Ur-version of the Hollywood revenge flick). In Book 17, Athena has imposed a test on the suitors: let's see which of them will be kind to the traveling beggar who visits them (the beggar is Odysseus in disguise, of course), and which will not. The poet reminds us that Athena has no intention of sparing any of the suitors, not even the good ones, but she wants to test them nonetheless. Rather surprisingly, the suitors all pass the test, except for Antinous, their mean, malicious leader: they "fill [the beggar's] pouch with bread and meat."

If Homer had wanted to convince us that the suitors were all utter scoundrels, worthy of death, he could have done so. Instead, the poet emphasizes the unfairness of the goddess, and puts in a good word for the suitors. Subtly, he plants a doubt in our minds: perhaps the suitors are not so bad after all (nor are Lear's knights, despite what Goneril has to say). Almost every first-time reader, when asked about this scene, will say, erroneously, that the suitors as a group act just as Antinous does: that is, they all refuse to feed Odysseus and insult him instead. It's not true! We have been tricked by the narrator, who knows that we want the suitors to be all bad all the time, so much so that we ignore the actual facts of the story. Only if they are consistent fools—heartless, derogatory swaggerers—can their punishment be fully satisfying for us.

Homer wants us to suspect our impulse to see ethical consistency wherever we turn. The suitors are not all bad; and even Odysseus, our cherished hero, is overbold and shortsighted at times. After fleeing from Troy, he slaughters in an offhanded, pitiless way: he sacks the first city he comes to (in the land of the Cicones), kills the men, and enslaves the women. Odysseus's taunting of the Cyclops after he blinds him, when he announces his name, allows Poseidon, the Cyclops's father, to pursue his vengeance against the Greek hero. Remember Nestor's shadowy reference in Book 3 to what the Greeks did wrong at Troy, where they were neither prudent nor just: does that include Odysseus? We're tempted to see Odysseus as a white hat surrounded by black ones (his slow-witted, irresponsible crew; those parasitic suitors), but in the Cyclops episode, his curiosity and daring get his men killed: it's Odysseus who decides to investigate the monster's lair. It's a central part of the beauty of Homer's great poem that he holds up for us the difficult moral dynamics of the Trojan War and Odysseus's voyage home. The difficulty makes the poem more thrilling, not less. With Homer as with many other authors, the reader's suspicions increase her awareness of the book's rich complexity, its capacity to test its readers as it tests its characters.

Rule Eleven: Find the Parts

Finding the parts of a book (or story, or poem, or essay) will allow you to get an idea of its structure, of the significant turns in its argument. (Even a poem has an argument, as I will explain in Rule Thirteen, "Explore Different Paths," which gives an account of Robert Frost's "Design.") The reader must understand how a book is organized, even if she has read only a few pages of it so far. Like a good detective, the reader needs to stay alert, and follow clues to the work's overall intent. Machiavelli's *Prince,* which I've already mentioned several times, is a tough book to read. If you feel lost in a mass of confusing historical anecdotes, or find that it's hard to see anything in this blizzard of unfamiliar names, battles, political intrigues and advice . . . then let me reassure you. I know just how you feel. The answer is to construct a map of the book's sections, to see how and why it progresses from one stage to the next.

In this rule, I show how a piece of writing has a structure that readers are able to discover, once they have learned to slow down and notice details. It's important to find the significant changes in a work: transformations of topic, or time and place (in a novel or story), or atmosphere (in a poem). Readers should be able to pick out the key sentence that announces such a change, or that heralds the beginning of a new part of the book (or poem, story, or essay). I will focus on just one example, but the technique of analysis I will use can be applied to a variety of other works.

"Gooseberries" is one of Anton Chekhov's most beloved stories. In the next few pages we will take it apart and see how it works. Chekhov's story depends on narrative pivots, crucial moments of transition. A master storyteller, he gives the reader a subtle sense of the shape of "Gooseberries," its adept, beautiful design. Chekhov's method may seem casual, but his stories are in fact ordered, even symmetrical. We'll see exactly how this works. You will need to pay attention to key motifs, words, and images that the author relies on to make you sit up and notice that you have entered a new phase of his tale. Chekhov's tug on your sleeve may be gentle or strong, but it is always felt.

Like much of Chekhov, "Gooseberries" conveys an odd blend of sadness and health: it stimulates us to think restlessly, but also to accept the way of the world. Chekhov is attracted both to being discontented and to saying yes to the way things are. The power of his short stories and plays is hard to define, but this power becomes a part of every reader. Chekhov in his books has created his own country, with a bittersweet climate and a landscape full of unsettled, unexpected joys.

In "Gooseberries," two characters, the veterinarian Ivan Ivanych and his friend Burkin, a schoolteacher, take a long walk in the countryside. It starts to rain, and they seek shelter in the house of Alekhin, a prosperous farmer. Ivan Ivanych (whom I will call Ivan from now on) tells a story about his younger brother, Nikolai, who worked for years in a city office but dreamed of retiring to the country. Ivan describes how Nikolai finally achieved the rural life he desired, and how this new life changed him. There are four main characters in "Gooseberries": the two travelers Ivan and Burkin; their host Alekhin; and Ivan's brother Nikolai, who appears only in the story-within-a-story that Ivan tells about him. These four balance one another. Chekhov plays the restless Ivan off against the much more contented Burkin. He also plays the two landowners, Alekhin and Nikolai, off against each other: Nikolai claims to be satisfied with his life, but Alekhin truly is satisfied.

So much for the bare-bones plot of "Gooseberries" and its chief characters. To really understand Chekhov's story, though, we need to find its structure. Since "Gooseberries" is only a few pages long, it's easy to outline it in a way that shows how Chekhov tells his tale. Here is my rather extensive recounting of the story's parts. (I rely on the translation by Richard Pevear and Larissa Volokhonsky.)

A "Gooseberries" begins with a description of the weather. Ivan and Burkin know that the rain will come, but they are too exhilarated to stop their trek through the countryside. Tired and happy, they feel "love for these fields, and both thought how great, how beautiful this land was."

B Ivan is about to begin the story of his brother, but the rain has now begun, and so the two men must seek shelter first. (The brother, or rather Ivan's feelings about him, takes center stage in parts D through G, the climax of "Gooseberries.") Ivan and Burkin take cover at Alekhin's estate, which has a mill, a pond, and a bathing house. Alekhin looks like a professor or an artist rather than what he is, a wealthy landowner. He wears a dirty white shirt and muddy boots, and is covered with dust. He lives frugally, and rarely goes upstairs to the beautiful rooms where he receives guests.

C Ivan and Burkin go inside Alekhin's house and are met by Alekhin's maid, a girl whose youthful beauty stuns them. The maid brings towels and soap, and all three men go to the bathing house (where the scruffy Alekhin has not been for a long time, he confesses). Even though it is raining, Ivan exultantly swims in the pond, talks to some peasants on the bank, and is so distracted with happiness that he has to be called back to the house by Alekhin and Burkin.

D Now the three men are upstairs in Alekhin's rarely-visited drawing room. Washed, dressed and comfortable, they sit at their tea, served by the beautiful maid. Now Ivan finally begins his story of his brother. He says that he and his brother spent their carefree childhood in the countryside on a small estate, which had to be sold to pay debts after their father's death. The brother, Nikolai, imprisoned in an office job, saved his money fanatically, and never stopped fantasizing about the country estate he would one day be able to buy, with its servants' quarters, its garden . . . and its gooseberries. (Gooseberries resemble grapes, though they are more tart than grapes; they grow especially well in the Caucasus.) Still scheming for his retirement, Nikolai married an "ugly old widow," forcing her to live in poverty with him. After her death, Nikolai used her money as well as his own to buy his three hundred acres in the countryside. There he settled down, hired his servants, and planted his gooseberry bushes.

E Ivan's story of his brother Nikolai culminates with the visit that Ivan made to the brother's estate the previous year. He found Nikolai sitting in bed, "grown old, fat, flabby." The brothers embraced and, crying with joy, were sad too, as they thought about how young they were once, how old they were now, and how "it was time to die."

F Ivan describes, with disapproval, his brother's behavior as
country landowner: Nikolai is offended when the peasants fail
to show him proper respect, and he does his good deeds for
them "not simply but imposingly": treating the peasants for
their ailments, and giving them each a half-bucket of vodka on
his own name day, the feast day of Saint Nicholas. Ivan identifies
his brother with the typical "fat landowner" of rural Russia,
who usually exploits and punishes his peasants, but occasionally
rewards them, earning their servile loyalty. For Ivan, Nikolai
is the emblem of a broken social system. Nikolai fancies himself
a nobleman, Ivan complains, "though our grandfather was a
peasant and our father a soldier."

G Ivan presents the culmination of his story, the crucial event that
occurred during his visit to his brother: the arrival of a plate of
gooseberries from Nikolai's garden. Nikolai, intensely moved,
looked at the gooseberries with tears in his eyes, and ate them
with a child's excitement. Ivan reports that "they were tough and
sour," but to Nikolai, delicious. Such illusions do what truth
cannot: Nikolai, Ivan realized, is the completely happy, because
completely deluded, man. This discovery overcame Ivan with
"an oppressive feeling close to despair." Trying to sleep that
night, Ivan heard his brother snacking on gooseberries. Now, in
Alekhin's drawing room, Ivan recounts his insomniac thoughts
as he lay on the bed in his brother's house: there are so many
contented people, yet the horrors of poverty, oppression, and
hypocrisy go on behind the scenes. The happy man is only happy
because the unhappy suffer silently. Someone should stand at
the happy man's door tapping a little hammer, Ivan thinks, constantly reminding him that misery will come to him too, sooner
or later. That would ruin his complacency! But there is no man
with a hammer. The "petty cares" of life stir the happy man
"only slightly, as wind stirs an aspen—and everything is fine."

H Ever since that night on his brother's estate, Ivan concludes, he is enraged about the lack of progress toward freedom and education for the people. (Chekhov does not mention, but we are expected to know, that though Tsar Alexander II freed Russia's serfs in 1861, their condition was still miserable, and that Russian intellectuals concerned themselves intensely with the question of how to better the lot of these peasants.) Ivan confesses that living in town is a torment for him; he can't bear the sight of a happy family. "I'm old and not fit for struggle," he laments. "If only I were young." Ivan goes up to Alekhin, who is still young, and urges him not to let himself "fall asleep." Don't be content with your own happiness, he tells Alekhin: "do good." Ivan says this with "a pitiful, pleading smile, as if he were asking personally for himself."

I Ivan has finished his story and his ensuing reflections. Chekhov now returns us to the scene of the luxurious drawing room where the three men are sitting—and where Alekhin is, in fact, falling asleep. Chekhov tells us their thoughts: Neither Alekhin nor Burkin, the schoolteacher, is satisfied with Ivan's story, which they find boring and unsuitable to the beautiful drawing room, with its portraits of the "generals and ladies" who once sat and drank tea there. They decide that the room itself, and the beautiful maid who serves them, are better than any story.

J The two guests, Ivan and Burkin, go to their bedroom, with its impressive wooden beds and fresh linen, and its ivory crucifix. Ivan utters one sentence, "Lord, forgive us sinners!"—and pulls the covers over his head. Burkin lies awake, trying to discover the source of a heavy scent in the room. It is Ivan's pipe, which he has left on the table. "Gooseberries" concludes: "Rain beat on the windows all night."

Now, here is a much more abbreviated outline of Chekhov's story:

- Ivan and Burkin on their walk through the fields; rain
- Alekhin's estate; bathing
- Ivan's story about his brother Nikolai; gooseberries
- Ivan's commentary on life; the drawing room
- Ivan and Burkin in the bedroom; the pipe and the rain

Note that, in this second, concentrated diagram of "Gooseberries," I have mentioned a few crucial signposts (see Rule Six, "Identify Signposts"). Each one provides a signature for a scene. The rain seals the story's first scene (Ivan and Burkin walking in the countryside); Ivan's pipe and the rain seal the final one (Ivan and Burkin going to bed at Alekhin's house). The depiction of the three men bathing caps the introduction to Alekhin and his estate; the tableau of the drawing room with its distinguished portraits sets off Ivan's polemic against society. Most important, Chekhov sums up Ivan's feelings about his brother when he shows Nikolai devouring the gooseberries. Chekhov divides his story into parts by stationing these resonant signposts at key moments in the tale.

Your version of the story will probably be closer to my second than to my first outline. That's a good thing: the first outline gives a full summary description, but the second outline is actually more useful, since it shows you how "Gooseberries" works—how Chekhov tags each of its movements with a significant signpost image.

The title of the story clues us in to the most prominent of Chekhov's images, the gooseberries. Humble as they are, they are crucial to Nikolai's dream of country life. The gooseberries may be sour, but Nikolai tastes only delight when he eats them. The eating of the gooseberries occurs at the center of the story, during Ivan's narration of his visit to his brother. The self-deception involved (a sour taste seems delicious, because thinking makes it so) comments on another, larger deception: Nikolai's noble posturing among his peasants. Nikolai thinks his country life is sweet, but in fact it shares in a rancid social system.

The gooseberries, then, provide Chekhov's key motif. Perhaps the story's other gratifications resemble Nikolai's gooseberries: that is, they might depend on a deceiving imagination to transform their unpleasant aspects into pleasures. Ivan chats happily with some peasants on the bank of Alekhin's pond: Chekhov doesn't let us hear their conversation, and we are left to wonder whether Ivan might not after all resemble his brother Nikolai, a man living a fantasy of country life surrounded by the common people, who are mere décor, a kind of accessory to that life. (The lovely maid who serves the three men is just a beautiful object, not a person to be considered in her own right.) Ivan shares in such superficiality: he heartily enjoys the countryside, as well as the hospitality of the gentleman farmer Alekhin. So maybe Ivan's complaints about the hypocrisy of the well off apply to himself too. His theatrical plunge into dissatisfaction near the end of the story might be less a spiritual awakening than a momentary twinge of conscience, an escape valve that lets him be critical and yet still enjoy himself. He's a familiar type, the leftist rebel who savors the good life. After all, Ivan is happy for most of "Gooseberries," until he begins his condemnation of his brother in the drawing room scene. The image of the gooseberries, the object of pleasure that covers up some sourness, some disagreeable fact, radiates throughout Chekhov's story, and it applies to both brothers, not just Nikolai.

Before we begin to discuss the purpose of Chekhov's key images (the rain, bathing, the gooseberries, the drawing room, and the pipe), we can ask some basic questions about the structure of the story. Think about the author's choices. Chekhov could have had Ivan tell the story of his brother while he and Burkin walk through the fields at the story's beginning, or as he swims in the pond, taking in the countryside's pleasures. Instead he waits until Ivan and Burkin are in Alekhin's beautiful drawing room, sitting over tea. The portrait of Nikolai requires as its counterpoint a portrait of Alekhin, the grimy, hardworking gentleman farmer, and the comforts that he offers his guests. Ivan's commentary on the evils of the typical Russian landowner, and the need to wake up and correct social ills, comes only near the end of the story, when Alekhin is getting sleepy and all three men are about to go to bed—that is, when Ivan faces a bored and indifferent audience.

Why does Chekhov structure "Gooseberries" as he does? Ivan's story has to be told in Alekhin's presence because Chekhov wants to underline a contrast between Alekhin and Ivan's brother Nikolai, the subject of the story. Both are country landowners, managers of busy estates. But Alekhin labors while Nikolai is sluggish (Ivan finds his brother sitting in bed, overweight and idle). Nikolai spouts opinions about the common people, and cherishes his self-invented role as a generous yet strict nobleman, a father to his peasants. Alekhin seems uninterested in such role-playing; he is free from the realm of illusory self-satisfaction that Nikolai dwells in. But Alekhin is also indifferent to the social ills that agitate Ivan so profoundly: he dozes off while Ivan denounces social hypocrisy. Significantly, Chekhov's detailed depiction of the drawing room overshadows Ivan's talk. The evils that pain Ivan so profoundly might be less memorable than the room itself—than the artful impression made by its fine portraits of generals and ladies, who while they were alive led a refined existence there.

When Alekhin and Burkin lounge, drink tea, and half-listen to Ivan's passionate, confused speech, are we to think that

Chekhov sides with them or with Ivan? Do we share their drowsy satisfaction, or do we instead embrace the hotheaded Ivan? Every reader must decide this question for herself, and Chekhov makes the decision as hard as he can. There is something callous in us if we simply reject Ivan's anger, for so much of what he says is true. Yet Ivan also fails to own up to his own tastes: he too enjoys the pleasures of Alekhin's estate. Does knowing society's ills mean turning away from the sensual comforts of nature—and from Alekhin's plush, sophisticated drawing room?

"Gooseberries" ends in the kind of bedroom that every weary traveler yearns for. We can almost feel ourselves sinking into those welcoming beds with their wonderfully fresh linen sheets. Ivan has told the others to wake up instead of sinking into sleep, but he can't explain to them how to demonstrate their wakefulness—how they might correct social ills. Chekhov could conclude his story with a reminder of Ivan's critique, but he does not. Instead, by focusing on the snug, dozing Burkin, he returns us to the physical pleasures we all share. Like Burkin and Alekhin, we have become uninterested in Ivan's Hamlet-like denunciation of the lies that lurk within our lives. We too drift toward sleep, tired and happy.

Chekhov's way of arranging his story as a sequence of parts makes Ivan's invective, which loudly occupies the center of the tale, fade away at its conclusion. The beginning of "Gooseberries" presents a hearty, full-blooded appreciation of the countryside. Its conclusion describes a similarly memorable solace. Though the ending is colored by a fading memory of Ivan's discontented story, the palpable coziness of the bedroom overcomes such discontent. Both beginning and ending focus on the sensual, at the expense of the heated intellectual polemic that Ivan delivers in the middle. (See Rule Five, "Notice Beginnings and Endings.") Chekhov structures "Gooseberries" this way in order to press us to decide how, and how much, Ivan's denunciation matters.

Why does the story end with Burkin's insomnia, his smelling of Ivan's pipe, and the sound of the rain? Here we need to speculate. For one thing, Burkin's sleeplessness clearly harks back to Ivan's sleeplessness on his brother's estate. The two men are both kept awake by subtle things: the odor of Ivan's pipe parallels the noise of Nikolai eating gooseberries in the kitchen. What Burkin broods over at the end is not the content of Ivan's talk, but rather a sensual detail, the odor of the pipe smoke, which lingers long after Ivan's words have faded. Whereas Ivan was kept awake by a symbol of his brother's deluded life in the country (gooseberries), and as a result composes an angry diatribe while lying on his bed, Burkin is kept awake by a simple, curious fact, the tobacco smell that outlasts Ivan's brief lecture. The physical world is more interesting to Burkin than debates about society. The rain returns as it always will, no matter what people discuss and argue about. Weather and landscape are more primal and persistent than the ambition to achieve one's dream (as Nikolai wants to) or to change one's life and the life of one's country (as Ivan wants to). The rain falls outside, a mere gentle sound. The story's characters have luxurious shelter, unlike the impoverished masses for whose sake Ivan broods: the suffering ones who live in the wind and rain, exposed to the harsh elements of life.

The fact that Ivan remains frustrated, stymied in his wish to get the world to wake up, suggests that his aggressive speeches spring from a distressed soul. He seems unsure whether he is more disturbed by his own existence or by that of the rich landowners he decries. Alekhin and Burkin are simply uninterested in diagnosing Ivan—or his brother Nikolai. Instead, they remain attached to the consoling realities of life: a bath, tea in front of a fire, and a warm bed. As we finish the story, our sym-

pathies are divided between these two camps: the troublemaker
Ivan and the calm realists, Burkin and Alekhin. If the latter two
incline too much toward indifference, the former seems self-
thwarting, an unquiet spirit.

If we know something about Chekhov's own life, we gain
deeper insight into "Gooseberries." Chekhov bought a country
house for his family in 1892 in Melikhovo, south of Moscow.
Janet Malcolm, in her marvelous book *Reading Chekhov*, notes
that "the purchase of Melikhovo was a culminating product of
Chekhov's literary success—and of the illusion (one that Russian writers, Chekhov included, are particularly good at mocking) that life in the country is a solution to the problem of
living." Chekhov knew that the redeeming power of the countryside was an illusion, yet he shared in that illusion. "Gooseberries" was written about three years before Chekhov bought
his country estate; he must have been comparing himself to
Nikolai, the cooped-up brother who looks forward to a liberating rural existence. There is a further twist: Chekhov's own
brother, who died before Chekhov wrote "Gooseberries," was
named Nikolai. Chekhov wrote a famous letter to his brother
accusing him of vulgar habits (bossing others around, fits of
temper) and telling him to change his life. So Chekhov apparently identified too with the Ivan of "Gooseberries," who sees
and condemns a crass egotism in his brother. Yet Ivan is far
from the hero of Chekhov's story, as we have seen. By making
Ivan a figure whose strength remains doubtful, Chekhov casts
doubt on the worth of his own preaching in his letter to his
brother.

Knowing these biographical details enriches our perception
of "Gooseberries." And if we read the two other short stories
that Chekhov wrote featuring the characters Ivan and Burkin
("The Man in the Case" and "About Love"), our sense of
"Gooseberries" will deepen further. But we have explored the

story in great depth without the aid of the other stories; and it can be read, too, without the knowledge of Chekhov's life I have just given you. More important than such background is the impulse to investigate how Chekhov divides his story into parts: how he makes his ending respond to the beginning, how he centers his story with his two set-pieces (the bathing scene, Ivan's long speech), and how he places the gooseberries at the middle of his tale, as symbol of Nikolai's illusory yet deeply desired enjoyment. I have given a rather detailed dissection of "Gooseberries," not to suggest that you should examine the structure of every literary work with such microscopic attention, but to show how far you can go if you want, and the benefit you will get from thinking about how a work's parts function together. The more you understand about how an author orchestrates a book (or story, or poem), putting everything in its right place, and making the scenes and images answer one another, the more pleasure you will get from your reading.

Rule Twelve: Write It Down

When you practice the art of slow reading, you will find it helpful to jot down your impressions in the book's margins or in a notebook (or in the electronic margins provided by an e-book's note-taking feature). Here you can respond directly to the book in several ways: by summarizing one of its points, or by showing where the book has led you, the spur it has given your mind. But you must keep an eye on the author's stance and style. The give-and-take between author and reader takes place on a two-way street. In this imaginary but essential conversation, the reader has a responsibility to keep the author interested. You will refine your perceptions, and become a better interpreter, the more time you spend trying to do justice to a book, rather than too quickly making it into something of your own. The book has something to say, and you are obliged to listen carefully before talking back.

Writing a few notes is better than writing none. I give an example of exceptionally thorough note-taking, but you need not become an obsessive annotator in order to read more deeply.

Your notes are a kind of conversation with yourself, and may substitute, to a degree, for the presence of fellow readers with whom you can study a book. You have an advantage if you discuss what you read with others, whether in a class or a book group. Students in a classroom can rely on the comments of a teacher or another student to feel sure of themselves, and to advance their insights. When you read alone rather than with a class or in a group, you develop your responses to a book in a different way: by talking to yourself, evaluating your reactions in order to make them richer and more involved.

If you compare your earlier reactions to a book with your later ones and keep a record of them, you will find that headscratchings have been replaced by interesting observations, and baffled questions by more substantial ones. In a few pages, I give a (purely imaginary) example of such a "reading diary," about Alfred, Lord Tennyson's poem "The Kraken," and I explain how and why this reader has made progress.

When you become an avid note-taker, you will have some august company. The English Romantic poet Samuel Taylor Coleridge, author of "Kubla Khan" and *The Rime of the Ancient Mariner,* was undoubtedly the most impressive scribbler of marginalia in literary history. His collected marginalia have been published, and they stretch to thousands of pages: a treasure trove of glorious sidebars, by turns crabby, appreciative, puzzled, and full of wonder. The enthralling essayist Charles Lamb, a close friend of Coleridge, remarked, "Lend thy books; but let it be to such a one as S. T. C.—he will return them . . . with usury; enriched with annotations, tripling their value." The minor poet Robert Southey, another friend of Coleridge, traced over Coleridge's penciled marginal comments in ink so that they wouldn't be lost.

Coleridge is just one of the accomplished note-takers among famous writers. Joseph Conrad, the Polish seaman and future novelist, bored during one of his voyages in the 1890s, retreated as he usually did into solitary reading. He began filling the margins of Flaubert's *Madame Bovary* with comments, and his kibbitzing gradually evolved into his first novel, *Almayer's Folly.* William Blake, the wildest and most intensely prophetic of the Romantics, was another distinguished author of marginal comments, for the most part highly combative. When Blake confronted the staid champions of orthodox belief, he drew blood: his fire-breathing marginal thrusts are aimed directly at the normative reassurance provided by eighteenth-century worthies like Joshua Reynolds (whom Blake mocked as "this President of Fools").

A peculiar and alarming exhibit in the strange history of marginalia is the Rev. James Granger, who in 1769 published his *Biographical History of England,* which he illustrated by pillaging more than 14,000 engravings from other books. In later editions of his book, Granger introduced blank pages, and invited his readers to do as he had done: steal illustrations from the books in their libraries and paste them into their copy of Granger. The fashion of personalizing a book by mutilating other books caught on, and became known as Grangerism; in some readers' hands, the stolen illustrations could be an eccentric riposte to or else a way of egging on the original text. Grangerism was, in effect, a form of marginal commentary in visual form. Thankfully, the rapacious habit Granger promoted, which became the scourge of libraries as well as private collections, has faded in popularity.

Virginia Woolf disdained marginal annotation: she used notebooks instead. In an unpublished essay populated by a rogue's gallery of marginal scribblers, Woolf imagines (so H. J. Jackson reports in her book *Marginalia*), "A crusty Colonel venting his rage in the 'violated margin' of a book; a timid clergyman contributing literary parallels; a sentimental lady making 'thick lachrymose lines' against poems about early death, and pressing flowers between the pages; and a pedant correcting typographical errors." Woolf is in a distinct minority; most authors, like most readers, have been enthusiastic writers of marginalia. Nabokov thickly annotated his copies of Flaubert, Joyce, and Kafka, and used these comments for his lectures on literature at Cornell (which were later published in book form). He noted in his copy of Kafka that the Czech author, no entomologist, had made a mistake about the kind of beetle into which Gregor Samsa was transformed in *The Metamorphosis:* it actually has wings, and so poor Gregor could have flown away, escaping his scandalized family.

Perhaps the most intriguing marginalia are those of John Keats, in his copy of Milton's *Paradise Lost* (the subject of an entire book by scholar Beth Lau). Keats's scribblings show an inspired, vastly imaginative mind at work, but they can also guide us mere mortals. When Satan enters the serpent in Book 9 of *Paradise Lost,* Milton adds, "but his sleep / Disturbed not" (9.190–91). Keats, an expert noticer of small things, draws attention to this detail. Focused on the pathos of Satan at this moment, he comments, "Whose spirit does not ache at the smothering and confinement—the unwilling stillness—the *'waiting close'*?" Keats draws our attention to the dour and resentful, yet suffering sensibility of Satan, who has chosen a house of mortal clay, and who must keep quiet so as not to awaken the slithering reptile he inhabits.

When he reads the opening of *Paradise Lost*, Keats remembers the first pages of two other famous works: Dante's *Inferno* and Shakespeare's *Hamlet*. Why these two? we may ask. Dante, like Milton, begins his sacred poem in hell, not heaven; and the story of *Hamlet* commences on the dread battlements of Elsinore, which are haunted by the ghost of Hamlet's father. The reference to Dante is rather obvious; Keats's thought of *Hamlet* is less so. But then we start to think: perhaps Milton's Satan resembles Hamlet's father, scorched by penal fire and bound to rehearse his own sins. Old Hamlet begs his son, the gloomy and charismatic prince, for revenge; Satan in *Paradise Lost* is like both old and young Hamlet, the father who requires and the son who pursues vengeance. Alone and damned, with the tedious ambrosial surfeitings of Milton's heaven lost to him forever, Satan claims authorship of himself; he becomes an avenger, and his deeds redound upon his own too-wily head. Satan and his fallen angels spend much of *Paradise Lost*'s first two books debating the most effective way to get back at God. Young Hamlet spends most of his play in similar pondering, as he tries to invent a fitting revenge. He could kill his uncle Claudius, but instead he delays in order to fashion a plot that will answer to the dizzying, uncanny height of his imagination.

Keats might be implying that Hamlet's fantasy is devilish like Satan's. Hamlet is not just a thinker of unrivalled nimbleness, brooding yet lightning-quick, not just supremely funny and lacerating in his ironies, but also a man with a strong taste for violence. "Now could I drink hot blood," he crows. He stabs Polonius without regret. Hamlet's rancor, like Satan's, remains unappeased even at the play's end, and when he dies he takes down with him many of his fellow characters. Unlike Satan, though, Hamlet is not diminished but further exalted as his story goes on.

In his marginal note, Keats doesn't say anything like what I've just said. He merely notes a comparison between the beginnings of *Paradise Lost* and *Hamlet*. But the suggestive power of the comparison makes it a nearly limitless source of interest, allowing me to offer a gloss on Keats's gloss. Your marginal notes may not be as fascinating as Keats's, but they will be useful to you, and that's the point.

Let's use as our text to illustrate note-taking "The Kraken," one of the earliest canonical poems by the sublime Tennyson, who was only twenty-one when he wrote it. Once you've read "The Kraken," you remember it; it is among the poet's most thrilling and accessible works. The poem stars a strange sea-creature that Tennyson found in Norse mythology, and he creates an ominous, haunted atmosphere around its bulking presence. First, here is the poem:

Below the thunders of the upper deep;
Far, far beneath in the abysmal sea,
His ancient, dreamless, uninvaded sleep
The Kraken sleepeth: faintest sunlights flee
About his shadowy sides: above him swell
Huge sponges of millennial growth and height;
And far away into the sickly light,
From many a wondrous grot and secret cell
Unnumbered and enormous polypi
Winnow with giant arms the slumbering green.
There hath he lain for ages and will lie
Battening upon huge sea-worms in his sleep,
Until the latter fire shall heat the deep;
Then once by man and angels to be seen,
In roaring he shall rise and on the surface die.

Now here are a series of notes that might be written by a reader who approaches the poem cold. Before using the dictionary or mulling over Tennyson's words, this reader's first impression might look something like this. (In her helpful book *Poems Poets Poetry*, Helen Vendler gives several examples of similar notebook jottings.)

Below the thunders of the upper deep;
[why the "upper" deep? Where is that? And what's "below" it?
    What are the "thunders"?]
Far, far beneath in the abysmal sea,
[what does "abysmal" mean here? It can't have its usual
    meaning . . .]
His ancient, dreamless, uninvaded sleep
[why "uninvaded"? who might invade it?]
The Kraken sleepeth: faintest sunlights flee
[what's a Kraken? why "sunlights" in plural rather than
    singular? Strange idea: sunlights fleeing . . .]
About his shadowy sides: above him swell
["Shadowy" is right—it's hard for me to make out what the
    Kraken actually looks like . . .]
Huge sponges of millennial growth and height;
["Millennial" = ?]
And far away into the sickly light,
From many a wondrous grot and secret cell
["grot" must mean "grotto," right?]
Unnumbered and enormous polypi
Winnow with giant arms the slumbering green.
[What does "winnow" mean? "Slumbering" reminds me of the
    sleeping Kraken . . .]
There hath he lain for ages and will lie
Battening upon huge sea-worms in his sleep,
["Battening"? Again he's sleeping . . . does this monster never
    wake up?]
Until the latter fire shall heat the deep;

[The "latter fire"? what's that?]

Then once by man and angels to be seen,

[Not just man but angels too? Why does Tennyson add the angels?]

In roaring he shall rise and on the surface die.

[Not much of a career for this monster: as soon as he wakes up he dies. Or does he wake up?]

Okay, let's try that again. After a few visits to a good dictionary (preferably the OED) and some serious thought (see Rule Seven, "Use the Dictionary"), our reader returns to the poem, and reads it again slowly, aloud, several times. Patience, as I advised in Rule One, is needed for slow reading. The reader's first reactions were not wrong, but they required development. Her notes might now look something like this:

Below the thunders of the upper deep;

[Tennyson starts the poem by describing a place, but he makes its location murky . . . the "deep" is the ocean, my dictionary tells me, and so perhaps the "thunders" are the noises made by ships?]

Far, far beneath in the abysmal sea,

[the poem is going down even further: not just below the upper deep, as in line one, but far, far beneath it. "Abysmal" comes from "abyss": the ocean's depths seem bottomless]

His ancient, dreamless, uninvaded sleep

[That's three adjectives in a row—what's known as a tricolon crescendo, where the most important term is always the third, last one. We haven't yet gotten to the subject of the sentence, which Tennyson defers until the next line, the center of the poem. We know, though, that he is very old and "dreamless": does he have a mind at all? The series culminates in the strangest of the three words: "uninvaded." This creature's sleep is closed off, defended as if against an invasion.]

The Kraken sleepeth: faintest sunlights flee

[The Kraken must be a legendary monster . . . Tennyson says that he "sleepeth" his "sleep," and the repetition seems to indicate that sleeping is his essential activity, if you can call it an activity. "Sunlights" is plural because these are very faint, fragmented traces, refracted from the sea's surface . . . and they "flee" from the Kraken, as if he has some extraordinary power to frighten away anything that approaches him, including feeble rays of light.]

About his shadowy sides: above him swell

[That's the second line in a row with a colon in the middle—what experienced readers of verse know as a caesura. The two halves of the line start with "about" and "Above," respectively—more location markers, as in the poem's first two lines. "Shadowy sides" is vague—shadowy—in order to suggest that it's hard to find the difference between the Kraken himself and what surrounds him. We still don't know what the sides look like.]

Huge sponges of millennial growth and height;

[The sponges almost seem like part of the Kraken—his sides are about him and the sponges are above him.]

And far away into the sickly light,

["Far away" is appealingly vague, almost reminiscent of fairy tales that take place in a land far, far away. "Sickly" sounds severe and strange—what an odd adjective to use with "light"!]

From many a wondrous grot and secret cell

["Wondrous" and "secret" give a magical atmosphere. . . . I seem to remember "grot" from Keats's "La Belle Dame Sans Merci": "She took me to her elfin grot"]

Unnumbered and enormous polypi

[Like "uninvaded," "unnumbered" describes the Kraken with a negative word; here, the poet suggests that we can't see the true number of the polypi—there are just too many of them.

"Enormous" means vast, but how vast? The Kraken still seems shadowy, undefined]

Winnow with giant arms the slumbering green.

[Winnowing is what farmers do at harvest time: they separate the wheat from the chaff, the valuable from the useless. The "green" here is not a field, but the ocean algae. It too "slumbers," just like the Kraken: the monster seems to produce a sleep-inducing force field. The polypi now look like arms.]

There hath he lain for ages and will lie

Battening upon huge sea-worms in his sleep,

[There's sleep again . . . and more emphasis on vastness (the "huge sea-worms"). "Battening" means feeding, growing fat.]

Until the latter fire shall heat the deep;

[Seems to be a reference to an apocalypse, when fire burns the world up. "Heat" is interesting: Tennyson could have said "boil" or "scorch," but instead he uses something more moderate, a word that carries a lulling vowel assonance with "deep."]

Then once by man and angels to be seen,

[Angels: it must be the end of time, as in the Book of Revelation. We finally get to see the Kraken only once, at the end of time—a counter to the seeming endlessness of his deep-sea existence.]

In roaring he shall rise and on the surface die.

[The last line has two verbs, "rise" and "die" (they almost rhyme!), and they are coordinated: rising is dying for this beast. The last half of the line comes as a surprise: we might have expected that the Kraken would wake up to a flamboyant career as an apocalyptic beast. But he doesn't seem to wake up at all; he just reacts fiercely for one spectacular, final moment. Roaring implies the creature's pain, but also the fact that he is still fearsome: lions roar to terrify their prey. The poem's last word is "die": was the Kraken ever really alive? He seemed eternally oblivious; only one event affected him, and that one killed him. Did he even know what happened?]

You may not share this reader's suddenly acquired knowledge of literary forms (caesura, tricolon crescendo) and earlier texts (Keats, Revelation). But, if you've spent enough time with Tennyson's "Kraken," if you've cultivated your patience (see Rule One), you will develop something like this level of sensitivity to the poem's nature. You will be able to make detailed, insightful remarks like the ones I've recorded. Importantly, too, you'll begin to understand the mood of the poem, as well as the creature at its center. The universe of the Kraken is torpid, inert, deprived of actual experience. To this pallid beast, the surface world we know so well is barely visible, the slightest of shadows. When reality finally touches him, he bursts into a lethal howl and expires.

"The Kraken" lacks drama, and in this respect it is characteristic. Tennyson's poems are often conspicuously languid. Stasis enraptures this poet, and his audience too: a dreamlike, gorgeously dense atmosphere captivates the reader of "The Kraken." The more you study Tennyson's haunting vignette, the more you find yourself absorbed into its shadowy undersea world. And the notes you take along the way will give you a firmer sense of your response. You will know how you are reading the poem, what you see in it and why. The same will be true of any text that you take notes on.

One final word of advice on note-taking. If the book is your own, you will probably want to annotate it in pencil rather than pen (I always do); otherwise, you'll feel like you're competing with the author, rather than pursuing the author's meaning.

And now a serious warning: don't write in a library book. Vladimir Nabokov's effervescent novel *Pnin* depicts a hapless émigré professor, Timofey Pnin. Here Pnin encounters the coming of the new semester at Waindell College (modeled on Wellesley and Cornell, where Nabokov himself taught): "Again in the margins of library books earnest freshmen inscribed such helpful glosses as 'Description of nature,' or 'Irony'; and in a pretty edition of Mallarmé's poems an especially able scholiast had already underlined in violet ink the difficult word *oiseaux* and scrawled above it 'birds.'"

The marginal annotator sometimes outsmarts himself—a good reason not to annotate in public. Frank Kermode remembered that he once found, "in a university library, a copy of Wordsworth's *Prelude* in which the editor, in a rare flight of fancy, remarked in his preface that he detected 'celestial ichor' running through the poem's veins. A reader had corrected this (in ink) to read 'celestial choir.'" (Ichor is what runs in the Greek gods' veins.) There's nothing worse than anticipating refuge in a book, only to find it adorned with someone's yellow pen-swathes and crude underlinings, or comments of the kind that Nabokov and Kermode lampoon. While in graduate school in the 1980s, I noticed that many of the books on English literature in Yale's Cross Campus Library, especially those on the eighteenth century, had been defaced by an aggrieved reader. This person, presumably a fellow graduate student, liked to make snarky marginal remarks in ink, always in spidery, upright letters. These "clever," cozily superior comments were a rude way of elbowing into a book and trying to steal the show from the author.

Rather than scratching and clawing your way through an author's work, it's best to use your marginal notes as a way of tracking your responses, and so getting closer to a book; to become the book's partner, rather than giving it battle scars. The point of note-taking is not to get the better of a book, but to understand it; to ponder an author's way of working, not to throw a wrench in the works.

Rule Thirteen: Explore Different Paths

Revision, the writer's most basic tool, is also important for the reader. It's always a useful exercise to imagine how the author might have begun or ended a work differently, or changed a crucial moment in its plot. Develop a sense of the decisions a writer makes by practicing thought experiments: what would the work you're reading be like without a key character? What difference would it make if it lacked this or that scene? You will gain a new knowledge of how writers work, the choices they make. Books weren't born perfect, with every trait set in stone from the beginning. They were reworked and rearranged, and they bear the traces of their creators' second thoughts. This is true even of writers who cultivate an air of improvisation, like Cervantes or Dostoevsky. W. H. Auden remarked in a lecture (recorded by Alan Ansen) that "when we read Dostoevsky, we feel, yes, this is wonderful, this is marvelous, now go home and write it all over again. And yet if he did, the effect might well be lost." Dostoevsky's pell-mell storytelling is in fact a carefully produced effect, rather than evidence of a rush job.

Our preliminary, untutored feelings about how a book might have been different tend to be vague wishes rather than full-fledged acts of imagination. We might wish, for example, that Chekhov had not killed off Kostya, his brooding, youthful hero, at the end of *The Seagull;* or that Dreiser had spared Hurstwood the long, slow process of degradation to which he subjects him in *Sister Carrie.* These reactions shy away from the book, rather than encountering it. There's a better way. If the reader actively uses her imagination to envision an alternative ending, one that the writer might have, but did not, pursue— Kostya a successful playwright, Hurstwood happily united with Carrie—then she will begin to understand why Chekhov and Dreiser wrote what they did. Dreiser's Carrie is an anti–Emma

Bovary, whose fantasies, unlike Emma's, are successful because she knowingly acquires the "passivity of soul" that an actress needs; Hurstwood too is a Romantic yearner, but he is antitheatrical, in contrast to Carrie. He rejects role-playing, instead becoming more dismally and narrowly his worst self. Carrie and Hurstwood are in fact opposites, and their savagely contrasting fates bring out this difference. To unite them would be to lie about the radically separated choices that life consists of in Dreiser's works.

Some authors—Samuel Beckett and Thomas Hardy, say— seem to have a nearly sadistic relation to their readers: they want to punish us for hoping. If we dislike this trait, we are merely protesting against the basic thought of the author (see Rule Nine, "Find the Author's Basic Thought"). We will not get anywhere looking for happy endings in Beckett and Hardy. Instead, we must appreciate the uncompromising brilliance of their pessimistic vision. Our imaginary rewrites of an author must attend to the author's own sensibility, rather than trying to exchange it for something more congenial.

It is always valuable to consider an author's own revisions, and to ask what and why the author decided to change. Some famous works exist in several different versions: in the case of Wordsworth's *Prelude,* you will want to compare all three, the *Two-Part Prelude* of 1798 and the later versions of 1805 and 1850. At every turn, Wordsworth's changes of mind are instructive; you will be forced to ask yourself which version of the poem you prefer and why. *The Two-Part Prelude* is a stunningly powerful and concentrated work; yet the expansive later *Preludes* span much more, showing us Wordsworth's sublime imagination at full stretch. If you love Whitman's "Crossing Brooklyn Ferry," you will see the poem with fresh eyes after reading "Sun-Down Poem," its first version, from the second (1856) edition of *Leaves of Grass.* A study of revision gives us a glimpse into how a book is put together, a behind-the-scenes look at the writer's job.

In a 1956 interview with *The Paris Review*, Ernest Hemingway said that he rewrote the last page of his novel *A Farewell to Arms* thirty-nine times before he was satisfied with it. Vladimir Nabokov once remarked, "I have rewritten—often several times—every word I have ever published. My pencils outlast their erasers." (Nabokov always wrote with pencils on index cards, which he rearranged to make his finished text.) Gustave Flaubert, that monastic, masochistic disciple of rewriting, announced, "I love my work with a frenetic and perverted love, as the ascetic loves the hair shirt that scratches his belly." Ceaseless reformation is the writer's art: turning sentences around. Oscar Wilde burlesqued the process of revision when he described his work day to guests at dinner: "Before luncheon, I took a comma out. After luncheon I put the comma back." Wilde, like every good writer, was a perfectionist, a fanatic of the word.

Here are two fascinating examples of works that the author revised in a dramatic, thoroughgoing way: F. Scott Fitzgerald's *The Great Gatsby* and Robert Frost's "Design." In both cases, considering the author's choices leads to increased respect for that author's vision. It also lets you see how writing is an active process, just like reading. A book may seem set in stone, but it was actually chiseled and rechiseled. A writer's false starts and second thoughts give us the chance to see how a book works, how its parts are necessary to one another. Every book, and especially every great book, could have been different.

Fitzgerald's thoroughgoing revision of *The Great Gatsby* is a famous case, and an instructive one. In this passage, Daisy, Gatsby's beloved, recounts to the book's narrator, Nick Carraway, a shocking snapshot from her marriage to the brutish Tom Buchanan. Here is Fitzgerald's earlier version:

"Listen, Nick," she broke out suddenly, "did you ever hear what I said when my child was born?"

"No, Daisy."

"Well, she was less than an hour old and Tom was God knows where. I woke up out of the ether with an utterly abandoned feeling as if I'd been raped by a company of soldiers and left out in a field to die."

Fitzgerald altered Daisy's lines to read this way:

"Well she was less than an hour old and Tom was God knows where. I woke up out of the ether with an utterly abandoned feeling . . . I said: 'I hope she'll be a fool—that's the best thing a girl can be in this world, a beautiful little fool.'"

Fitzgerald's revision improves the novel. Instead of voicing a violent and aimless comparison (being raped by soldiers), Daisy speaks of her abandonment more frailly and pathetically, murmuring the harshly ironic hope that her daughter will be like herself, a "beautiful little fool" (as she is for marrying Tom). The new line is *echt* Daisy; the old one was flailing and crude, frantic enough but otherwise unfitting for Daisy's wan, fantasy-driven persona. The revised line is much more painful, because in it Fitzgerald puts Daisy's sense of herself on display.

Frost's sonnet "Design" offers another intriguing lesson in revision. Here is Frost's early version of "Design," which he titled "In White":

A dented spider like a snowdrop white
On a white Heal-all, holding up a moth
Like a white piece of lifeless satin cloth—
Saw ever curious eye so strange a sight?—
Portent in little, assorted death and blight
Like the ingredients of a witches' broth?—

The beady spider, the flower like a froth,
And the moth carried like a paper kite.

What had that flower to do with being white,
The blue Brunella every child's delight.
What brought the kindred spider to that height?
(Make we no thesis of the miller's plight.)
What but design of darkness and of night?
Design, design! Do I use the word aright?

Compare Frost's final version of the poem "Design" (from his book *A Further Range*):

I found a dimpled spider, fat and white,
On a white heal-all, holding up a moth
Like a white piece of rigid satin cloth—
Assorted characters of death and blight
Mixed ready to begin the morning right,
Like the ingredients of a witches' broth—
A snow-drop spider, a flower like a froth
And dead wings carried like a paper kite.

What had that flower to do with being white,
The wayside blue and innocent heal-all?
What brought the kindred spider to that height,
Then steered the white moth thither in the night?
What but design of darkness to appall?—
If design govern in a thing so small.

Frost, when he rewrote the poem, made a few changes in order to streamline it: he dropped the distracting line in parentheses about the "miller" (the miller-moth), as well as the reference to the "curious eye" of the speaker. But his most important changes are to the beginning and end of "Design." He replaced the original first line, "A dented spider like a snowdrop white," with "I found a dimpled spider, fat and white." In addition to putting an "I" in the poem (the only one in all twelve lines), Frost's revision makes his spider a grotesque. The neutral "dented" changes to "dimpled," which suggests a childlike face with dimples—a hideous, evocative mismatch. The spider is now "fat and white," not a "snowdrop" (a word Frost saves for later on, in the new version of the poem).

Frost has decided to disgust the reader in the very first line of his rewritten sonnet: he presents a minute monster, obese and pallid. As the poem goes on, this opening note of repugnance continues with the new image of the "witches' broth." Frost mixes a repellent potion, composed of the sickening spider, its victim the moth, and the heal-all (a flower that is usually blue, but rarely, as here, white). The spider is the pale, dead-looking crab spider, which often hides against a white background. (A quick Googling will reveal the horrible aspect of this particular spider; it is truly stomach-churning, dimples and all.)

In his revised version, then, Frost accentuates the decadent and gruesome character of his scene. He also strongly underlines the argument of the poem, which concerns the place of design, or governing intent, in the universe (as the new title suggests). If you know William Blake's "Tyger," you know what's behind Frost's question in "Design." Blake asks whether God, the creator of goodness, could possibly delight in creation's sublime evils, like that perfect predatory machine, the fearsome tiger ("Did he smile his work to see? / Did he who made the lamb make thee?"). How can good and evil coexist? What kind of God wants both? Blake's question, in turn, derives from the towering and terrifying conclusion of the Book of Job, as well as Isaiah 44, which names God as the creator of both good and evil.

These are high precedents. Frost incongruously applies them to a tiny particular: a design or composition of white on white, eater and eaten. *Design* means both a composed thing or pattern and a ruling direction. In our day the desperately anti-Darwinian proponents of "intelligent design" use the word in this sense, to mean the workings of a superior power shown in nature. Darwin too saw design, but he drained it of intent, whether benevolent or malevolent. We may be at the mercy of a looming fierceness like that of Blake's tiger or Job's leviathan, but this fact does not argue for a treacherous or tainted universe. God does not impose suffering or blessing on us, Darwin argued; biology has its own order, which remains indifferent to morals. Frost stands ambivalent on the issue of whether design governs all: whether a horrifying scene proves malicious intent behind the universe. The thought of such planned terror is perversely tempting. Yet to indulge the thought fully would be morbid, fantastic. This is merely a spider and a moth, after all.

Frost's "Design" culminates in a piercing question: what brought the "kindred spider" to its "height"; what led it to devour the moth, a prey so close to it in color and nature? The answer, which takes the form of more questions, varies starkly in the poem's two versions. Frost originally wrote, "What but design of darkness and of night? / Design, design! Do I use the word aright?" This early ending seems histrionic, with its thrice-repeated "design"; and it stumbles in its final question, which sounds abrupt rather than, as it should, portentous. The final version delivers the portent with a proper solemnity: "What but design of darkness to appall?— / If design govern in a thing so small."

Frost here returns to the smallness of the scene, which might be proof to a sufficiently grim mind that darkness extends all the way down to nature's finest details. He also adds, brilliantly, the word "appall," linked by etymology to "pale," and to the pallor that fear brings. Melville in *Moby-Dick* speaks of whiteness as the most confounding, and the final, shade of evil: darkness's paradoxical epitome. Like Frost with his white spider, Melville with his white whale was thinking of Macbeth, his face drained of blood after he murders King Duncan. "How is't with me that every noise appalls me?" Macbeth asks.

Perhaps Frost's more frightening thought is that there is no design after all, that the universe is mere anarchy, and the spider's work mayhem in miniature. Frost has been fantasizing, playing with a possibility. At the end, he leaves the question open: Do we want to see a malevolent pattern planned by God, or a cosmos even more dire, one self-shaping in its darkness? The latter would be not innocent in the Darwinian fashion, but tending radically toward an evil that would reach down pitilessly to the smallest corners of the created world.

Revision doesn't always work as brilliantly as it does in the case of Frost's "Design." And, though rarely, writers' work can even become worse in revision. Sometimes an editor is the culprit. Raymond Carver's editor Gordon Lish made Carver's stories lean and minimal, but diminished their florid impact. W. H. Auden revised his own poems assiduously, and some of his decisions are questionable. In his elegy "In Memory of W. B. Yeats," Auden originally wrote, "O all the instruments agree / The day of his death was a dark cold day." He later changed the first of these lines to "What instruments we have agree." The revision makes the statement qualified and prosaic, determinedly dry. Before, it was an outcry; now, it is a careful measuring.

Revision can happen in the mind of the reader as well as that of the writer. As we read, we fantasize about paths the author might take, or that we wish the author would take. Sometimes we are disappointed, so much so that we spurn the whole book.

What happens when a reader wants a book to be different from what it is? There are famous cases of readers who have objected to a book's ending: for instance, Dr. Samuel Johnson on *King Lear*. Confronted with the infinitely painful death of Cordelia, Johnson rebelled. He turned away, refusing for many years to read the ending of Shakespeare's play. The stage tradition of Johnson's time turned away too: a revision of Shakespeare's play by Nahum Tate in which Cordelia survives (and marries Edgar!) held the stage for over a hundred years.

What do we do when, like Johnson, we find an author's decision hard to bear? We should avoid Johnson's way of warding off what he didn't like. The more sympathetically we think about a writer's choices, the closer we come to the writer, and to the book's vision. But we also need to find our voice as readers: simply mimicking the author's words and thoughts is not a conversation. A reader can develop a point of view and, paradoxically, "be herself" the more she yields to an author's vision. Such yielding is not surrender, but rather an admiring, respectful struggle with the author. An author might antagonize us for a good reason; might even, like Shakespeare in *Lear*, put us through something close to hell. We ought to face the author's vision, rather than turning away to substitute a milder, more compatible work of our own.

Rule Fourteen: Find Another Book

What is the conversation like between author and reader? This is the question that colors all of the rules I've given you so far. I've emphasized the patience (Rule One) and the care that the reader needs to exercise in order to listen to what the author has to say, and to talk back. There's a further step: we can consider the dialogue that books engage in, the conversations that their authors have with one another.

Books talk to one another; in cases of influence, most obviously, but not only then. We broaden the dialogue between author and reader when we bring in unexpected books and make them argue with each other. A volume of lyric poetry might be answered by a work of philosophy, or a history of Europe by a Kafka novel. Books speak to each other across the lines of genre, era, nation, and culture. Often, their conversation reveals their radical disagreement. Plato referred to "the ancient quarrel between philosophy and poetry." Common experiences like growing up, falling in love, and coping with death take on stunningly divergent aspects in different kinds of books. A philosopher, a poet, a biologist, and a theologian will all express contrasting opinions about love, and the contrast will have much to do with the distinctive worlds they have built in their books. These worlds are never simply alien, however. Books depend on each other even when they disagree. Every poet knows that, by writing a poem, he is turning aside from a radically different way of thinking about the world: the way of political speeches or of the realist novel, for instance.

There are more apparent, more easily discussable cases of books talking to books: for instance, when a poet responds to an earlier poet, through allusion or echo. Here is a small example to begin with, by a poet, the late Samuel Menashe, all of whose poems are small. "Time and again" in Menashe's poetry, Christopher Ricks writes, "there is this teasing of levity against gravity." Teasing is just right: Menashe has gentle, at times childlike fun with some of the most serious matters, while still giving the serious its full weight. Here he measures his idea of death against a famous passage from Shakespeare:

Full Fathom Five

Each new death opens
Old graves and digs
My own grave deeper
The dead, unbound, rise

Wave after wave
I dive for pearls
That were his eyes
But touch bedrock—
Not a coral reef—
Where my father lies
I come to grief

Menashe sends us back to the song that Shakespeare's Ariel sings in *The Tempest* to taunt Ferdinand, who thinks his father has been drowned (father and son are wondrously reunited later in the play):

Full fathom five thy father lies
Of his bones are coral made
Those are pearls that were his eyes
Nothing of him that doth fade
But doth suffer a sea change
Into something rich and strange.

In Menashe's quick verse, the father is not a fable but a fact, sheer "bedrock." He trades the fantastic illusions that Shakespeare flourishes in *The Tempest* for an unmagical, compact, stonelike poem. To "come to grief" means, idiomatically, to come to ruin: we might say that our plans have come to grief. Here, though, the phrase means to arrive at grief, to discover a proper feeling for the way death places things (that is, people). Still, Menashe lightly touches the usual, idiomatic meaning of "come to grief."

In Menashe's poem, the dead rise, "wave after wave," in memory; and the living man descends, reminded of his own oncoming death. This seems like leaden subject matter, but Menashe gives it an enduring swiftness and slightness. So he raises his poem to a calm, open-eyed recognition of grief, quizzical and well-made: a contrast to Shakespeare's ghostly, hypnotic lines. Menashe dispels the Shakespearean magic in order to offer something of his own.

Another instance of conversation between a poem and its precursors is Robert Frost's sonnet "Never Again Would Birds' Song Be the Same," which reacts to the Bible and to Milton's *Paradise Lost*. Frost's poem answers the tradition of literature about the Fall of Adam and Eve: most prominently, the opening chapters of Genesis and *Paradise Lost*. But there is no Fall in Frost's "Never Again," and the relation between Adam and Eve is vastly different than in any earlier account: in Frost, Adam appreciates the "daylong voice of Eve," which softly influences the birds of Eden. (I discuss Frost's poem fully in *The Art of the Sonnet*, co-written with Stephen Burt.) When we correctly identify the earlier works that Frost responds to in "Never Again Would Birds' Song Be the Same," and when we realize how thoroughly he differs from them, we learn to read the poem anew. We see this one short poem as part of a lively argument taking place over the course of centuries. The same is true of most books you pick up; the more worthwhile ones will be conscious of their ancestry, and ready to explore it.

Sometimes, as in T. S. Eliot, such delving into literary ancestry becomes a daring confrontation. Eliot's *The Waste Land* begins,

> April is the cruellest month, breeding
> Lilacs out of the dead land, mixing
> Memory and desire, stirring
> Dull roots with spring rain.

Eliot gestures back six centuries to the great progenitor of English verse, Geoffrey Chaucer, who starts off his Canterbury Tales with a praise of April's lively powers:

Whan that Aprille with his shoures soote
The droghte of Marche hath perced to the roote,
And bathed every veyne in swich licour,
Of which vertu engendred is the flour . . .

Eliot's allusion to Chaucer is unmistakable, since Chaucer's lines are among the most well-known in English; and it is sheer irony. The "shoures soote" (sweet showers) of Chaucer's gentle April, which resurrect the earth after freezing winter, become, in Eliot's modernist masterpiece, the slate-cold rain that intrudes on what should stay buried, "mixing / Memory and desire." Eliot's rain engenders a shuddering, claustrophobic world shot though with pangs of Eros and flashes of revelation—the world of *The Waste Land*.

John Milton in *Paradise Lost* poses himself against the Hebrew Bible, not to contradict it, as Eliot does with Chaucer, but to rival it. In his sonorous and expansive Book 7, Milton outdoes the compact Genesis account of creation. And in the Invocation to Book 3 of his poem, he honors and at the same time contends with this most authoritative of all precursor texts. Here Milton describes the first moments of creation, when light strikes "The rising world of waters dark and deep, / Won from the void and formless infinite." I remember that, when I first read these lines as a teenager, I would walk around repeating them to myself. I couldn't get them out of my head. I was entranced in part by the alliteration of "world of waters" and "dark and deep," and by the majestic phrase "void and formless infinite" (a bold revision of the King James Bible's "the earth was without form and void"). Milton adds the soaring sense of infinity to the biblical depiction of the chaos before creation. In his lines, it seems that creation happens of its own accord: the waters rise in grandeur, in a sublime motion that has something a little ominous about it, because of that "dark and deep."

(Wagner at the beginning of his *Ring* produces a comparably dense and magical effect in the wordless realm of music.) The august splendor of Milton's idea of creation becomes all the more striking when we consider that he places beside it his knowledge of his own dark personal world. Milton's Invocation to Book 3 of *Paradise Lost* feelingly describes his blindness: he is sealed off from all visual experience, from "flocks and herds and human face divine."

In *Paradise Lost*'s Book 7, Milton gives an equally stunning account of the first moment of creation. He shows the Father and the Son looking out over a "vast immeasurable abyss / Outrageous as a sea, dark, wasteful, wild"—and then comes the divine word: "Silence, ye troubled waves, and thou deep, peace." My graduate school teacher Leslie Brisman used to ask us in class where creation occurs in this magnificent line. The answer: between "deep" and "peace." Milton gives us a caesura (a pause or break) in the final foot of the line, its last two syllables: a very rare event in English, as in Latin and Greek, poetry. The suspense this pause engenders, heightened by the identical consonant sound p and the identical vowel sounds of *deep* and *peace,* conveys not only solemnity but also a radical and exciting newness. Peace, as Milton the consummate scholar well knew, is in Hebrew *shalom:* completeness, harmony. This harmony occurs over a sharp, silent edge: the caesura that communicates divine tension and divine energy. Milton competes with the ultimate source text, the opening of Genesis, and he produces something just as uncannily memorable.

The more you learn about the rich and complicated society of books, how they compete for our interest, and talk to each other as well as to us, the better reading becomes. Books argue with each other: finding another book sometimes means finding one that contradicts the one you just read. Some authors present themselves as opposing pathways. Among readers of poetry, there are few who are equally fond of Byron and Shelley, or Ezra Pound and Wallace Stevens; and Stevens said that he and T. S. Eliot were "dead opposites." W. H. Auden loved the agile, socially adept Byron, with his virtuoso lightness; he hated Shelley, whose visionary intensity Auden found clumsy, mistaken, and self-serving. What's important is not Auden's inability to respond to Shelley's true strength, but his wonderfully expert appreciation of Byron (and his lovely verse homage to his precursor, *Letter to Lord Byron*).

There are more complicated cases. One writer's aversion to another may be real, but counterbalanced by a profound, messy involvement in his work. Nabokov claimed to detest Dostoevsky: I say "claimed," because the later Russian writer clearly paid close attention to the ice-cold, calculating Svidrigailov of *Crime and Punishment,* who is practically a Nabokov hero *avant la lettre.* Nabokov also scorned Thomas Mann, whom he grouped with Conrad and Dostoevsky: all three, for Nabokov, were ploddingly devoted to ideas, which they pursued at the expense of the beautiful aesthetic structures on which Nabokov prided himself. But Mann's *Felix Krull* seems eminently Nabokovian in its delightful, deceptive manner; and the more one thinks about Mann's and Nabokov's characteristic heroes and themes, the closer they seem to one another. Nabokov too has his ideas—about corruption, self-invention, authoritarian societies—cunningly hidden beneath his claims to an aesthetic of pure pleasure. Both Nabokov and Mann meditate on decayed aesthetes; both dream of classical purity; both write haunted fables. In Mann's *Death in Venice* as in Nabokov's *Lolita,* sexual obsession, the love for an innocent youth, poisons the soul of a connoisseur.

There are some contentions between authors that are harder to patch up. Emerson said about Jane Austen in his Journal,

"I am at a loss to understand why people hold Miss Austen's novels at so high a rate, which seem to me vulgar in tone, sterile in invention, imprisoned in the wretched conventions of English society, without genius, wit, or knowledge of the world. Never was life so pinched & narrow." After reading *Pride and Prejudice* and *Persuasion,* Emerson groused, "The one problem in the mind of the writer . . . is marriageableness. . . . Suicide is more respectable." Clearly, something about Austen drove Emerson up the wall (as it did Mark Twain, who also hated her novels). Instead of freedom, she seemed to him to espouse comfort and security: values antithetical to true imagination. As Emerson correctly sensed, Austen was no bold American individualist, ready to face the universe alone. But her vision is no less capacious and vital because she adheres to the firm limits of respectable, propertied life. Austen is in her distinct way just as knowing as Emerson, just as alive to the possibilities of soul. She merely believes in the virtues of constraint and the beauties of convention as he does not. We have a real argument between two authors here. It is certainly possible to be passionately attached to the works of both Emerson and Austen; but they do present us with a clear choice. Emerson is finely conscious of society's claims, but can assert himself against the social world as Austen cannot—as she does not want to, not even for a moment. For her, happiness is a reflection of how you understand your connection to other people, and marriage is the highest, most established form that such understanding can take.

The combat between Austen and Emerson reminds us that authors' differences from one another are sometimes irreconcilable. You, the reader, may not be able to bring them together; nor should you, since you want to allow each book its distinct weight. You must acknowledge the unbridgeable chasms, the interplanetary distances, that sometimes separate authors. But you can stretch your sensibility by appreciating the radically diverse worlds they have brought into being for you. Then you will realize that what one author embraces fully and vividly is often anathema to another. The battle of the books will continue as long as books are written or read—*vive le combat!*

Reading Short Stories

The short story wants to stop time. The novel is like a feature film; the short story, a snapshot. In its brief span, a short story frequently spurns us by denying our wish to get to know its characters the way we do when we read a novel. We don't identify with the people in a short story as we do with the central figures of a novel. Instead, we peer at them from a distance, through a finely crafted glass. Often, they are frozen in an attitude, a moment, a gesture. The short story tends to give us portraits of the unfinished life, or the life already over: hard vignettes of regret and loss. It can also be joking and anecdotal, and imply a comic resilience. In every case, though, the short story makes brevity work for it. All is encapsulated, made memorable, in less than an hour of reading.

The short story's economy, its concentrated force, makes readers rely on Rule Five ("Notice Beginnings and Endings") and Rule Six ("Identify Signposts"). The opening and the conclusion of a short story are often implied in each other; and many short stories are organized by signposts, by central images and scenes. Rule Eleven, "Find the Parts," is also of key importance (in Rule Eleven I analyzed the structure of Chekhov's story "Gooseberries"). A tightly coherent structure governs many short stories, though this sometimes comes as a surprise: Chekhov's stories, for instance, seem to move in a casual or meandering way, but they are in fact precisely designed (as we saw with "Gooseberries"). Because a short story may resemble an anecdote or a tale, it might appear to lack art. The opposite is usually the case. Artfulness lurks beneath the surface; the short story writer practices a discipline of concealment.

The Irish writer Frank O'Connor sees in the short story "the purity of an art form that is motivated by its own necessities rather than our convenience." The short story writer often resists us, not least by leaving us wanting more at the story's end. O'Connor adds that "there is in the short story at its most characteristic something we do not often find in the novel—an intense awareness of human loneliness." Isolated individuals are suited to a form that stands apart, less eager to please us than the novel.

In this chapter I give an account of six short stories (by Eudora Welty, Nathaniel Hawthorne, D. H. Lawrence, Jorge Luis Borges, Alice Munro, and Stephen Crane). Each of the writers takes a stance toward the solitary individual featured in his or her story; each has a different sense of how much freedom to give the lonely protagonist. The author's final mastery over the central character's fate vies with the character's effort to perform an act of rebellious or dreamy or simply resistant imagination. This competition between the author's control and the character's independent will can sharpen into a tense combat, when the author insists on domination; or it can relax into an easy partnership between author and character. At times, the short story's hero proves reluctant to yield to the strict limits that this literary form imposes. "The Author's Basic Thought" (Rule Nine) at the core of each story that I discuss here has something to do with the strife between author and character, and with the author's anxiety or satisfaction or mixed feelings about presiding over the most curtailed and definitive of narrative forms, the short story.

Eudora Welty's "Death of a Traveling Salesman," her first published story, is a beautiful instance of O'Connor's idea that the short story is a pure kind of art driven by its knowledge of human aloneness; and it exemplifies too the author's will to mastery over her hero. Welty gives us the short story as image of the isolated, unfinished life. The title character, whose car has run into a ditch somewhere in remote Mississippi, receives food and shelter from a taciturn woman and man in a country hut. The salesman sees the couple from outside and fantasizes about their life together. He wants to enter this life, but knows that he cannot. His surprised realization that the woman is the man's wife, not his mother, and that she is pregnant, marks the pivot in Welty's story. Suddenly the salesman realizes that the woman is an object of romantic love; she represents a complete, swelling life. The story begins with a near disaster, the car crash, and ends with a certain disaster: the salesman's death, which was announced already in Welty's title.

Why does "Death of a Traveling Salesman" affect us so? The answer lies in the way Welty makes the salesman know his own incompleteness. At the end, the salesman seems to move with full consciousness toward his destiny, his early death, after a glimpse of the fulfilled life that he must not have. He receives the sentence of the storyteller with a moving equanimity. She has already foreseen his death in her title; we've known it from the beginning. Yet the salesman understands nothing of why he has been given just this fate, and in this respect he is exactly like us when we think about our own lives. Our sense that the hero of a short story has an essential anonymity, that he could have been anyone else, reaches its apex in "Death of a Traveling Salesman." Welty and her main character collaborate in a silent, absolutely concerted way; she leads him willingly toward his end.

Let's take a look at a few sentences from the opening paragraph of "Death of a Traveling Salesman." Welty introduces her salesman, R. J. Bowman, to us:

> R. J. Bowman, who for fourteen years had traveled for a shoe company through Mississippi, drove his Ford along a rutted dirt path. It was a long day! . . . The sun, keeping its strength here even in winter, stayed at the top of the sky, and every time Bowman stuck his head out of the dusty car to stare up the road, it seemed to reach a long arm down and push against the top of his head, right through his hat—like the practical joke of an old drummer, long on the road.

The long arm of the sun is also the long arm of Welty the author-manipulator, and her story does in fact read as a rather grim practical joke. Bowman tries to climb out of his ditch and into a glimpsed world of love; Welty pushes him back down. She is like the drummer who, "long on the road," metes out a hard, sardonic stroke. Welty lets it remain unclear whether the signpost image of the malevolent sun as drummer is Bowman's thought as well, or just her own: we don't know how far the character shares his author's knowledge. By the end of the story, we are sure he is stumbling toward that knowledge.

When Bowman first enters the couple's hut—the woman is standing in the doorway—Welty writes,

> all of a sudden his heart began to behave strangely. Like a rocket set off, it began to leap and expand into uneven patterns of beats which showered into his brain, and he could not think. But in scattering and falling it made no noise. It shot up with great power, almost elation, and fell gently, like acrobats into nets.

This epiphany, a deep puzzle to Bowman, blocks him even as it displays, like the fine acrobat, a strong finesse, even grace. The image of Bowman's beating heart as acrobats falling into nets is another signpost, like the joking drummer of the story's beginning: both suggest comic, adroit feats; but the acrobats have a beauty that the drummer doesn't. The acrobats, with their lightness and control, tame the image that directly precedes them, the disruptive, random launch of the rocket. Though the acrobats have stumbled, they are saved by the nets; their fall is gentle, a tender part of their performance. The acrobats hint that Bowman's coming death might participate in a form of grace (it will look like being caught, rather than like crashing to the ground); but the earlier image of the drummer tells us that the joke's on the salesman, and that his death will be a mockery, not a fulfillment. The two signposts argue against each other; as we read, we wait and see which one will win out.

When Bowman leaves the couple's hut and goes out alone into the night, Welty tells us, "The cold of the air seemed to lift him bodily. The moon was in the sky." The stark empty scene mirrors the salesman's revelation that he is forever barred from the love he sees, or imagines, in the couple's house; he can perceive that love only because he is excluded from it. The couple, close-mouthed, apparently grudging, yet kindly, offer him food, drink, and a place to stay the night. But Bowman wants more—he wants their love to fill the "deep lake" of his heart, which, he feels, "should be holding love like other hearts. It should be flooded with love."

The epiphany of urgent need that Bowman feels when he sees the couple is echoed at the end of the story, when the salesman runs into a dark night, feels his heart pound, and experiences his fatal seizure. Now, the feverish salesman's heart is exploding "like a rifle, bang bang bang," announcing the approach of the end. "He felt as if all this had happened before," Welty writes. "He covered his heart with both hands to keep anyone from hearing the noise it made."

In "Death of a Traveling Salesman," Welty plays the author as lawgiver: she draws the end of the salesman's short life, giving him the death he must have. Yet we intuit her sympathy for Bowman, her kinship with him as an outsider who observes and yearns. Welty has misgivings about her own capacity to rule her character's fate, to determine it from above. The basic thought in "Death of a Traveling Salesman" is Welty's worry about how to describe a person's life within the narrow confines of the short story. For a short story writer, portraying a character means putting him in his place; but, as Welty recognizes, a character like the salesman, in his hapless wanting, eludes the tight limits that the story draws around him. There is something unruly about Bowman's desire, which is as obscure to us as it is to him. Making death the answer to his unsettled nature, as Welty does, is more a cruel joke (the act of a malicious drummer) than a fitting or satisfying gesture. Her lethal punch line, Welty knows, is no graceful epiphany, despite her captivating image of the acrobats, with its overtone of neat, safely cushioned destiny.

In "Death of a Traveling Salesman," Welty meditates on the power of the author to make her character her victim. Other short stories show no such concern, since in them hero and author are in harmony. Welty preys on her salesman; Nathaniel Hawthorne, America's greatest short story writer, collaborates with his protagonist in his strangely memorable, laconic story "Wakefield." An interest in being held by one's circumstances, defined within exquisitely, even fatally, narrow limits, unites Hawthorne and his Wakefield (there is a similar bond between author and character in many of Kafka's works). Hawthorne produced many small masterpieces in his two volumes of *Twice Told Tales;* "Wakefield," my own favorite among them, is remarkable for its understated force. In "Wakefield," Hawthorne tells the tale of a man in London who, on a whim, leaves his wife and his home. He takes up residence in a neighboring street, disguises himself with a red wig, and embarks on his experiment: to discover what his life would be like without him. For over twenty years, he stays away from home. He lives alongside his previous existence; his wife is convinced he is dead. He periodically thinks of returning home, but he doesn't. Once, still in disguise, he meets his wife by chance in the street; she has a momentary, uncanny feeling, but fails to recognize him. Hawthorne ends his story at the moment when Wakefield prepares to enter his home again after his lost decades: all seems the same to him as he ascends the stairs, and yet all is irrevocably changed.

What tempts Wakefield is the notion of making himself absent. Is this curiosity, properly speaking, or something infinitely more fundamental, more corrosive? What does Wakefield hope to find? Hawthorne has an answer: Wakefield wants to measure his own significance, or lack of it, by going missing, by making himself invisible.

Wakefield is like Herman Melville's Bartleby in "Bartleby, the Scrivener": he simply prefers not to. "By stepping aside for a moment, a man exposes a fearful risk of losing his place forever," Hawthorne writes. Wakefield thinks that he can halt time and pick up where he left off. It seems to him that only a few days have passed, not twenty years. But his dead-even complacency alarms his author, and us. With sudden intensity, Hawthorne calls out to Wakefield, his consummately odd protagonist: "He ascends the steps—heavily!—for twenty years have stiffened his legs since he came down—but he knows it not. Stay, Wakefield! Would you go to the sole home that is left you? Then step into your grave. The door opens." Hawthorne concludes "Wakefield" by reminding us "that, by stepping aside for a moment, a man exposes himself to a fearful risk of losing his place forever. Like Wakefield, he may become, as it were, the Outcast of the

Universe." So Hawthorne's "Wakefield" ends: the place that Wakefield has returned to is no longer his home; only the grave would welcome him now.

Like Welty's "Death of a Traveling Salesman," Hawthorne's "Wakefield" puts us on guard to "Notice Beginnings and Endings" (Rule Five). Hawthorne begins "Wakefield" by recounting a story he had read "in some old magazine or newspaper" of a man who mysteriously left his wife for twenty years, lived in a neighboring street, and then returned one evening "quietly, as from a day's absence, and became a loving spouse until death." This vaguely remembered—or invented—news story, of a genre that used to be called "human interest," provides the spur for Hawthorne's tale; but Hawthorne deprives his hero of the eerily uneventful reunion described in this opening, bare-bones version of his plot. When Wakefield, pages later, ascends the steps of his home after twenty years' absence (the same amount of time that Odysseus is separated from Penelope), Hawthorne abruptly departs: he will never tell us what happened next.

"Stay, Wakefield!" This cry from the usually restrained Hawthorne pierces the tale he has told: Wakefield should have remained invisible. And, in fact, Hawthorne saves Wakefield from his blunder, from his decision to return to his old life, by simply refusing to describe the meeting with his long-lost wife (to whom, Hawthorne tells us, Wakefield has remained faithful, while he has gradually faded from her mind). When Hawthorne shuts us out at the end, refusing to show us the final scene we've been waiting for, he has the satisfaction of keeping Wakefield hidden. He expresses his sympathy with Wakefield by guarding his privacy: this is a secretive move in Wakefield's own style. Yet Hawthorne, who sees himself in Wakefield, also hints at his conviction that Wakefield's existence has been a determined exercise in futility, really a living death.

Wakefield's absence effects a "great moral change" in him, Hawthorne writes, but this change remains "a secret from himself," and Hawthorne keeps Wakefield's secret for him. Wakefield will never know why he did what he did: to him it always seems a "little joke."

Wakefield's curiosity is like his author's: he pursues the question of his life from the outside. His wish is to be the third-person observer of his story, the arm's-length narrator rather than the hero. Wakefield merely wants to see what his world is like without him; and sure enough, that world goes on undisturbed. On one occasion the madness of his idea breaks on him, and, Hawthorne comments, "all the miserable strangeness of his life is revealed to him at a glance." Wakefield's reticent madness is also Hawthorne's genius: to look at life from a remote, estranging perspective, the "view from nowhere," as the philosopher Thomas Nagel calls it. Alfred Kazin remarks that Hawthorne himself is a kind of alien. In Hawthorne's final period, surrounded by unfinished work, "his own characters became unreal to him," writes Kazin. (Hawthorne's marvelous notebooks are filled with ideas for stories he never wrote; each page is tantalizing, fantastic.)

Hawthorne's final, anxious sense of the unreality of the world he describes is already hinted at in an early tale like "Wakefield," where Hawthorne shares his hero's gingerly effort to ward off significance. The author, like Wakefield, avoids a denouement. He breaks off his story before the climactic moment of recognition between Wakefield and his long-lost wife, as if to declare that the most pivotal events are mere whims (and this too is why he describes Wakefield's act as "stepping aside for a moment").

Yet Hawthorne himself is never shaken, always centered: his voice remains solid and continuous. In much of Hawthorne's work, the disoriented insight into a day-to-day existence that suddenly comes to seem dreamlike, deathly, or artificial rather than truly alive is strangely matched by the author's sage assurance. As Kazin writes, Hawthorne "tells us a great deal, and always in the same grave voice." Kazin adds that "Hawthorne *knows*, he seems to know, because to him the activity of the soul is not complicated; it is just fatally deep. Everything counts, everything tells, every action is fateful in the unraveling of the knot of which we are made." Hawthorne calmly tells us the facts of our fate; who we are turns out to be disturbingly identical with the law-abiding meaning we serve.

D. H. Lawrence, like Hawthorne, values the fateful, seeing in it the deepest proof of our existence. And Lawrence, like Hawthorne, demonstrates the importance of voice in the short story. These writers, who sound so radically different from each other, bring together Rule Three ("Identify the Voice") and Rule Four ("Get a Sense of Style"), since their way of writing and their perspective are so closely wedded. Lawrence, better known as a novelist, may be the most remarkable short story writer in English in the twentieth century: ungainly, tenacious, sublimely concentrated. (He is also an extraordinary poet.) Lawrence shows his art at its best in "A Fragment of Stained Glass." Lawrence's story is never brutal, despite its ruthless energy. His characters have the force of nature in them: in Eudora Welty's admiring description, they speak "not conversationally, not to one another," but "are playing like fountains or radiating like the moon or storming like the sea," and when they are silent, it is "the silence of wicked rocks."

Lawrence's "Fragment of Stained Glass" is narrated by the friend of a quiet country parson, the vicar of Beauvale. The vicar says he is "compiling a Bible of the English people—the Bible of their hearts—their exclamations in presence of the unknown." The vicar begins Lawrence's tale by reading a paragraph he has found in a medieval chronicle, what he describes as "a jump at

God from Beauvale." In the chronicle, monks are singing vespers at their devotion in Beauvale's church:

> Then, while we chanted, came a crackling at the window, at the great east window, where hung our Lord on the Cross. It was a malicious covetous Devil wrathed by us, rended the lovely image of the glass. We saw the iron clutches of the fiend pick the window, and a face flaming red like fire in a basket did glower down on us.

The chronicle continues, reporting,

> When the sun uprose, and it was morning, some went out in dread upon the thin snow. There the figure of our Saint was broken and thrown down, whilst in the window was a wicked hole as from the Holy Wounds the Blessed Blood was run out at the touch of the Fiend, and on the snow was the Blood, sparkling like gold. Some gathered it up for the joy of this House.

The medieval monk's reminiscence (invented, of course, by Lawrence) shows a ferocious imagination, one of the most memorable I have encountered in any piece of fiction. What could be the story behind the sentences in the monk's chronicle, behind such a potent, awestruck illumination? The vicar invents this story, and, miraculously, adds even more to the power of the uncanny fragment he has discovered. The vicar's inspired fantasia is itself a fragment, a picturing of a dire and intense long-ago life. As in Hawthorne's "Wakefield," the tale is made up from whole cloth, but it answers splendidly to our imaginative need; and Lawrence, like Hawthorne, becomes his hero's partner as he urges his story on.

The vicar, still speaking to Lawrence's narrator, talks into being a miserable serf, master of the stables on a medieval estate. The life of the serf as the vicar imagines it is impulsive, drastic, yet vital and sensual, full of strange power. Flogged nearly to death for killing a horse that has bitten him ("an old enemy of mine," he says), the serf burns his master's barn and house, and flees into the harsh winter night. The bright glow of the fire that the fleeing man sets recurs throughout Lawrence's story as a "Signpost" (Rule Six): the red is the red of his blood; of the hair of his lover, the miller's daughter who shelters him; and of the stained glass window he bursts through in his ragged desperation. He has never before seen stained glass, which Lawrence marvelously describes as "a door of light," "open for a red and brave issuing like fires." Thinking the stained glass window is divine light incarnate, the serf reaches up to partake of its terrifying magic, and shatters it. "Looking through I saw below as it were white stunted angels, with sad faces lifted in fear," he says. These are the monks within, who have just glimpsed someone closer to God than they are, someone more eager and passionate, driven by a fiery dread.

Lawrence's entire story is one fast, raging blaze; there couldn't be a clearer contrast to the meditative, slowly coiled Hawthorne. The violent breaking of the window becomes a sacrament more real, more full of life, than the church ritual it interrupts within. The serf may seem to the monks a devil, but he is instead a hero who runs for his life, and who reaches out insistently for more life, even if it means lightning-quick ruin. With the miller's daughter, he escapes for a few days, hearing behind him his master's dogs hunting him down, along with the noise of wolves.

We know that this doomed pair are near the climax of their brief lives. The morning after they crash through the church window, the serf holds up to his beloved a bit of the "red and shining" stained glass—reason for fear and for awe—and announces, "It is my blood." The woman answers: "'Give it,' she commanded, low." Lawrence here plays aggressively on the meaning of the Christian Eucharist, in which Jesus becomes real sustenance, bread and wine. The serf, like Jesus, is man at his most extreme and most glorious, stretched toward godlike passion. He offers himself to us as to the miller's daughter. He jumps at God, just as the vicar has claimed, this relentless, reckless figure whose agony sums up his whole life. Hawthorne's Wakefield retreats from life, and Welty's traveling salesman is broken by it; but Lawrence's serf defiantly seizes life. Lawrence's "Fragment of Stained Glass" is a breathless wonder, too little-known among Lawrence's short stories.

Jorge Luis Borges, in contrast to Lawrence, deals in careful, cryptic designs rather than bursts of feeling. But just as much as Lawrence, he relies on the form of the short story to give us a glimpse of difficult existence, a life captured in a moment. Borges, more than Lawrence, asks us to "Find the Parts" (Rule Eleven), to study how he arranges his compact fictions. Characteristically, the beginnings and endings of his stories are folded together (Rule Five, "Notice Beginnings and Endings"). Borges's "Secret Miracle" is a gemlike story about an invented Jewish writer, Jaromir Hladik, who is arrested by the Nazis in Prague in March 1939 (the Nazi invasion of Prague was, of course, all too real). Borges published the story in February 1943, gripped by fear of a fascist coup in Argentina (the coup in fact took place in June).

"The Secret Miracle" opens with a dream. Before the Germans march into Prague, Hladik dreams he is playing a chess game that has lasted for centuries. Suddenly, in his dream, he is running across "the sands of a rainy desert," and he discovers he has forgotten the rules of chess. When Hladik wakes at dawn, German tanks are entering Prague. Arrested and sentenced to death, Hladik spends his time imagining his execution, and hopes that this will ward off the death that awaits him: if he lays claim to it in imagination—so he hopes—it won't happen in reality. (There is a similarity here to Wakefield's strategy of substituting thought for life; Borges was a great admirer of Hawthorne's story.) Hladik also broods over the obscure verse drama that he is currently writing. This drama, called *Enemies,* is another strange dream: the "circular delirium" of a jilted suitor who fantasizes that he is actually his rival, the man who has won his beloved's hand. Finally, Hladik reveals, the play's plot exists only in the mind of the suitor, a certain Jaroslav Kubin. The mad, unsuccessful suitor represents Hladik himself (as well as Borges, who in 1943 was on the losing end of a romantic triangle). Borges hardly makes us eager to read Hladik's grand opus for the stage, which sounds colossally, tiresomely ornate. Borges's point is to contrast his own compressed, perfectly made "The Secret Miracle" with the obsessive and disheveled work of the figure at the tale's center, the obscurely preoccupied, ever self-revising *Luftmensch* Hladik. In some ways the disappointed lover and scholar Hladik stands in for Borges himself; a student of kabbalah, he shares the Argentine writer's mystic preoccupations. But Hladik lacks his creator's power to concentrate and summon all in a brief span—he could never be a short story writer, let alone one of genius like Borges.

Soon to face his Nazi executioners, Hladik addresses God and asks for a reprieve: another year in which to finish his play. Exhausted, he sleeps, and has a final dream. In the dream, a librarian in dark glasses tells him that God is in one of the letters in one of the 400,000 volumes of the Clementine Library in the Vatican; the librarian has gone blind looking for that letter. In the dream, Hladik instantly finds the divine letter, and is rewarded with the additional year he has asked for. The next morning, the dream proves true. Hladik is led before the firing squad, but when the Germans' guns are raised and ready, and a drop of rain rolls down his cheek . . . time stops. Hladik remains surrounded by German soldiers, who are frozen in place.

For the next year, motionless and still at the center of this same scene, he occupies himself with refining his great work. If we find the parts of Borges's "Secret Miracle," we can compare Hladik's dreams to one another: we see how the dream of the library represents an advance beyond the earlier dream of the chess game, and how this in turn leads to the final dream of perfection at the story's end, the vision of stopped time.

Now, as Borges's story concludes, Hladik takes advantage of a supreme opportunity to compose himself: he completes his work, the play *Enemies*. He does so, in part, by incorporating into that work the smallest details: the drop of rain on his cheek, the face of the soldier who guards him. The baroque, contorted drama that Hladik has been laboring over acquires some of Borges's own elegant concentration as it meets a small-scale, final reality, this courtyard, these men with their poised guns. Hladik revises: "He omitted, condensed, amplified," Borges tells us. In an astonishing moment of inspiration on Borges's part, Hladik longs to communicate with the soldiers who are about to murder him; they become part of his achieved solipsism. "He grew to love the courtyard, the barracks," Borges writes. "One of the faces endlessly confronting him made him modify his conception of Roemerstadt's character." (Roemerstadt is the protagonist of Hladik's play, the fantasy alter ego of the play's deluded "author," Hladik's double Kubin.)

Uncannily, Hladik spends his year of stopped time reenvisioning not his actual life, but the play he is writing, in which he depicts himself as a man who has dreamed a world into being. Such fantasies are prevalent in Borges. His tour de force "Tlön, Uqbar, Orbis Tertius" tells the bizarre story of a reclusive millionaire who commissions the encyclopedia of a fictive world; eventually, the invented objects from that world begin to infiltrate our own.

In "The Secret Miracle," Borges confronts, and argues with, the reductive habits of the short story. In many short stories, a life becomes something that can be told in just a few minutes, with all the stunning luck and the potential for inhumanity that fact implies. But—Borges suggests—what if one gave the story's hero the chance to design his own life, instead of rendering him, like Welty's salesman, the captive of the storyteller's bleak art? So the writer Hladik gives birth to a mirror-like version of himself, an alter ego he is at leisure to invent. This is Borges's own fantasy of the writer's privilege, a privilege so generous that it extends to his characters. Like a minor-league Richard Burton (whose *Arabian Nights* translation Borges cherished) or Thomas Browne, or Robert Burton, author of the voluminous *Anatomy of Melancholy,* Hladik finds himself luckily caught by his own mental extravagance, tangled in the creeping vines of his fancy. "Meticulous, unmoving, secretive, he wove his lofty invisible labyrinth in time," Borges says of Hladik, who dies satisfied.

In "The Secret Miracle" we see what Harold Bloom calls Borges's "addiction to the self-protective economy and overt knowingness of his art": his adherence to symmetries, and to the consoling power of a final recognition. Again, Borges tells us to find the parts of his work, to see how perfectly it mirrors itself. Borges the ascetic, economical writer, rather than Hladik the rampant, showy one, controls "The Secret Miracle." Through his control he disciplines his earlier baroque self: Borges began his career as the owner of a young man's lavish, hyperactive writing style, though he was never as outrageously bad as Hladik. But Borges still ennobles Hladik, in spite of the fact that he rejects Hladik's false artistry. God (or Borges?) has given Hladik space and time to construct his existence, to hold it up as a pattern, the way a man holds up a beautiful specimen. Hladik creates a perfect written world, one that makes the proper place for his death and his life, even in the midst of the catastrophic violence of the Nazis. He holds that violence at bay as he builds his tableau. He is like Lawrence's serf, but in a vastly different tempo; unlike the serf, he relies on art rather than hurtling, reckless life. Borges, a brave, convinced opponent of Nazism as well as its Argentine allies, imagines a reprieve from Nazi barbarism furnished by the realm of art, and by the sheltering gesture of a God who looks out for writers. But the reader's knowledge that the German mass murderers will not be stopped, even if history were to pause for a whole year, remains heartbreaking.

Paul de Man summed up Borges's art as follows: "a man loses himself in the image he has created." In the case of "The Secret Miracle," the loss is a happy one. The other side of the Borgesian coin is the dystopian landscape that the author so often explores, as in his story "The Library of Babel" (which I discussed in an earlier chapter, "The Problem," where I saw Babel as an apt symbol of the ever-expanding, overreaching Internet). In Borges's Babel, an endless library contains all possible books, even senseless, unreadable ones. Here a dangerous infinity overtakes the diminished, hapless self. The choiceless vertigo of a library without limits is the nightmare; Borges recovers from it by means of his exquisite, self-contained craft. The library of Babel, Borges chillingly remarks, is "illuminated, solitary, infinite, perfectly immovable, filled with precious volumes, useless, incorruptible, secret" (in Anthony Kerrigan's translation). An art that exhausts all possibilities, like that of Babel's library, prevents us from discovering as Hladik does the divine letter that speaks to us. Babel writing becomes no art at all, but rather "useless, incorruptible," deadly in its spaciousness. Borges, a definitive master of the short story, exploits the form's centripetal power with nearly otherworldly mastery; his heroes quest for the key, the one moment that governs all. For

Spanish language writers, Borges himself is the Word: the essayist Ilan Stavans remembers learning pages of his stories by heart. Rather miraculously, a canonical simplicity dwells within Borges's mystic contrivances.

The Canadian short story writer Alice Munro's voice couldn't be more different from Borges's, yet she has something in common with him: she furnishes ample space and time for her characters to inhabit their fantasies of themselves. Through such fantasies, Munro endows the people she creates with the springing, subtle possibility of new life. Like Hawthorne, she promotes her characters' strange wishes; but she rejects Hawthorne's draconian, decisive way of closing in on his characters. Munro suggests that no drastic solutions can or should be attempted in a crisis; instead, she shows an interest in the tricky, self-deluding but also self-nurturing things we tell ourselves, and a strong sympathy for the tellers. In this respect, she resembles a more cautious Chekhov, reticent but not unhopeful about the happiness of her characters.

Munro often balances one character's imagination against another's in the course of a story: here we must be attentive to "Competing Voices" (see Rule Three). In her story "Wild Swans," she begins with the hysterical cautions of Flo, a stepmother (as Munro reveals in other stories featuring the same characters) sending the young, perhaps teenage, Rose off on a brief trip to Toronto; the two women live in a sleepy rural Canadian town. In her first few pages, Munro gives us a quiet yet spectacular account of Flo's fear that "White Slavers" will abduct Rose. Flo describes a retired undertaker who rides around town in a hearse, and who (so says Flo) plies unsuspecting women with gum and candy:

> Flo said he had been seen, he had been heard. In mild weather he drove with the windows down, singing, to himself or to somebody out of sight in the back.

> *"Her brow is like the snowdrift*
> *Her throat is like the swan . . ."*

> Flo imitated him singing. Gently overtaking some woman
> walking on a back road, or resting at a country crossroads. All
> compliments and courtesy and chocolate bars, offering a ride.

Rose is properly skeptical of Flo's florid imagination, noticing that Flo seems to relish the lurid details (which she has,
needless to say, invented) of the ex-undertaker's seductions. Yet
there is something haunting about poor Flo's vivid fantasy; the
fairy tale purity of the undertaker's song takes hold of us.

The song's gentle images of snow and swan are a "Signpost"
moment (Rule Six); the images recur soon, as Rose, on the
train to Toronto, meets a middle-aged minister. The minister
(not an undertaker, but close), who sits next to her, comments
on the "snows," and then tells her about a glorious sight he has
seen recently: a group of wild swans ascending from the puddle
in a field. The minister, placid and healthful, unfolds his newspaper, reclines and closes his eyes. Rose then feels what she
can't quite believe is the minister's hand, shielded by the newspaper, traveling very slowly over her leg. (Flo was right!) "She
thought for some time that it was the paper," Munro writes.
"Then she said to herself, What if it is a hand? That was the
kind of thing she could imagine." Rose is alternately disgusted
and, rather despite herself, enticed by the strange minister's
hand, as she decides not to protest against its "most delicate, . . .
most timid, pressures and investigations." She takes dreamlike
control. In her own response she detects curiosity, a wish "just
to see what will happen."

As "Wild Swans" continues, Rose secretly collaborates with
the molesting minister by opening her legs; she expresses her
sense of what she is doing with a supple ambivalence far beyond
Flo's picture of lust in action, which Munro gave us at the story's

opening (Rule Five, "Notice Beginnings and Endings," is relevant here). Rose laments to herself,

> This was disgrace, this was beggary. But what harm in that, we say to ourselves at such moments, what harm in anything, the worse the better, as we ride the cold wave of greed, of greedy assent. A stranger's hand, or root vegetables or humble kitchen tools that people tell jokes about; the world is tumbling with innocent-seeming objects ready to declare themselves, slippery and obliging. She was careful of her breathing. She could not believe this.

In this calmly virtuosic passage, Munro shows a tender consideration for Rose's consciousness, her frightened, yet exhilarated state. Rose, with the author at her side, wanders into a wild, crude humor (the kitchen tools) and then returns to an inward tension of soul.

"Wild Swans" is a story of sexual awakening, of initiation. It ends in a mood of quiet imagining, as Rose remembers Flo's friend, a waitress who went on vacation and pretended, successfully, to be the actress Frances Farmer (who, we are perhaps meant to remember, led a tragic, psychically battered existence: the unspoken counterpoint to the waitress's easy role-playing). With the anecdote about the waitress, Munro invokes a grown-up masquerade: the unfinished life as reason for hope. Any working-class girl can become an incognito movie star. You can be satisfied in your own illusion, Munro argues; others won't call you on it, even when you act it out. (Rose too will become an actress in Munro's later stories about her.) Rose's strength is that she relies on mystery, the memory of the train journey that both incites and protects her. Rose's fantasized, remembered life wins out over the gossipy imagination of Flo because her way is more inward, more focused than Flo's. (This, in "Wild Swans," is Munro's "Basic Thought" [Rule Nine].) Welty's

"Death of a Traveling Salesman" sees in the unfinished life an abortive, frustrated thing; Lawrence, in "A Fragment of Stained Glass," sees in it a leap at God, a disastrous triumph. In Munro's "Wild Swans" there is no taste for brutal exposure, as there is in Welty, but also none of Hawthorne's emphatic reticence. Munro yields to her character Rose, who in effect writes her own story; she gives Rose's dreamy voice a thoughtful dominion over memory. Rose will recall the sexual incident on the train, which began as a stranger's molestation, but which became her property; she will return to it as to a refuge, a home, later in her life. Remember the signpost, shown already in the story's title. Those wild swans, whose ultimate source is Yeats's achingly nostalgic poem "The Wild Swans at Coole," are rare beauty, an epiphanic glimpse of something tranquil, hidden, and all one's own.

Munro has said that for her a short story is like a house; in it, author and reader should be able to wander around. Few other short story writers would think of this image for their work: instead of paring down to a single slice of time, an isolated event or moment, Munro spreads her stories out. She is unafraid of ramifications, vague branchings out.

Munro embodies the short story's ability to glimpse a limitless world, one open to a character's fantasy; and so, in a very different mode, does Borges. Stephen Crane, my final example of the short story writer, insists, by contrast, on pitiless limits. Crane clamps down on his characters, more ardently than even Welty or Hawthorne.

Crane's "The Open Boat" is spare and stark, a seemingly heartless tale about four men stranded in a dinghy after a shipwreck. (It is based on Crane's own experience of being shipwrecked en route to Cuba in 1897.) The men spend days on the open sea, trying to get to land, and several times come within tantalizing sight of safety, only to have their hopes dashed.

Exhausted with the constant effort required to keep their boat from capsizing, they give themselves false hope, then come near to despair. Crane plays with his four men, and with his reader, like a cat with a mouse. We are often convinced that they will all die in the cruelest manner, after the author has taunted them with the prospect of salvation. In the end, Crane lets them all, except one, survive. In the last pages of the story, the men are finally swimming to shore, and Crane enters the mind of one of them, the correspondent (who clearly stands in for Crane himself). Within a few minutes of land, the correspondent finds himself struggling "in the grip of this strange new enemy—a current":

> He thought: "I am going to drown? Can it be possible? Can it be possible? Can it be possible?" Perhaps an individual must consider his own death to be the final phenomenon of nature.
>
> But later a wave perhaps whirled him out of this small deadly current, for he found suddenly that he could again make progress toward the shore.

Crane's odd "perhaps" in this last sentence testifies to his agnostic feeling about such an apparently lucky turn of events: perhaps there really was nothing there to help the correspondent, no wave, no sudden good fortune. (Or if there was, it meant nothing.) Just before this, Crane utters another "perhaps": "Perhaps an individual must consider his own death to be the final phenomenon of nature." This poised and impeccable sentence proclaims Crane's cold realism. A piece of strangely alienated philosophizing, it shows us that Crane is unfailingly precise. Death seems impossible to the dying, he says, since it resembles the end of everything, even nature itself. The captain, who is still holding onto the boat, calls the correspondent to him. Crane goes on to describe this climactic moment, and he once again voices the correspondent's thoughts:

In his struggle to reach the captain and the boat, he reflected that when one gets properly wearied drowning must really be a comfortable arrangement—a cessation of hostilities accompanied by a large degree of relief; and he was glad of it, for the main thing in his mind for some moments had been horror of the temporary agony. He did not wish to be hurt.

Approaching the now empty dinghy, Crane writes, the correspondent

performed his one little marvel of the voyage. A large wave caught him and flung him with ease and supreme speed completely over the boat and far beyond it. It struck him even then as an event in gymnastics and a true miracle of the sea.

Here Crane drops his chilly "perhaps," which cast doubt on such miracles; he yields to the correspondent's imaginative exertions. When we arrive at the ultimate fact of "The Open Boat," the "little marvel" of the wave that rescues the correspondent, Crane names its beauty gymnastic. Here at last his beleaguered protagonist is allowed a jump of power: Crane credits him with having "performed" what is actually, and obviously, the result of a random, blind surge of water. Yet this respite, when Crane lets the correspondent enjoy for a moment his astounded, grateful perspective, is temporary. Crane retains his customary accuracy in the final line of "The Open Boat," which looks with remote irony on the saved men's new conviction that they know the ways of the sea: "When it came night, the white waves paced to and fro in the moonlight, and the wind brought the sound of the great sea's voice to the men on shore, and they felt that they could then be interpreters."

This is piercing irony: Crane, as a victim of shipwreck himself, knows that the men's experience has brought them no new wisdom. They can interpret no better than anyone else the stochastic, unrelenting waves that nearly killed them (and that did kill one of their number, the oiler). As Emerson wrote in his essay "Fate" of a shipwrecked crew, "Well, they had a right to their eye-beams, and all the rest was Fate." Crane goes further than Emerson. The crew of the open boat are all prey to a strictly meaningless fate, and the author for the most part denies them even their eye-beams, their wished-for perspective on their escape from death.

There is an athletic quality to Crane's style, in its streamlined, balanced approach to what proves decisive. One rapid shift of water changes everything: the correspondent could easily have died, but instead he lives; and the difference is best seen, so Crane implies, with a cold eye. The miracle, for Crane, is dumb: it tells us nothing about the intentions of nature, the character of men, the fate of a life.

When "The Open Boat" finally comes to a halt on shore, with a crowd of civilians bringing the men blankets, clothes, flasks, and coffeepots, our relief is immense after the nearly asphyxiating tension of the action; but we are not rewarded with any lessons about comradeship or tenacity. The men's persistence, their wish not to die, seems more inevitable than brave. And when the correspondent, close to drowning, does for a moment wish to die, to reach "a cessation of hostilities," his impulse is just as honorable as his usual desire to save himself. An opposite ending to "The Open Boat," drowning rather than survival, would have been just as apt. In Rule Thirteen, "Explore Different Paths," I suggested that readers experiment with alternative endings for the work they are reading. Crane makes the experiment for us, by taunting us with the possibility of death instead of survival.

Crane teaches us that even the most fraught and consequential moment can be implacably resistant to our desire to make meaning out of it. The abruptness of the short story, its interest in a curtailed, fixed action, suits Crane perfectly. We find out nothing about the men's lives before the shipwreck, and nothing about what happens to them after they get to shore. All that matters is those few days in the boat, when what might happen next seems both utterly open and utterly closed, and in any case, blank. Crane's approach in "The Open Boat" is like the sea he describes: bare, tense, and forbidding.

Of all the short stories I have discussed in this chapter, "The Open Boat" presents the most drastic tension between author and solitary protagonist. Crane is determined to cast doubt on his hero's slightest twinge of freedom, even though, unlike Welty in "Death of a Traveling Salesman," he lets his man live. At the opposite end of the spectrum, Munro in "Wild Swans" gladly advances the inward power of her heroine's imagination; and Borges in "The Secret Miracle" gives cosmic scope to Hladik's inventions. Hawthorne's "Wakefield" and Lawrence's "A Fragment of Stained Glass" demonstrate, in their different ways, how a writer can elaborate a fictional fate for his character, giving him either liberated energy, as in Lawrence, or a powerful drive toward inhibition, as in Hawthorne.

The string-pulling contours of destiny are also the limits of the short story, which always underlines the role of the author as director of events. In Welty, Hawthorne, Lawrence, Borges, Munro, Crane, and many others, author and reader together must accept the strict boundaries of the form. Yet we are also moved, in our own loneliness, by the lonely capabilities of the story's hero. Brevity makes the short story decisive, but also full of possibilities, so that we speculate, and judge, and sympathize, all at once—like Borges's Hladik, caught in a bubble of time.

Reading Novels

More than any other literary form, the novel asks us to identify with its characters. We get to know the novel's hero from inside; we sink into someone else's identity, utterly absorbed by a new, fascinating person. Short stories force us to keep our distance from the characters; novels bring us closer to them. E. M. Forster, in his pioneering work *Aspects of the Novel,* wrote, "The final test of a novel will be our affection for it, as it is the test of our friends, and of anything else which we cannot define." A favorite novel, as Forster intuits, is like someone who is dear to us; we feel for the persons depicted within it.

Novels don't just feed our desire for identification. They also make it complicated. One way they do this is by playing characters off one another. Novels trade in competing voices (see Rule Three, "Identify the Voice," where I discussed Balzac's *Père Goriot*). The author makes central characters balance, or argue against, each other, and poses them against minor characters. In this way the novel distinguishes itself from the short story, all of whose characters are, in a crucial sense, minor, because they don't demand our sympathy as a novel's hero does.

We meditate on characters when a book becomes close to our heart, at least if the book is a novel, whether the characters are boldly perverse like Melville's Ahab or hidden and enticing like Henry James's Daisy Miller. In the lyric poem and the essay, the author's voice speaks to the reader; often in these genres, author and reader stand in for each other without the need for intermediary characters. But in novels, character is all: invented people confront us directly.

In this chapter I give you a quick tour of some remarkable novels that depend on the reader's desire to identify with a hero: Willa Cather's *The Professor's House,* Henry James's *Daisy Miller,* Philip Roth's *American Pastoral,* Herman Melville's *Moby-Dick,* Ralph Ellison's *Invisible Man,* and Leo Tolstoy's *Anna Karenina.* In each case, the author explores the reader's sense of identification with the hero, and then plays that sense off against other characters in the book, who serve as foils. This is a lesson in structure that nearly every novel teaches: we are meant to pull back from our fervent impulse to identify with the figure at the center, and to think instead about the other characters who populate the novel. We must "Ask the Right Questions" (Rule Two) and "Identify Signposts" (Rule Six) in order to see how the novelist guides us toward a mature assessment of the hero. We can also benefit from following Rule Ten, "Write It Down": taking a few notes on the structure of a novel will help make clearer the viewpoints it offers on its central characters. The experience of seeing the hero from different sides, knowing the other lives that surround her or him, makes our feelings deeper. The intimacy we enjoy with our favorite character isn't ruined, but instead qualified: made richer, more ambivalent.

Willa Cather's *The Professor's House* focuses on a central hero, the Professor, but balances him with others, most notably the young man Tom Outland, whose story inspires the Professor and us. Cather's remarkable *The Song of the Lark* is a bildungs-roman, a novel of education about a young woman on the cusp of adulthood. *The Professor's House* is also a kind of bildungsro-man; it portrays its hero's growth into new consciousness. The Professor is a middle-aged man with grown children, but he recovers the inward strength of his boyhood, and with it the core of his quiet, self-assured imaginative life. Cather here shows herself a follower of Wordsworth. The return to the mood of childhood, when one was a stranger to society and a vibrant miniature visionary, nurturing oneself through high instinct, is a signal theme of Wordsworth's poetry; it's hard to imagine a novel like Cather's without Wordsworth's *Immortality Ode,* which pictures the child as lone hero of the imagination.

Cather was an American original, and American geography is fundamental to her work. The intimate bond between voice and sense of place is the key to this novelist (Dickens is a comparable case, as I argued in Rule Three). Cather's early life plays a role here. Transplanted from Virginia to Nebraska at the age of ten, the shocked girl faced the harsh openness of the Great Plains. The lesson Cather learned was that even as a child you are a stranger, an exile, and that the grown-up writer needs to draw on this early, alien feeling. "Art, like Nebraska, is a journey into thin air, a walk into whiteness, where you lose everything but yourself," Joan Acocella movingly writes. What Acocella accurately describes as Cather's "plain and pure" prose is probably the most beautiful in American letters. It rises in front of the reader, offering no solace but that of the solitary imagination.

The Professor's House is about a Midwestern professor of Spanish history, Godfrey St. Pierre, who decides to spend the summer alone in his small town rather than voyaging to Europe with his family. The Professor passes his time in his garden and his study, in a house that the family has moved out of. Refusing to follow them, he continues his scholarly work in the house's nearly empty rooms. He looks at Lake Michigan in the distance, a lake he has known since he was a boy. Cather's picture of the lake that the Professor watches so steadily tells us something important about the man—reluctant, stoic, yet yearning and cultivated—and brings us close to him. "The great fact in life," she writes,

> the always possible escape from dullness, was the lake. The sun rose out of it, the day began there; it was like an open door that nobody could shut. You had only to look at the lake, and you knew you would soon be free . . . it ran through the days like the weather, not a thing thought about, but a part of consciousness itself.

Cather's picture of the blank, isolate sublimity of Lake Michigan may have influenced Wallace Stevens's vision of his native landscape, in Stevens's poem "The River of Rivers in Connecticut" and in his prose evocation of Connecticut, "Connecticut Composed." In the latter piece, Stevens wrote,

> The man who loves New England and particularly the spare region of Connecticut loves it precisely because of the spare colors, the thin lights, the delicacy and beauty of the place. . . . When the spring was at its height we should have a water-color not an oil and we should all feel that we had had a hand in the painting of it, if only in choosing to live there where it existed.

Like Stevens's Connecticut, Cather's equally austere Lake Michigan promises, strangely, freedom. The Professor is a born solitary, in spite of his deeply courteous nature and his sympathy for others; and for Cather, being alone in the world makes you free.

The Professor's House is something very unusual: a novel about working alone. The professor is most himself when he is absorbed in the task of putting words to paper. This inclination he shares with his creator, and with any great author. His wife's worldliness—her interest in fine things, her "willingness to get the most out of occasions and people"—seems to Godfrey uncomfortable and rather unnatural. Closer to Godfrey than his wife is his son-in-law, the enterprising Louie Marsellus, whose humane generosity and high spirits are unmatched by anyone else in Cather's novel; but Marsellus's considerable verve seems to Godfrey to be somehow beside the point. Marsellus cannot know the bare self as the Professor does.

Cather tests her people against one another, and so discovers their integrity. She presents a study in minor characters, the Professor's wife, daughters and sons-in-law, as a way of framing the struggles of her protagonist. These flanking characters set off the Professor's own quest, which takes place not only in the lonely experience of writing, but in his connection to his students, and to one student in particular, Tom Outland. Tom came as a young man to the St. Pierre household, courted one of Godfrey's daughters, and then died in World War I, soon after developing an invention that, patented by Louie Marsellus (who marries the daughter), proves wildly lucrative.

Tom Outland's true love was archaeology, and that love is at the center of Cather's novel, along with the Professor's love for his own work. Tom is a minor character, but an intensely memorable one; he buttresses the Professor of the book's title. The most extraordinary section of *The Professor's House* is "Tom Outland's Story," and like the Professor's story, Tom's is about the joy of solitude. Godfrey remembers the tale of the dead young man as he sits alone in his house, during that summer many years later.

This is Tom Outland's story. A few years before he arrives at the St. Pierre household, Tom stumbles upon the remains of an ancient Indian village in New Mexico: a whole vanished world perfectly preserved, unknown to anyone. After a futile trip to Washington, where he tries and fails to interest the Smithsonian in an excavation of the settlement, Tom returns to New Mexico and discovers to his shock that his companion on the exploring trip has sold the Indian artifacts en masse to a trader. The village is now empty of tools and blankets and pottery, its rich culture erased forever. Tom is devastated by this news, but then decides to spend the summer alone on the mesa, in the empty village (which is like Godfrey's empty house): once again with his long-lost, now doubly lost, Indian tribe.

Here, at the end of Tom Outland's story, Cather reaches the peak of her achievement in *The Professor's House*. Tom says,

> I remember these things, because, in a sense, that was the first night I was ever really on the mesa at all—the first night that all of me was there. This was the first time I ever saw it as a whole. It all came together in my understanding, as a series of experiments do when you are beginning to see where they are leading. Something had happened in me that made it possible for me to co-ordinate and simplify, and that process, going on in my mind, brought with it great happiness. It was possession.

Tom stays on the mesa until November, studying Virgil and Spanish grammar, and "tidying up the ruins to wait another hundred years, maybe, for the right explorer." He wants to explain his illumination:

> I can scarcely hope that life will give me another summer like that one. It was my high tide. Every morning, when the sun's rays first hit the mesa top, while the rest of the world was in shadow, I wakened with the feeling that I had found everything, instead of having lost everything. Nothing tired me. Up there alone, a close neighbor to the sun, I seemed to get the solar energy in some direct way. And at night, when I watched it drop down behind the edge of the plain below me, I used to feel that I couldn't have borne another hour of that consuming light, that I was full to the brim, and needed dark and sleep.

Tom concludes, "Happiness is something one can't explain. You must take my word for it. Troubles enough came afterward, but there was that summer, high and blue, a life in itself."

In the absolute exhilaration of these lines, all the more powerful for their calmness of statement, Cather shows the essence of the American resilience that Ralph Waldo Emerson invented: when we are defeated, we possess our axis more strongly, and therefore win. A later American writer, John Ashbery, remembered Cather's passage when he wrote in his poem "Evening in the Country," "My resolve to win further I have / Thrown out, and am charged by the thrill / Of the sun coming up." But Ashbery remains deeply disconsolate beneath the strong surface of his lines, whereas Cather's Tom Outland tells of pure, serene victory. The loss of what mattered most to him, his Indian artifacts, has given him his chance. He comes sublimely early, not late, to his mesa. (There is a similarly exalted epiphany in Cather's *Song of the Lark:* the singer Thea Kronberg, Cather's hero, discovers her vocation during a sojourn in Arizona, surrounded by the glorious emptiness of Navajo territory.)

Acocella writes that Tom Outland's story is "driven like a wedge" into *The Professor's House*. When we "Find the Parts" of the novel (Rule Eleven), we see how this one epiphanic high pitch supports and raises the whole. Tom's story is a purer form of the Professor's own quest; Tom's marriage to Godfrey's daughter and his talent as an inventor are mere afterthoughts. The real point is that one high summer, revived by the Professor many years later as he too sits alone, leaning late and reading there, and regaining the strength of Tom's earliness. Tom sustains the Professor's desire, makes it truer. His voice is a shining youthful version of the Professor's; finally, the two blend into one.

Cather's novels are private and modest like her Professor, but also healthily bleak; not pessimistic in the high modernist fashion, but not cheerful either. Her writing has an absolute feel: to read Cather is to gain a sense of life lived alone, at its most essential. She refuses the social graces, the barbed, complex strategies that give Henry James his material and allow for Tolstoy's vividly orchestrated set pieces. She is out for something narrower and, as she sees it, more real.

James's slender early novella *Daisy Miller* presents a questing protagonist, like Cather's Professor. (The novella, or short novel, is a distinguished subgenre, stretching from the Greek prose romances of late antiquity to late modernist monologues like Thomas Bernhard's *The Loser* and Roberto Bolaño's *By Night in Chile*.) Cather set her hero free of society, but James in contrast supplies a frame that constrains Daisy: the busy, often rigid social censors that surround her. With due ambivalence, James studies this constraint. He presses hard, and shows the damage that society can inflict on the innocent self; yet he is unwilling to forsake society's way of arranging and evaluating our lives. The "Basic Thought" (Rule Nine) of James in *Daisy Miller* concerns what is lost when habits of social scrutiny are applied to the young and the free; but also how youth and freedom are incapable of defining themselves, and reach out, inevitably, for a frame that only society can provide.

A young American girl on the verge of adult life, almost, but not quite, ready for courtship and marriage, Daisy is traveling in Europe for the first time. In Geneva and then in Rome, she encounters another American, Winterbourne, the rather stiff yet reflective character who tells Daisy's story. Whereas Cather's Tom Outland strengthens the Professor's inner life, James's Winterbourne sets an ironic limit to Daisy's selfhood. Daisy is free-spirited, frank, flirtatious, and completely winning; Winterbourne, more than half in love with her and afraid to admit it, feels compelled to find her secret. Is she really as naïve as she seems, or could she be manipulative, sexually experienced, disappointingly worldly? The immensely attractive Daisy charms every reader: she's a natural. But as James's novella goes on we start to think of Daisy as Winterbourne does, as a puzzle to be solved. Willy-nilly, we identify with Winterbourne, the inveterate observer, the man fascinated by Daisy's supremely fresh character. Daisy flirtatiously teases Winterbourne, and he, James writes, "was divided between amazement at the rapidity of her induction and amusement at the frankness of her *persiflage*. She seemed to him, in all this, an extraordinary mixture of innocence and crudity." Later on, Winterbourne puzzles that Daisy "continued to present herself as an inscrutable combination of audacity and innocence." He is a reader of people just as we are: we are reading James's book out of a curiosity like his. But we differ, too, from James's staid young man. Daisy delights in provoking Winterbourne, and at these moments we identify with her: we rebel against Winterbourne's hidebound interest in respectability, the way he touts conventional appearance. When Daisy takes up with a Roman companion, Giovanelli, Winterbourne and his entourage are scandalized. Could she be having an affair, flouting all the norms of her social set? Winterbourne is convinced that she is ("a clever little reprobate," he fumes; "how smartly she played at injured innocence"), but he finds out that he is wrong after Daisy's tragic death (recklessly, she has caught "Roman fever"—malaria—on a dangerous visit she makes with Giovanelli to the Colosseum). She was, after all, innocent.

Winterbourne's portrait of Daisy is faulty; James's severe irony reveals him as an inadequate narrator. But the irony touches Daisy too. Her statement that Europe is "perfectly sweet" indicates that she can't even begin to perceive the depth and the darkness of the old civilization she is journeying through. For her, the Colosseum seems a romantic, moonlit place; she does not realize it is really an emblem of the ancient, and modern,

Rome that can ruin its victims, meting out disease, death, or disgrace. Daisy is one of those victims, and we, her readers, see her from an enormous distance: we are older, more knowing. We are seduced by her, but we are also influenced by the mature perspective of James the author. With James as our guide, we begin to understand the workings of rumor, and we grasp what society can do to people. Daisy can't escape completely from the grip of social attitude embodied in Winterbourne. He sets the terms of her story; he pronounces judgment on her. Even though he is finally wrong about her, his misjudgment of Daisy does not make him swerve from his accomplished, assured manner. At the end of *Daisy Miller,* Winterbourne is the same person he was at the beginning; Daisy is a memory for him, not a lesson. The two characters remain forever joined yet permanently distinct, an odd duo indeed. There is something of James in both Daisy and Winterbourne, and the reader shares the author's ambivalence. Here we have a stark contrast to Cather's *The Professor's House,* in which the Professor supports and strengthens himself by remembering Tom Outland, whose voice sounds very much like his own. Cather is unlike James, who, as so often in his work, depends in *Daisy Miller* on competing voices (see Rule Three, "Identify the Voice").

James, in many of his fictions, presents a reader-observer figure (like Winterbourne), and another character who (like Daisy) embodies an enigma facing that narrator or observer. Philip Roth's *American Pastoral* conforms to this Jamesian pattern. Here, as in *Daisy Miller,* respectability is played off against something more threatening, as a father tries to understand his more-than-difficult daughter. In *American Pastoral* more than in *Daisy Miller,* the respectable becomes an object of puzzlement, as fragile in its way as the radical protest against it.

Roth's narrator (a nearly invisible observer, absent from the novel's plot) begins by brooding over the respectable father: his admired friend Swede Levov, a gleaming high school athlete turned middle-aged businessman. The Swede, whose real given name is Seymour, has moved from Newark to well-heeled, rural New Jersey, where he lives a seemingly perfect family life. The only flaw in that life is his daughter, arrested for blowing up the local post office at the height of the Vietnam War. The narrator ends up imagining the Swede's traumatic, agonized relationship with his daughter Merry, who becomes a left-wing extremist, a terrorist on the run, and finally an emaciated fanatic living in a dirty, dangerous apartment in Newark. The Swede owns a glove factory inherited from his father, and Roth devotes a loving, lengthy passage to the Swede's description of the intricate techniques required in glovemaking. (He is talking to a young student named Rita Cohen, whom he will later discover is Merry's comrade, another raving, dangerous revolutionary.) " 'See the seams?' " the Swede asks Rita.

> "The width of the sewing at the edge of the leather—that's where the quality workmanship is. This margin is probably about a thirty-second of an inch between the stitching and the edge. And that requires a high skill level, far higher than normal. . . . Look at how straight these seams are. This is why a Newark Maid glove is a good glove, Rita. . . . Close your hand, make a fist," the Swede said. "Feel how the glove expands where your hand expands and nicely adjusts to your size? That's what the cutter does when he does his job right—no stretch left in the length, he's pulled that all out at the table because you don't want the fingers to stretch, but an exactly measured amount of hidden stretch left in the width. That stretch in the width is a precise calculation."

Here is *American Pastoral*'s true object of nostalgia: an old-fashioned concern for work. Such craftsmanship is the Swede's as well as the narrator's métier: the careful effort to understand

and to report resembles the making of a fine glove, artfully designed to suit the hand of its wearer. Roth serves up a deliberately repellent contrast: in a shocking scene midway through *American Pastoral,* the beautiful working of a glove's stitching over the palm and the fingers is balanced by the obscene gesture of Merry's fellow radical Rita Cohen, whose rudely displayed hand stretches open her vagina, as Rita taunts the Swede by announcing that his missing daughter hates him. Rita's vulgar spectacle is linked in turn to Merry's gaunt, nauseating appearance when the Swede finally finds her. As a Jain (or, rather, her own fantastic version of one), she refuses to wash or brush her teeth, and her stinking mouth testifies to a perverse purity sought in the realm of filth. As a teenager, Merry, who is afflicted by a stutter, shouts at the politicians on television. "The impediment became the machete with which to mow all the bastard liars down," Roth writes, as he depicts Merry screaming at the image of Lyndon Johnson: "You f-f-fucking madman! You heartless mi-mi-mi-miserable m-monster!" Nothing could be further from the calm, orderly voice of her father, Swede Levov.

Roth gives us two competing voices locked in combat: the Swede and his daughter Merry. Some readers feel that the deck is stacked against Merry; but the Swede also falls short. In *American Pastoral* we identify with the Swede, but by the end of the book we are forced to realize that repression is both his means and his end, and that Merry's rebellion against her father, brutal and misguided as it is, aims at a real, and significant, target: the sheer intolerable stone wall of the American pastoral, with its maddening niceness. In many of his books, Roth specializes in chopping away at that wall with broadly sardonic, lusty strokes. In what is probably his greatest novel, *Sabbath's Theater,* he celebrates the benefits of the rude and the obscene, which have a vigorous, desperate energy that convention can't reach. But in *American Pastoral,* rebellion has a depressingly limited scope (as it does in some of Roth's other works, like his recent fable *Indignation*). The book asks an unanswered question about suburban American life: what does this life repress, and why? As we read Roth's painful diagnosis of the malady within American success, we identify with the good-hearted Swede Levov, who is as kind a fictional character as one can think of. But Roth makes us aware that such kindness also means deliberate ignorance: a will to exclude suffering, so that misery becomes unacceptable, unfathomable. We are with the Swede all the way, we feel for him; but we want to know more than he does. In the end, Roth persuades us to value the knowledge of our unease over the Swede's kindness, even when this knowledge terrifies. In doing so he alerts us to a disquieting aspect of the Jamesian tradition: the taste for diagnosis, no matter how disturbing or even cruel its results, over the decency we rely on in everyday life.

James's *Daisy Miller* is a sophisticated exploration of naïveté and knowingness; Roth in *American Pastoral* doesn't allow himself such sophistication, since for him the way we entrench ourselves in a choice of life is always naïve, never sufficiently knowing. He depicts a father who falls in love with social convention, prompting his daughter's insane rebellion, and Roth displays as he tells the story a capacity for both the straight-laced and the furious: he suits himself to both father and daughter, in their rival blindnesses.

If Roth, like James, balances competing identifications against each other, Herman Melville exerts all his mighty authorial passion to make us identify with a single dangerous hero, against our better judgment. In *Moby-Dick,* Melville's magnificent prose epic, he puts us inside the mad Captain Ahab, and makes us sympathize profoundly with Ahab's lunatic search for the white whale that has maimed him. We are ready to be helpless before Ahab's sublimity, the way he both invokes and defies the grand powers that rule the universe, and that—he proclaims—lurk in his dreaded whale.

Yet *Moby-Dick* also sets its two major characters against each other. Ishmael, the novel's yarn-spinning, slowly ruminating narrator, counterbalances fast, wild Ahab, who is bent on ruin and power. Melville poses Ahab's huge thunderings against Ishmael's quieter, inwardly questing sensibility. We align ourselves with both Ahab and Ishmael; and we see that Ishmael's sympathy for Ahab is the attraction to an opposite, an opposing, elated, and tormented power. Ahab awakens not just curiosity in others, but something submerged and recklessly vital. His magnetic hold over his men, and over Melville's readers, defies resistance. His mate Starbuck tries to withstand Ahab, praying "Stand by me, hold me, bind me, O ye blessed influences!" (words that echo poignantly in the work of one of Melville's chief inheritors, Hart Crane). Starbuck's plea is heartfelt and deeply touching, but will prove ineffectual.

In Chapter 35 of *Moby-Dick*, Ishmael rests "a dreamy meditative man" atop the masthead, so intent on philosophical reverie that he fails to notice any sign of whales. The ensuing Chapter 36, "The Quarter-Deck," demonstrates the susceptibility of Ishmael's thoughtful nature to Ahab's demonic strength. Here, Ahab musters his crew and reveals to them the purpose of his voyage: the hunt for Moby Dick, his grand enemy, the whale that has taken his leg. When Starbuck balks, suggesting that "vengeance on a dumb brute" would be blasphemy, not justice, Ahab gives his most sublime oration. Ominous, visionary, he promises Starbuck a "little lower layer": "All visible objects, man, are but as pasteboard masks. . . . Who's over me? Truth hath no confines."

"If man will strike, strike through the mask!" Ahab shouts. "How can the prisoner reach outside except by thrusting through the wall? To me, the white whale is that wall, shoved near to me. Sometimes I think there's naught beyond. But 'tis enough. He tasks me; he heaps me." There may in fact be "naught beyond" the white whale, and not much even to the whale itself (which is a visible object like any other, and therefore a pasteboard deceit too). Instead of a malicious devil, Moby Dick may be a dumb brute—we cannot tell. But what Melville calls Ahab's "intense bigotry of purpose" admits no other option than heroic vengeance, even if it ends, as it does, in the death of himself and his whole crew (with the single exception of Ishmael, who survives to tell the tale). Ahab defies the gods themselves, picturing himself in a boxing match with these puny pugilists. "Ahab's compliments to ye," the mad captain cries to his imagined deities: "Come and see if ye can swerve me. Swerve me? Ye cannot swerve me, else ye swerve yourselves!" Ahab is convinced that his quest was inscribed by fate from the very beginning of time. "Ahab is forever Ahab, man," he resoundingly tells Starbuck. "This whole act's immutably decreed. 'Twas rehearsed by thee and me a billion years before this ocean rolled."

Moby-Dick is the novel as encyclopedic voyage, a great, roiling prose poem. Melville absorbed what he calls the "bold and nervous lofty language" of Nantucket sea captains and made it his own. Alfred Kazin's description of *Moby-Dick*'s brio cannot be bettered: "It sweeps everything before it; it gives us the happiness that only great vigor inspires." Kazin goes on to note that Melville's great novel is "primitive, fatalistic, and merciless," but also focused on the experience of the self, its tentative human search for significance. Ishmael's inability to come to a conclusion, his unsatisfiable contemplations, restless and striving, set him off from the monolithic, single-minded Ahab, the huge dark force at the center of *Moby-Dick*. Ishmael wants to find out meaning; but, Kazin writes, "Ahab's drive is to *prove,* not to discover." Ishmael's speculations about whales, like his musings on the world, are endless, probing, fascinated; he cannot come to a fitting verdict about these grandest of creatures. Melville finally sides with Ishmael rather than Ahab, in that he wants to discover rather than prove; but he is far more extreme than his creation, the gentle Ishmael. The author of *Moby-Dick* is violence-prone, apocalyptic. "What Melville does is to speak for the whirlwind, for the watery waste, for the sharks," Kazin notes. Melville has a taste for ruin; he drowns men in torrents. And even Ishmael quietly sides with destruction, at one key point in the novel. At the beginning of Chapter 41 ("Moby Dick"), after hearing Ahab's terrible challenge to his men, he confesses,

> I, Ishmael, was one of that crew; my shouts had gone up with the rest; my oath had been welded with theirs; and stronger I shouted, and more did I hammer and clinch my oath, because of the dread in my soul. A wild, mystical, sympathetical feeling was in me; Ahab's quenchless feud seemed mine.

Early on in *Moby-Dick*, Ishmael, in New Bedford before his voyage, hears a sermon in a sailors' chapel on the biblical Jonah. Father Mapple, the venerable and robust parson who delivers the sermon, condemns Jonah for fleeing from his appointed mission to warn the sinful city of Nineveh. By emphasizing solely Jonah's desire to avoid the task that God has charged him with, Father Mapple skirts the most troubling aspect of the Jonah story: when he finally does embrace his prophetic mission, Jonah becomes thirsty for destruction, so that he is gravely disappointed when God decides to spare Nineveh. Melville has a similarly catastrophic thirst.

"Find Another Book" (Rule Fourteen) suggests that you follow up your reading of one literary work with another that answers it. Ralph Ellison had Melville's rough epic *Moby-Dick* in mind when he wrote *Invisible Man,* which pursues an extravagance of language close to Melville's own. (Ellison was also thinking about Melville's shrewd tale of racial battle, *Benito Cereno,* which supplies the novel's epigraph.) In his prologue's vigorous preaching about the "blackness of blackness," Ellison gives us a sublime, raucous homage to Melville's sermon on the appalling power of whiteness, which for him is the blank, all-meaning color of colors, transcendent and terrible. Both novels share in what Richard Chase called the "poetics of disorder" that inhabits much American fiction. Such disorder is not a malady but a source of ungovernable, threatening energy; it feeds both Melville's white whale and his Ahab. But Ellison rejects Melville's wish to give the stage to the sublime forces of ruin: the near-anonymous Invisible Man, who resembles Ishmael, is the strangely meek center of the novel, and like Ishmael he is acted upon far more than he acts. There are no true apocalyptic threats, no Ahab, in *Invisible Man* (the black radical Ras the Destroyer, who appears near the end of the novel, is oddly cartoonlike rather than terrifying).

Like *Moby-Dick,* Ellison's *Invisible Man* is haunted by the Jonah story. Ellison tunes his novel to the biblical tale of the reluctant prophet who is by turns desperate, escapist, and vengeful, as he waits and watches for the ruin of the mighty city of Nineveh. Thinking of Jonah, Ellison enfolds *Invisible Man* with a parable: in the book's beginning and end we see Ellison's unnamed protagonist in his basement (his lair, his whale), surrounded by thousands of lightbulbs, listening to Louis Armstrong's brilliant, heartrending version of the Andy Razaf song "What Did I Do to Be So Black and Blue?" The Invisible Man represents the fate and fortune of African Americans, unseen by the white world, and concealed in that world like a poison, a strange benefit, a mute explosion. The vivid energies of Ellison's narrative make it the central postwar American novel, the most encompassing portrait of our racially divided social being. Ellison's protagonist lives through an odyssey of black history, from the respectable bootstrap days of Booker T. Washington (who figures in the novel as the legendary Founder), to an involvement with the communist-leaning American Left (the Brotherhood) to an angry, undirected black militancy (represented by Ras the Destroyer). Through it all, the Invisible Man remains a decent, rather self-effacing narrator: like Jonah a prophetic laggard, prone to shying away in the face of the many strident, full-blooded combats that Ellison depicts.

Ellison does offer us one powerful competing voice, who overshadows for a few pages the wily yet naïve persistence of his nameless Invisible Man: the wild, disturbing Jim Trueblood. Trueblood appears early in the novel, during the Invisible Man's youthful days at a college closely based on Tuskegee Institute, which Ellison himself attended. The Invisible Man has clumsily led a wealthy white donor to the shack of the incestuous sharecropper Trueblood, who scandalously became the father of his own daughter's child. Anyone with doubts about Ellison's strength as a writer need only read Trueblood's hypnotic, uncannily thoughtful monologue, the intense aria of explanation that he presents to the Invisible Man and the white donor Norton. In the middle of a dream, Trueblood says, he found himself having sex with his daughter, who was sleeping next to him and his wife:

> But once a man gits hisself in a tight spot like that there ain't much he can do. It ain't up to him no longer. There I was, tryin' to git away with all my might, yet having to move *without* movin'. I flew in but I had to walk out. I had to move without movin'. I done thought 'bout it since a heap, and when you think right hard you see that that's the way things is always been with me. That's just about been my life.

To move without moving is Trueblood's condition as he understands it (Ellison's words here are rooted in the great blues song "You Got to Move"). The Invisible Man, by contrast, is always too mobile, in his flight from the Deep South to Harlem, from humorless self-improvement to fashionable, bohemian leftism. He scarcely pauses, from fear of the malady that the siren Trueblood represents: an authentic voice that will not budge from its own sickness, that has no interest in excuses, no shame before the white world, and no higher goal, but instead muses powerfully on its own depths. Trueblood, an immensely potent minor character, acts as a danger sign to Ellison's protagonist. As his name suggests, Trueblood cares nothing for the freedom of new circumstances because he is too profoundly centered in himself.

The Invisible Man refuses Trueblood's temptation. Instead of reconciling himself with his sticky fate, he follows another competing voice: his grandfather's advice, delivered to the Invisible Man in the novel's first chapter. "Live with your head in the lion's mouth," the grandfather, on his deathbed, tells the hero. "I want you to overcome 'em with yeses, undermine 'em with grins, agree 'em to death and destruction, let 'em swoller you till they vomit or bust wide open." (Another take on the signpost Jonah image.) The Invisible Man takes his grandfather's daredevil counsel to heart. He knows that he "yam what he yam," but also that he will be what he will be. (In a delectable interlude, Ellison's hero devours a hot yam on the streets of New York and meditates on Popeye's axiom.)

Ellison's tricky, capacious *Invisible Man* is always on the move, but its hero finally returns back to the basement where he started, an underground man. (Remember Rule Five, "Notice Beginnings and Endings.") And now he announces that he is ready to come out of hibernation. He has had the patient cunning to store his energy, as if all his actions so far have been

merely spurious, and the whole novel a prelude to some unnamed future. In the final line of *Invisible Man,* the reader is
buttonholed by Ellison's famous question: "Who knows but
that, on the lower frequencies, I speak for you?" We might
recall here the "little lower layer" that Ahab describes to Starbuck, the truth beneath the masks. Are you attuned? How can
you tell? We try to hear what the Invisible Man has been sub-
liminally broadcasting: not a call for action like Ras the Destroyer's or the Brotherhood's, but a call for recognition of how,
in black and white America, we are divided within, and against,
and together with ourselves.

Ellison gives us a cryptic protagonist who is hard to identify
with; by contrast, Leo Tolstoy, the greatest realist of all, offers a
range of characters who reach out for our sympathy. Tolstoy's
Anna Karenina is one of the most memorable and most provocative of all novels, in part for the way it tests our wish to
identify with its characters. It helps to think of the doomed,
adulterous Anna and the obligation-bound, ascetic Levin as the
contrasting poles of Tolstoy's novel. But Tolstoy makes the contrast a similarity as well: both Anna and Levin are talented so-
lipsists who build and live in their own worlds. We may feel that
Anna is a martyr, that she suffers bravely for her love; or that
she is a narcissist, a destroyer of her family who cares only for an
unreal fantasy of passion, the adulterous affair with Vronsky
that she so quickly finds disappointing. Whatever we think of
her, Levin strikes us as just the opposite of Anna: a hearty, up-
standing man, ethically unimpeachable in his devotion to family and to honest work. Yet Tolstoy tells us that Levin thinks
only about his own picture of the world, and that he is a poor
judge of people—he worships his beloved Kitty, whom he
courts and eventually marries, but knows little about her. The
responsible Levin is perhaps not so different from the fast-living
Anna as we think. We need to "Be Suspicious" (Rule Ten) and

resist our impulse to embrace Levin, to see in him only pure, simple virtue.

   Beginnings are important in Tolstoy (see Rule Five, "Notice Beginnings and Endings"). Tolstoy begins his novel by introducing us to Stiva Oblonsky, Anna's louche and personable brother. Stiva is married to Dolly, the sister of Levin's Kitty. We learn in the first few pages of *Anna Karenina* that Stiva is cheating on Dolly; he has been having an affair with the family's governess. Why does Tolstoy show us Stiva's love affair before he shows us Anna's? This question about structure is also a profound matter of novelistic argument; when we "Find the Parts" (Rule Eleven) we learn something about Tolstoy's method. Stiva Oblonsky is immensely appealing: he is generous, even noble, yet morally weak. Tolstoy is adept at showing Stiva to us through his own eyes. His sex life is undoubtedly sordid, yet it never seems so to us (as John Bayley, one of Tolstoy's best critics, notes). Tolstoy's superhuman powers of sympathy as a writer are here on full display. What goes along with Tolstoyan sympathy is a tendency for each of his characters to remain locked in his or her own world. In Part 1 of *Anna Karenina,* Tolstoy describes a friendly yet strained lunch between Stiva and Levin: "To each of them it seemed that the life he led was the only real life, and the one his friend led was a mere illusion." Stiva lives in a realm of simple enjoyment; in his mind, he is always innocent. And Levin, in his way, is just as willfully innocent. Levin inclines toward the glorious and unreal; he elevates Kitty into a goddess-like stature that simply doesn't fit her. In matters of love, Levin can seem a purist affronted by the touch of reality.

   In their lunch meeting, Stiva criticizes Levin for his high-minded idealism: he says, "You also want . . . that love and family life always be one. And that doesn't happen. All the variety, all the charm, all the beauty of life are made up of light and shade." Tolstoy is doing something very interesting here. As we eavesdrop on the conversation between Levin and Stiva, we know that Stiva's talk of "light and shade" is a mere evasion of the facts: he is an immoral sneak who has cheated on his wife and quarreled with her as a result, and who will lie to her in the future, claiming that he has reformed. Yet we also, strangely, look with favor on Stiva's ability to see in his own faults a picturesque enhancement, part of the "variety" of his life. He forgives others, we must remember, in exactly the same way he forgives himself. No one in Tolstoy's novel is more humane than Stiva. A good fellow and a true friend, he has us on his side. We appreciate his tender concern for Anna as well as his kindness to Alexei, Anna's suffering husband; and when he proves instrumental to the reunion of Kitty and Levin at a dinner party, some time after Kitty has rejected Levin's proposal, he seems (so Bayley writes) like the hero of the novel. Yet we know, too, that he is a man of appetites, and one for whom his own comfort matters a great deal. Sacrifice and hardship are not his way. His talk of light and shade is a paltry, transparent excuse—a shabby lie, really. When he hears Stiva's words, Levin feels a million miles away from him. Yet Levin too avoids a difficult matter: focusing on his love for Kitty, which he thinks of as an external force that possesses him, he has neglected his sick brother Nikolai. Perhaps Stiva and Levin are more similar than they realize. Before his wedding to Kitty in Part 5 of the novel, Tolstoy tells us Levin is convinced that "he and his happiness constituted the chief and only goal of all that existed."

By the end of Part 1, very early in *Anna Karenina,* Stiva and Dolly have been reconciled. And Anna, without realizing it yet, has fallen for Vronsky; her love for him is still just a stray thought that bothers her (the first meeting of the pair occurs when a man is crushed beneath a train—an ominous foretelling of Anna's suicide). Kitty is drawn toward Anna, but she is also frightened by her: she sees something cruel in Anna's intense, rapturous face. So Tolstoy gives us Anna and Kitty as foils, too. Part 1 offers another foil, Vronsky. The dashing Count who has enchanted Anna falls short: he comes off in Tolstoy's telling as a shallow character. Vronsky, we are told, scorns "the banal, stupid and above all, ridiculous" people: those loyal to conventional morality, who care about family and social obligation. "But there was another sort of people," Vronsky thinks, "the real ones . . . for whom one had, above all, to be elegant, handsome, magnanimous, bold, gay, to give oneself to every passion without blushing and laugh at everything else" (in the translation by Richard Pevear and Larissa Volokhonsky). Vronsky's ideal is an adolescent one; he is the greenest, the most callow, of *Anna Karenina*'s characters.

Levin and Anna are foils; so are Stiva and Anna; and so are Levin and Vronsky. Levin as the lover of Kitty, and Vronsky as Anna's lover, have their work cut out for them. Bayley writes astutely that Levin has by far the easier job: Vronsky has to embody love, Levin only has to represent it. Even Vronsky's "solicitude irritates" Anna, Bayley remarks, "for it is without intuition."

Encouraged by Dolly to try again with Kitty, Levin tells her that she doesn't understand how shattered he was by her rejection of him: "It's the same as if your child were dead, and you were told he would have been like this or that, and he might have lived, and you would have rejoiced over him." *Anna Karenina* counters Levin's moving, but overwrought and clearly fictive, image of a dead child with an actual dead child. Much later in the novel, Dolly remembers her dead little boy with his "innocent, surprised mouth," lying in his open coffin. The passage is brief, but it stings like nothing else in Tolstoy's novel. When we read these words, which are among the most painful descriptions in literature, we are startled by the sheer invisibility of Dolly's grief; no one else can feel what she does, and her added sorrow is that no one tries. Children suffer in *Anna Karenina:* they are shoved aside by the adult world, treated as props for a grown-up's sense of identity rather than persons in themselves. The world of love affairs, politics, and social action ignores their presence, their real existence. Yet, Tolstoy emphasizes, children are independent beings, the centers of their own worlds: Seryozha, Anna's son from her marriage, is one of the most vivid characters in the book, and we see his life as he sees it. The immensely tormenting scene in which Anna is reunited for a few minutes with her beloved Seryozha reminds us that she can never be a true mother to this son, and that Seryozha will have to forget her. In the midst of a novel about romantic love, Tolstoy reminds us of what such love excludes: children, who are cruelly seen as mere obstacles or pawns. Perhaps most disappointing of all to us is Anna's neglect of the daughter she has with Vronsky: Anna cannot even pretend to love her. The grown-ups' passions make them lose sight of another world, the foil to their own: the realm of childhood where they once themselves lived, innocent and vulnerable.

Anna's death scene, her sudden choice to kill herself by throwing herself under the wheels of a train, seems curiously mistaken. In a basic and unavoidable sense, of course, any suicide is a tragic mistake; but this is especially or purely the case with Anna's death. Suicide seems particularly futile in Tolstoy's universe, in which you cannot finally sway others through any action, no matter how radical—even death. Tolstoy's lesson—his "Basic Thought" (see Rule Nine)—is that it is your own world you must attend to; your existence is your own, not a tool for manipulating others. When Anna begins to see herself as someone whose only meaning lies in her effect on others, whether Vronsky, Alexei, or Seryozha—or her lack of such effect on them—we know she is doomed. Anna's wish to punish

Vronsky through her death is merely pathetic, and utterly futile.

All of Tolstoy's characters are innocent, and all of them are worldly; they have freedom. This is why Anna's suicide is a whim, not a compulsion. It strikes her suddenly as the path to take—and when she changes her mind, it is too late. In the weeks before her death Anna is never tormented by her irrational impulse to die; she has successfully hidden from herself the thought of taking her own life, and Tolstoy collaborates with her in this. Tolstoy lets his characters shield themselves with rationalization, excuse, forgetting.

The ending of *Anna Karenina* is a puzzle. Nabokov, in a lecture on *Anna Karenina,* commented that the novel's final paragraphs read like a page from the author's mystic diary: Levin, who has also contemplated suicide, recognizes as the novel ends the goodness of life, its God-given sufficiency. We marvel at the depth of Tolstoy's identification with Levin, and wonder for a moment whether the author thinks that he has finally chosen this one among his many heroes. Is this mere ventriloquism—does Tolstoy turn Levin into himself? He may do so for a page or two, but the vast dynamics of *Anna Karenina* speak against any such collapsing of author into character. Novelists are always tempted to sink into an identification with one of their characters, just as it is our temptation as readers to become one with a novel's hero. But the art of the novel counters such impulses: this art fights against the powerful pull toward the hero, and shows us instead the huge spectrum of life, displayed in an array of characters. In Cather's *The Professor's House,* Godfrey's son-in-law Louie Marsellus, who exemplifies social virtues at their best and kindest, is needed to set off Godfrey's need for isolation; the Professor does not ally himself with Marsellus, but with the lonely passion of the dead Tom Outland. In *Daisy Miller,* James places us between Daisy's reckless innocence and Winterbourne's practiced but callow way of showing his loyalty to society; in *American Pastoral,* Roth gives us, in Merry Levov, the rage that answers a father like the Swede, who is too composed, too intent on order. Melville, Ellison, and Tolstoy, too, balance voices: Levin against Stiva or Anna, Ishmael against Ahab, the Invisible Man against Trueblood (and, really, all of the other figures he encounters).

A novel's reader travels through hundreds of pages, moved, alert, compassionate, lost in the excitements of plot. Yet the reader must remain aware of her responsibility to measure characters, not just to "Identify the Voice" that prevails in a novel but to attend to competing voices (see Rule Three). The reader must think always of the author's demanding, contentious, nearly infinite project: to write a novel.

Reading Poetry

In his witty introduction to modern poetry, *Beautiful & Pointless,* David Orr notes that "poetry" is one of the most popular Internet search terms. He also comments that many people pair, in their searches, the word "poetry" and the word "love." If you Google "I love poetry" you'll get enormously more hits than if you Google "I love politics," "I love travel," or "I love interior decorating." We are interested in, or else are bored by, politics (or travel, or interior decorating); but we love poetry. When we turn against poetry we tend to say, not that we hate it, but that we don't understand it. We are afraid of approaching a poem the wrong way and so missing its point: the true message which, we suspect, it offers only to the initiated. But we still love poetry, even when we can't grasp it completely.

Unlike readers of novels, essays, or short stories, readers of a poem find themselves constantly brought up against the question of the poem's meaning. They must, above all, "Be Patient" (Rule One); they must "Get a Sense of Style" (Rule Four) in order to intuit the mood and the argument of the poem; and they must, even more than with other genres, "Use the Dictionary" (Rule Seven) and "Track Key Words" (Rule Eight). Finally, it helps to "Write It Down" (Rule Twelve): take notes on your impressions and, by doing so, bring the character of the poem out into the open. When you articulate your feelings about a poem, you increase your enjoyment of it; when you revel in its details, and especially when you write them down, you expand your knowledge of how the poem works.

A reader might be impressed, even deeply moved, but still mystified by a poem. In just this way, reading a poem resembles falling in love: we're attracted by what we don't get. In both love and poetry, mystery and truthfulness appear strangely conjoined. The Polish poet Adam Zagajewski said in an interview, "In poetry I always have the feeling: I'm looking for truth, for some truth about the world, about myself." The poem leads us on; it directs us, and promises to tell us who we are.

What do we expect from a poem? Eloquence, heightened language, yes; but most of all, true feeling. Poetry bares the inner life; it is direct and vulnerable in a way that novels aren't. Yet poetry is also highly artful, shrewd in its reliance on disguise. Nakedness of expression is rarely a feature of poetry. Far more often poetry proves subtle and devious, in a way that makes us wonder where its verbal artifices are headed. When I walk into a classroom, as I often do, to teach the poems of Hart Crane, Emily Dickinson, or Wallace Stevens, I have to be prepared to reckon with these sublime poets' barrage of strategies, their spectacular cognitive feats, the ways that they keep the reader tangled in an intensity of thought and language that resists paraphrase. Very few poets are quite so wonderfully enfolded, and at the same time agile, in their style as Crane, Dickinson, or Stevens. But even when a poem appears accessible and plain-spoken, it nearly always harbors difficulty. We must not only attend to style, but also be alert to the relation between style and the author's "Basic Thought" (Rule Nine). Robert Frost is often considered an open and amiable, even simple writer; but in his thinking, in the hard, selective nuances of his words, he is as thorny and indirect as Crane. Frost's poems divide the reader who "Asks the Right Questions" (Rule Two) from the one who doesn't. Like the St. Mark he cites in his great quest poem "Directive," Frost likes to exclude, to build walls. If we can sense both the doom-laden side and the promising, pragmatically free side of Frost, and see how the two sides strangely interlock, we will have some inkling of what his basic thought is about. (It also has something to do with what work means to him, in life and in verse; and something to do with the benefits of being left out.) Like a good proverb, a Frost poem often turns back on itself: the chosen path in "The Road Less Traveled" looks almost exactly like the one not chosen, so what difference can the choice make—except that the poem's speaker has decided it makes an enormous, untellable difference?

Frost teaches us that a poem often has a sealed-off character: commanding us from the heights, it beckons even as it holds its ground. Poems are centripetal; they give everything to focus. (Even Walt Whitman, who has a reputation for passionate, far-flinging expression, is in fact judicious and inward, and keeps his own counsel.) What poetry must be, above all else, is memorable, because it is so concentrated a form, staking everything on a few moments in the life of words.

In her essay "How Should One Read a Book?" Virginia Woolf cites the unforgettable four-line medieval English lyric "Western Wind," which instantly transports us into the pained presence of its singer:

> Western wind, when wilt thou blow?
> The small rain down can rain.
> Christ, if my love were in my arms,
> And I in my bed again!

Woolf comments, "The impact of poetry is so hard and direct that for the moment there is no other sensation except that of the poem itself. What profound depths we visit then—how sudden and complete is our immersion! There is nothing here to catch hold of; nothing to stay us in our flight." Novels are different, she remarks: "The illusion of fiction is gradual; its effects are prepared." A poem like "Western Wind" (which may well be the first blues) hits the whole being, swiftly and utterly. There is no slow unfolding; instead, this short lyric ravishes us.

Poetry makes us fall in love with words, and with the passion behind them; a single word can seem to embody a whole world. Such is the case with the lapidary, provoking work of Emily Dickinson.

For Dickinson, poetry is not just a polished thing, but an ecstatic one, as a wider treatment of her work than I have time for here would make clear. No matter how minutely she teases words, her intensity is always electric. She once remarked in a letter, "If I read a book [and] it makes my whole body so cold no fire can ever warm me I know *that* is poetry." Dickinson gives us the same chill: her poems estrange and exhilarate the reader. She knows, too, the loneliness of both author and reader. Edward Hirsch compares the lyric poem to a message in a bottle: "It speaks out of a solitude to a solitude; it begins and ends in silence." Dickinson, so absolute, so separate in her poetic stance, would concur with Hirsch's observation.

I give two short poems by Dickinson to show how she bears down on meaning, how her playing with words can be a lonely revelation. First, Dickinson's Poem 185:

"Faith" is a fine invention
For gentlemen who *see,*
But *Microscopes* are prudent
In an emergency!

If we follow Rule Twelve ("Write It Down"), we might begin by contrasting the two halves of the poem, which are separated by Dickinson's "But." Our note may look something like this: "Faith / see vs. microscopes / emergency." These are some of the "Key Words" (Rule Eight) in Dickinson's Poem 185 (in such a short, compressed work, all the other nouns and adjectives—"fine," "invention," "gentlemen," and "prudent"—also count as key words). But let's begin with the four words we've written down first, and see how our first pair differs from the second. If we remember a biblical passage from Hebrews (11:1), "Now faith is the substance of things hoped for, the evidence of things not seen," we will get even further: Dickinson must be asking what kind of seeing is produced by faith—accurate and discerning, or merely invented? She suggests the latter option when she calls faith an "invention." Perhaps faith merely sees what it wants to, or how it wants to. In the second half of the poem, Dickinson refers to another invention, the microscope, which she says is useful in emergencies as faith is not. The two inventions are unlike: faith is a matter of belief, whereas microscopes are scientific instruments, and uncover actual, provable evidence (as opposed to the evidence of things not seen). Our first step has been to "Find the Parts" (Rule Eleven) of Dickinson's poem. It falls into two easily separated halves: an observation followed by a qualification; or, perhaps, a question (does faith really work, and if so, for whom, and how?) followed by an answer.

Dickinson's attitude in this small, cutting poem is skeptical. She begins by putting faith in quotation marks, a sign of her lifelong interrogation of the Christian beliefs that surrounded her. When it comes to God, Dickinson is always engaged, never merely diffident; no easy atheist, she wrestles with her inability to feel faith sufficiently. To call faith an invention, and beyond that a fine one, is to see it as a product of human ingenuity, rather than a response to God. "Fine" is a key word too: it retains its several meanings of intricate, subtle, precious and excellent; but we also remember that, when spoken in a sardonic tone, it accentuates a bad thing or situation, as in "a fine mess."

The "gentlemen who *see*" come off, in Dickinson's treatment, rather questionably. They would describe themselves as the ones with true insight. But we know that their faith is contrived, not a natural aptitude. Moreover, Dickinson tells us that faith falls short—it needs to be supplemented "in an emergency" by "Microscopes." That is, we need to look more closely, more clinically, perhaps more scientifically, than faith will allow. Above all, we need to look more "prudently." "Prudent" is another key word in Poem 185, and one that we ought to take a good look at: with this word, Dickinson casts doubt on her own solution. She's not entirely comfortable with the way that her poem moves from a problem in its first half (relying on faith) to a solution in its second half (relying on microscopes). Dickinson is, as she well knows, a poet of the microscope, one who rather myopically inspects the minute surfaces of the world. She does not have faith, but she has care. (And this is pressing: the single rhyme in Dickinson's quatrain, "see" and "emergency," implies that seeing properly is an urgent matter indeed.) But, she thinks, perhaps the close-up, sharp focus character of her achievement is a limitation: after all, prudence is not a heroic virtue. It is reasonable to attribute this self-ironizing reflection to Dickinson, even if we have to tease it out of her minuscule, glittering poem. She is more careful than she wants to be. How much more satisfying it would be to take the giant steps toward truth! As many of her other poems show, Dickinson has sublime appetites. When she denies herself sublimity, as she does in this little poem, it is in order to keep a covenant with something precise and searching in her nature. Elizabeth Bishop, one of Dickinson's heirs in American poetry, will show a similar fidelity when she refuses sloppy declarations in favor of high-stakes hints and nudges. Bishop often seems to be talking about something other than what she is directly describing (in her great, quizzical poem "The Monument," for example).

Another short, even more lethal Dickinson poem is 156:

> Surgeons must be very careful
> When they take the knife!
> Underneath their fine incisions
> Stirs the Culprit—Life!

In this quatrain, Dickinson again recommends a prudent approach. By "surgeons" she means not doctors performing an operation, but people who take an intellectual view, who examine the world and lay it open. Dickinson is herself one of the surgeons; her poetry has a lacerating, at times ruthless approach to existence. In her nearly 1,800 poems she observes grief, love, and loneliness with a clinical, sometimes icy eye. So her little poem is a piece of self-counseling, not merely a lesson to others. Surgeons (like her) must take care not to damage "Life," which lurks beneath their "fine incisions." She probably has in mind William Wordsworth's judgment that "we murder to dissect": that is, we kill in order to analyze, since analysis is what we love. Such surgery spoils life, hollowing out our experience and making it a mere datum for the empirical sensibility. Life is the "Culprit," the guilty perpetrator, or so the men with knives assume; the sharp rhyme of "knife" and "life" makes their point. But in charging life with such guilt, the scalpel wielders ignore its stirring and subtlety—and these are qualities that Dickinson expertly devotes herself to in her verse. Dickinson's poem is elusive because it plays with voice: we are forced to wonder whether it is Dickinson or the surgeons who name life a culprit. (Voice is often one of the hardest aspects of a poem to adjudicate, and one of the most crucial; see Rule Three, "Identify the Voice.") Surgeons are sworn to heal, not to kill; but when they become intellectual prosecutors, they make it hard for life to prove its innocence. They destroy the very thing that they set out to preserve.

Dickinson's two poems are epigrammatic: they deliver judgment, pronounce a truth with dry certainty. But, as we have seen, this truth must be interpreted, and, it seems, is never quite found: the reader is puzzled, provoked into thought, but not satisfied. Here, we must "Be Patient" (Rule One) and try to piece together the argument of the poem. If you like Dickinson's Poems 185 and 156, you may want to explore other epigrams. The tradition of the epigram is a long and diverse one: try Burton Raffel's versions of the ancient Greek poets who invented the form in his anthology *Pure Pagan,* or Guy Davenport's equally acerbic translations in his *7 Greeks.*

Let's turn now to another kind of epigram, one that, like Dickinson's poems, foregrounds the connection between style and argument: "To the Dead Owner of a Gym," by the British poet Thom Gunn. Written near the height of the AIDs epidemic, "To the Dead Owner of a Gym" has an epitaphic feel; it seems as if it ought to be engraved on its subject's tombstone. (Strictly speaking, it is an elegy: a poem addressed to and in memory of a dead person.)

To the Dead Owner of a Gym

I will remember well
The elegant decision
To that red line of tile
As margin round the showers
Of your gym, Norm,
In which so dashing a physique
As yours for several years
Gained muscle every week
With sharper definition.
Death on the other hand

Is rigid and,
Finally as it may define
An absence with its cutting line,
                    Alas,
                    Lacks class.

Gunn plays seriously with etymology, as we discover when we "Use the Dictionary" (Rule Seven)—one like the *Oxford English Dictionary* or the *American Heritage Dictionary,* which explain the foreign language roots of English words. "Elegant" comes from the Latin *eligere,* meaning to choose; and "decision" from the Latin *decidere,* meaning to fall dead. The "elegant decision" of the tile's red line signals the poem's own finely chosen dexterity, but also the fact of mortality that marks our lives' "margin." Gunn's poem presents itself as an act of definition, and it pursues that definition just as its subject, the perfectly named Norm, pursues better-defined muscles. A "cutting line" is a sharp witticism, and death, which always has the last word, is the best joker, as it coldly demolishes the ambitious human athlete's efforts to reshape his body. Gunn's poem strikes back against mortality, though. Its verdict on death is a Dorothy Parkeresque zinger: death, "Alas, / Lacks class," since it is "rigid," not "dashing" like Norm, whom it claims. But death displays formidable style, as Gunn is forced to admit: it is truly definitive as we, in our lives, are not. The chiseled tact of "To the Dead Owner of a Gym" ranks it on the side of death. The poem recognizes as it must our inevitable, fatal end; its honoring of its subject, the gym owner Norm, is ironically posed against this recognition. Death wins and we lose, and Gunn's poem must honor this fact, too, even as it remembers a lost friend.

I will use "To the Dead Owner of a Gym" as an opportunity to explore scansion. Scanning a poem is an exercise in how to "Write It Down" (Rule Twelve): think of it as a way of taking notes on an essential aspect of the poem. To scan verse means to mark its stresses (or accents), the syllables that a poem emphasizes over others. The first step is to notice natural speech stress. In Gunn's first line, "remember" has to be accented on its middle syllable, since we always do so when we speak; also in this first line, we say "I wíll" rather than "Í will," with the stress on the second rather than the first word of the phrase—we don't emphasize "I," since this is not the special case in which we want to imply "I rather than somebody else." (Only on rare occasions will a poem use "wrenched accent," which forces us to emphasize a syllable in violation of normal speech practice: a girl in a Scottish ballad may come "from a far countrée," but this is a very unusual instance.)

If we stay attuned to natural speech stress, we will see that Gunn's poem falls into an iambic pattern. The foot is the basic unit of verse within a line; an iambic foot consists of an unstressed followed by a stressed syllable (daDUM). The most common line of English verse is a five-beat iambic line: that is, a line with five stressed syllables, like Hamlet's "To bé / or nót / to bé: / Thát is the / Quéstion." Note that not all of this line's feet are iambs: the last two are a dactyl (DAdumdum, "Thát is the") and a trochee (DAdum: "Quéstion." But most are iambs, and so this is still iambic verse. Trochaic verse has quite a different feel: each foot begins with a beat. The trochaic line often seems to caper; trochees dance. So Ariel in *The Tempest* sings, "Fóot it / Féatly / Hére and / Thére."

Here is Gunn's "To the Dead Owner of a Gym" again; I have identified each stress with an accent mark (´) and divided the poem into feet with slash marks (/):

To the Dead Owner of a Gym

I wíll / remém- / ber wéll
The él- / egánt / decí- / sion

To thát / red líne / of tíle
As már- / gin róund / the shówers
Of your / gým, Nórm, /
In whích / so dásh- / ing á / physíque
As yóurs / for sév- / eral yéars
Gained mús- / cle év- / ery wéek
With shárp- / er dé- / finí- / tion.
Déath on / the óth- / er hánd
Is ríg- / id ánd,
Fínal- / ly ás / it máy / defíne
An áb- / sence wíth / its cút- / ting líne,

Alás,

Lácks cláss.

As you can see, the iamb, the basic unit of speech rhythm, usu-ally wins out, in Gunn's poem as in most English verse. There are exceptions, though: "several years" and "every week" end in anapests, a light, swift foot most often used to speed up a line (dadaDUM). The final two words of the poem are a spondee, a foot that stresses both syllables: "Lácks cláss." In contrast to the fleet anapest, the spondee gives a heavy, decisive air to any statement (think of the insult "Fúck yóu," a classic spondee). "Of your gym, Norm," is a very unusual line: a pyrrhic foot (two unstressed syllables) followed by a spondaic foot—and the spondaic foot contains a caesura, a sharp pause that here singles out and privileges the dead man's name (gym, ‖ Norm). For practical purposes, the "sion" and "tion" at the ends of "deci-sion" and "definition" are also pyrrhic feet (if one adopts a Brit-ish pronunciation, as Gunn, transplanted from England to San Francisco, probably would have done). The number of feet per line varies in Gunn's poem between four, three, two, and one—another unusual feature.

I have just hit you, very quickly, with quite a lot of technical information about English verse. If you are eager for more, I recommend a manual like John Hollander's lively *Rhyme's Reason*. The main thing, though, is to cultivate a sense of iambic rhythm, since the iamb is the soul of English-language poetry. A surprising amount of our prose, as well as our everyday conversation, is iambic; the popularity of this poetic foot depends on its living presence in our speech. But most of the time we don't talk in iambs, at least not for more than a few phrases at a time. Poems often make the iambic pace play against natural speech rhythm; if the two patterns coincide too completely, doggerel results. In the famous line from Shakespeare's *Macbeth*, "Tomór - / row ánd / tomór / -row ánd / tomórrow," no actor will give the two "and"s a stress as heavy as he gives the second syllable of "tomorrow," because "tomorrow" is accented on the second syllable in normal speech, whereas "and" is not. But the iambic rhythm emphasizes "and" as well: this is significant, because Shakespeare's theme is the endless series of "ands" that makes one day follow, and echo, another. "And" receives stress—just not as much as "tomorrow": "Tomorrow and tomorrow and tomorrow / Creeps in this petty pace from day to day, / To the last syllable of recorded time." (Note that Shakespeare's third "tomorrow" is what is called a hypermetric foot: it contains a final unaccented syllable, but it still counts as an iamb.)

Iambic form often appears even in "free verse" (that is, poetry emancipated from strict loyalty to accent). Let's take a look at a rhapsodic poem in free verse that relies, to marvelous effect, on iambs—Walt Whitman's "The Dalliance of the Eagles":

Skirting the river road, (my forenoon walk, my rest,)
Skyward in air a sudden muffled sound, the dalliance of the
    eagles,

The rushing amorous contact high in space together,
The clinching interlocking claws, a living, fierce, gyrating
    wheel,
Four beating wings, two beaks, a swirling mass tight
    grappling,
In tumbling turning clustering loops, straight downward
    falling,
Till o'er the river poised, the twain yet one, a moment's lull,
A motionless still balance in the air, then parting, talons
    loosing,
Upward again on slow-firm pinions slanting, their separate
    diverse flight,
She hers, he his, pursuing.

Trochees mark the beginnings of several lines in Whitman's poem, in each case giving a feeling of uplift (Skírting, Skýward, Úpward). All two-syllable gerunds are trochees, and we have plenty of them, too, in "The Dalliance of the Eagles": notice the high-sprung energy of "rushing," "clinching," "tumbling," "turning," "slanting." But Whitman also indulges an iambic rhythm in the opening line and a half of the poem:

"Skirting the river road, (my forenoon walk, my rest,)
Skyward in air a sudden muffled sound"

These lines settle into iambs after their trochaic beginnings: "(my fóre- / noon wálk, / my rést)," "a súd- / den múf- / fled sóund." There are phrases in "The Dalliance of the Eagles" that don't feel metrical, like "A motionless still balance in the air." But on the whole, Whitman's poem is happily indebted to the iambic foot.

I now want to take a look at the argument of "The Dalliance of the Eagles," Whitman's adroit feat of a poem. The argument centers itself around "Key Words" (Rule Eight). Whitman begins with "skirting" (the action of the poet, who is something of a bystander) and ends with "pursuing" (the action of the eagles, the poem's main actors). What do the eagles pursue but their singular selves, rather than each other? Like the eagles, each of us takes a "separate diverse flight." Here, solitude is solidarity. Dalliance usually suggests the irresponsible. But the eagles' skirting, tangential motions may be more committed, and more ecstatic too, than the lasting, explicit proclamations of the staid lover. Whitman's own promiscuous gaze as he visits the people and scenes he describes in his poems is just as serious a form of commitment.

Whitman begins with the sudden noise of the birds, and then follows them from below as they fly up. The glancing apex of his vision comes with "the twain yet one, a moment's lull." This momentary pause contains the recognition that union is actual, active, and therefore (this is Whitman's insight) passing. (This is the basic thought of "The Dalliance of the Eagles.") The "slow-firm pinions" buttress the two birds' independence. Whitman might be thinking of, in order to present a contrast with, Keats's image of Cupid and Psyche in his "Ode to Psyche": "Their wings embraced, and their pinions too." (A pinion is the primary feather, located at the outer rear edge of a bird's wing.) Instead of a sedentary amorous melding like Keats's, in which lovers sink into one another, Whitman gives us a wonderful word picture of desire as free flight. We salute others in our rapid, upward course, and this salute has a profound erotic dimension—it is, explicitly, a sexual tussle—but finally we are each alone, sensing only the self and the space around it.

Whitman's "Dalliance of the Eagles" is a pure lyric flight; it has no interest in a vision of personality. W. B. Yeats, by contrast, from first to last, depicts heroes who aim to find a conception equal to their desire, an integrated selfhood. Yeats's protagonists reach after a "Basic Thought" far different from

Whitman's praise of transitory, mounting energy. They want something steadier, more complete. They must remain awake and quarrelsome, since they are frustrated seekers after a unity that resists being found. Yeats embraces the striving after a whole, creative self. In Yeats, intellect on its own is not enough; the selfhood seeks a passionate oneness that will bring mind and emotion together.

Yeats's Fergus, in his early poem "Fergus and the Druid," is an example of undirected intellect, subject to every impetus, set adrift. In the poem's final stanza, Fergus says,

> I see my life go drifting like a river
> From change to change; I have been many things—
> A green drop in the surge, a gleam of light
> Upon a sword, a fir-tree on a hill,
> An old slave grinding at a heavy quern,
> A king sitting upon a chair of gold—
> And all these things were wonderful and great;
> But now I have grown nothing, knowing all.

The Druid has given Fergus a magical series of protean transformations, but they do not rise to the level of real experience; Fergus's mere knowing, without a passionate, thoughtful harmonizing of all these changes, leads to the gradual extinction of the self. Daniel O'Hara writes that Yeats in his *Autobiographies* was "imaginatively trying out possible self-images at the point of crisis to find the truly necessary one." This is exactly what Fergus, who remains a mere spectator, does not do; he feels neither crisis nor the pressure of necessity.

Early Yeats is haunted by surmise: a gentle fulfilling of imaginative fantasy, seen in Fergus's drifting from thing to thing, or the pleasant, echoing chant of Yeats's "Song of the Happy Shepherd," which he placed at the beginning of his *Collected Poems*. Whereas Keats and Shelley raised surmise to visionary heights, Yeats retains the difference between surmise and vision. He keeps pointing out that surmise, which for him is tentative and naïve by nature, falls short, and that vision instead is required. Vision, for Yeats, describes an absolute kind of poetic action, one that can unite knowledge and imagination. Yet, as Yeats's career continues, his protagonists time and again fail to achieve visionary perfection. They tend to lapse into bitter or disappointed states of being, as Cuchulain does in Yeats's sublime, very late poem "Cuchulain Comforted," composed two weeks before his death; they learn discontent rather than wisdom. They may be able to embody a truth, but for that very reason they cannot know it: this irony bars them from the wholeness, the devoted self-fashioning, that Yeats aspires to in the *Autobiographies*. (Yeats's ironic sense of the lack of knowledge that dogs committed and violent deeds, no matter how well such deeds embody their time, makes for his status as the twentieth century's best political poet in English: read his "Nineteen Hundred and Nineteen" and "Meditations in Time of Civil War.")

Love, too, fails to deliver the vision needed for unity of being. For Yeats, the tragedy of sexual love is the perpetual virginity of the soul (as I mentioned in my earlier account of Rule Nine, "Find the Author's Basic Thought"). Love's tumult may wrack us, but we are not truly metamorphosed by such passion. Stubbornly, inevitably adhering to our original selfhood, we never reach the enlightened realms that love promised us. Such was Yeats's own experience of his great love Maud Gonne: she was Muse, antagonist, and resentful, faulty prophet, and in all these roles she proved essential to Yeats. But her stature as ideal beloved posed a crucial problem: she was too much created by Yeats to truly change him.

In one late poem, "Beautiful Lofty Things," Yeats's heroes become themselves, and the bitterness of disappointed questing fades away. I have long loved this short poem, which in so many ways distinguishes itself from Yeats's usual kind of elevation. Instead of a tragic sense born of passionate intensity, it gives us a casual, poignant version of the heroic:

> Beautiful lofty things: O'Leary's noble head;
> My father upon the Abbey stage, before him a raging crowd:
> "This Land of Saints," and then as the applause died out,
> "Of plaster Saints"; his beautiful mischievous head thrown
>   back.
> Standish O'Grady supporting himself between the tables
> Speaking to a drunken audience high nonsensical words;
> Augusta Gregory seated at her great ormolu table,
> Her eightieth winter approaching: "Yesterday he threatened my
>   life.
> I told him that nightly from six to seven I sat at this table,
> The blinds drawn up"; Maud Gonne at Howth Station waiting
>   a train,
> Pallas Athene in that straight back and arrogant head:
> All the Olympians; a thing never known again.

We need to know something about Yeats's cast of characters so we can appreciate "Beautiful Lofty Things." In his brief, elegiac lyric (so different in tone and argument from Gunn's "To the Dead Owner of a Gym"), Yeats revisits the great Irish nationalist and orator John O'Leary, whom Yeats admired in his youth as a strong, passionate man of action; his father, the painter John Butler Yeats, who spoke, like his son, on the stage of the Abbey Theatre in defense of John Synge's *Playboy of the Western World,* which had scandalized its audience and sparked riots; Standish O'Grady, the independent-minded Dublin author and journalist; Lady Augusta Gregory, Yeats's patron, friend, and fellow author, who took a courageously moderate stance during the Irish Civil War, and received death threats as a result; and finally the restless Maud Gonne, who by this time (1938) had frightened Yeats with her increasingly fanatic temperament. In "Beautiful Lofty Things," the poet moves through a quick series of fond set pieces. He touches briefly on O'Leary before recounting his mischievous father's joke on the pious, irate crowd at the Abbey. We pass on from John Butler Yeats's witty words to O'Grady's high nonsensical ones, then to Lady Gregory's brave defiance, in quoted lines that effortlessly demonstrate her lofty superiority to her enemies. Finally, we see Maud Gonne, whom Yeats likens to the war goddess Pallas Athena. Maud, like O'Leary at the other end of the poem, is given a pose rather than an occasion—we are on guard here to "Notice Beginnings and Endings" (Rule Five). If O'Leary's handsome head sums him up, so that his noble nature needs no words, Maud's "straight back and arrogant head" show a different kind of sublimity, one marked by the wanton, highhanded ways of a Greek deity. What makes for nobility is the decision to show a superior profile, to raise oneself above others: whether one mounts the stage facing an angry crowd like J. B. Yeats, or moves in the thick of it like O'Grady, or sits calmly at one's table like Gregory. Yeats softly concludes, "All the Olympians: a thing never known again." These ones, at times petty like the Greek gods, and contentious among themselves, are gone: dead, dying or (like Maud Gonne) cracked; these moments, these people, will not come again—unlike the gods, who live forever.

In the course of a polemic against crude nationalism, Yeats once said, wonderfully, that he wanted Ireland to convince as a sleeping child convinces. "Beautiful Lofty Things" is convincing in an entirely different way; these people are grown ups, seen in daily action. Instead of the high poise of Yeats's "In Memory of Major Robert Gregory," which presents a similar gallery of characters, but with rapt, ceremonious care, "Beautiful Lofty

Things" feels elevated but loose, a reminiscence told among friends. It is familiar, conversational. It looks back to a past already gone, but one that still feels present. And this past remains completely separate from the swathes of aristocratic and folkloric tradition that Yeats so often relies on. Instead, we get the purely personal. Yeats engages here in the kind of remaking of loved ones into Olympians that Robert Lowell would later pursue to far more melodramatic effect.

Wallace Stevens is the modern American visionary poet who most closely rivals Yeats. Like Yeats, Stevens believes fervently in the imagination, and like Yeats, he tests imagination against the limits of reality. "We say God and the imagination are one . . . / How high that highest candle lights the dark," Stevens writes in a moving late poem, "Final Soliloquy of the Interior Paramour." Imagination is enough; it is one with whatever deity we can know, shining against the dark—the dark of reality, of death, of sober, limiting fact. The American poet James Merrill felt about Stevens's "Final Soliloquy," he said, the way other people feel about the twenty-third Psalm. "A scholar is a candle which the love & desire of all men shall light," Emerson remarked in his journal; and Stevens clearly had this statement in mind in "Final Soliloquy," an Emersonian poem if there ever was one.

In an early poem, "The Paltry Nude Starts on a Spring Voyage" (included in his first volume, *Harmonium*) Stevens invents a muse figure that he modestly describes as paltry, poor but his own. For the reader, though, she carries lyrical lightness, as well as bold spontaneity:

The Paltry Nude Starts on a Spring Voyage

But not on a shell, she starts,
Archaic, for the sea.
But on the first-found weed

She scuds the glitters,
Noiselessly, like one more wave.

She too is discontent
And would have purple stuff upon her arms,
Tired of the salty harbors,
Eager for the brine and bellowing
Of the high interiors of the sea.

The wind speeds her,
Blowing upon her hands
And watery back.
She touches the clouds, where she goes
In the circle of her traverse of the sea.

Yet this is meagre play
In the scurry and water-shine
As her heels foam—
Not as when the goldener nude
Of a later day

Will go, like the centre of sea-green pomp,
In an intenser calm,
Scullion of fate,
Across the spick torrent, ceaselessly,
Upon her irretrievable way.

Stevens's poem is a double annunciation: he first proclaims the
scudding goddess of the title, and then a new female deity
who will speed us in "an intenser calm" to a new day. Here the
reader can "Explore Different Paths" (Rule Thirteen): if the
poem had ended with the third stanza—if its last line had been
"In the circle of her traverse of the sea"—its argument would
be radically different. Stevens's last two stanzas make his paltry
heroine yield to a prospective, gleaming figure, the "goldener

nude" of the future. Abstract and smoothly mobile, a sign of alien grace, this future nude is less of a personality than the goddess of the title, who is "discontent," "tired," and "eager." If we "Find the Parts" of Stevens's poem (Rule Eleven) we will notice, first of all, the break that occurs after the third stanza, when Stevens exchanges one divinity for another.

Stevens's paltry nude rides not a shell like Botticelli's Venus, but the "first-found weed": she is ready, a resourcefully modern American goddess. She has a yearning for nature in its forceful extremes, "Eager for the brine and bellowing / Of the high interiors of the sea"—like the Malay ship's cook in Emerson's essay "Fate" who exhorts the winds during a gale, "Blow! . . . me do tell ye, blow!" But the nude has an inborn delicacy, too, as she reaches upward to touch the cloudy vault, and skims the waves that speed her on her way. This is, as the title informs us, a "Spring Voyage": spring is the natural start of the year, the reawakening from dead winter, time of new beginnings and new love.

In his two final stanzas, Stevens surprisingly discards his paltry nude, in spite of his obvious affection for her. He replaces her with the "goldener nude / Of a later day": a new and improved model, purer, more advanced. This futuristic madonna will be "scullion of fate," traveling without end over the "spick torrent." Stevens's piquant word choices spice his swift lyric. A "scullion" does menial tasks in a kitchen; "spick," a good Pennsylvania Dutch word from Stevens's own background, as in our "spick-and-span," means perfectly neat and clean. If we "Use the Dictionary" (Rule Seven) we will find treasures concealed in Stevens's intricate, sometimes overheated vocabulary.

Stevens in "Paltry Nude" responds to the directly preceding poem in his *Harmonium*, "In the Carolinas," in which the poet envisions a "timeless mother" whose "aspic nipples / For once vent honey." (Aspic lavender yields a pungent essential oil, whose sting is here counterbalanced by paradisiacal honey.) He replaces the languorous, somewhat druggy mood of "In the Carolinas," and its static maternal muse, with something gleaming and swift—a poem of spring's newer days, rather than sultry summer. The Stevens scholar Eleanor Cook has devoted detailed attention to the order of the poems in *Harmonium;* such study reveals to us that Stevens thought of individual poems as perspectives, meant to clash with or complement one another. We can "Find the Parts" that make up a collection of lyrics, its individual poems, as well as the parts of a particular poem. Cook's treatment of Stevens also reminds us to "Explore Different Paths" (Rule Thirteen), to think of a poem as a movement in a direction that might be answered by a countermovement.

Stevens's nude is a bit like Milton's unfallen Eve in Book 4 of *Paradise Lost:* "Not unattended, for on her as Queen / A pomp of winning graces waited still." Utterly self-contained, she attends herself, and needs no courtly apparatus. Stevens was probably also thinking of Henry Adams's words in *The Education of Henry Adams:* "The Woman had once been supreme; in France she still seemed potent, not merely as a sentiment, but as a force. Why was she unknown in America? . . . She was goddess because of her force; she was the animated dynamo . . . the greatest and most mysterious of all energies." Adams concluded that, "Symbol or energy, the Virgin had acted as the greatest force the Western world had ever felt." Is Stevens's nude Virgin or Venus?

For Stevens there is an imagination out there, already actual; imagination is no mere thing of thought, but a thing of life. In Stevens's darker poems he suggests that there is a reality inside us that resists imagination, a blankness of spirit; but "The Paltry Nude" is not one of those poems. "The Paltry Nude" is a poem of the imagination triumphant, with no sense of balking on the part of reality. Resistless, Stevens's current muse prepares

the way for the goldener nude of the future. And Stevens is unsure what that future will be like. The late man of letters Guy
Davenport wrote that Kipling, de Chirico, and Joyce (somewhat like Henry Adams) "saw a new world born in the dynamo
and the internal combustion engine, but did not know what
kind of soul would inhabit them." Davenport's contrast is with
the Italian Futurists, who praised the automobile as a violent
machine of destiny, just as they celebrated the weapons of modern war in which they saw new gods come to transform us forever, for good and ill. Stevens shares the element of uncertainty
that Davenport sees in Kipling, de Chirico, and Joyce, and rejects the facile cheerleading of the Futurists, who never met a
machine they didn't like. He is not cold and impersonal, but
sympathetic. He explores the coming soul with humanity and
tenderness, tutored by his awareness of our solitary fate as well
as our common questionings.

I will conclude this chapter on reading poetry with the unrivalled simplicity and compactness of the Hebrew Bible's Psalms,
which inspired Stevens as they have all Western poets—though
Stevens, seething with invention, moves beyond faith to the
novelties of imagination. Stevens brings in new divinities, and
composes hymns to the possible. The Psalms, by contrast, remain loyal to the one God of Israel; their reality-tested pledges
of comfort rely on the needs and hopes we all share. They speak
to the lonely, abandoned self, the self in a time of trouble, with
a beautifully available, heartening voice.

I give two Psalms here in versions by David Curzon (inspired
in part by the strong-stress meters of Anglo-Saxon poetry,
which Curzon sees as similar to the Psalms). Curzon's translations, in my view, give a more accurate sense than any others of
the near-physical ardor, the syncopated strength, of the Hebrew originals. The Psalms, which have provided sustenance

for thousands of years to religious believers, are profoundly integral and solid; dynamic and fervent, they console as no other poetry can, without denying the constant fact of human distress.

Here is Psalm 131, in Curzon's rendition:

A Song of Ascents, of David.

1 Lord, my heart
  is not haughty
  and my eyes are not
  raised, and I
  am not concerned
  with greatness, with
  what is beyond me.

2 I have aligned
  and quieted my
  desire, like
  a weaned child
  still with mother,
  my desire is like
  a weaned child.

3 From now until
  the end of days,
  Israel, have
  hope in the Lord.

Psalm 131 shifts from an address to God to an address to the nation of Israel; in between comes a movingly personal statement. This Psalm, like a few others, is headed "a song of ascents," but it refuses elevation. Instead, it trusts in a loving curtailment, a weaning, of human ambition. The first stanza, chastened, declares limits for the self. (Dickinson and Gunn too were interested in limits; but they seem to address the question from outside, the psalmist from inside.) The second stanza gives us its deeply affecting emblem for the speaker's self-humbling: he has "aligned / and quieted" his desire, which he compares to a child who has been weaned, but who still remains with its mother. (Curzon astutely translates the Hebrew *nafshi,* usually "my soul," "my life," or "my spirit," as "my desire.") To move on from the nourishing milk of infancy to the more difficult next phase, yet to remain with the God who comforts like a mother—not cast out alone into the world, but accompanied, however subtle and even disoriented the new relationship with God may be. Psalm 131 has a Wordsworthian commonness and simplicity, and a strength that resembles Wordsworth's too. The psychoanalyst D. W. Winnicott remarked that an independent self develops out of the capacity to be alone with one's mother. In Psalm 131, God is the mother, and we are the children who have learned to be alone, but still with God.

Psalm 131's final stanza asks a hard question: What is it to have hope in the Lord? Is it different from having hope in concrete, graspable things? The answer seems to be yes. Since the timeline suggested is so vast, "From now until / the end of days," perhaps the core consolation offered here is the command to take the immensely long view, to see from the end of days.

Psalm 114, like Psalm 131, also asks and answers. It proposes a calm and solemn reply to its question about the extraordinary destiny of the Israelites, who against all odds have accomplished their exodus from Egyptian slavery.

1 When Israel emerged from Egypt,
   the House of Jacob from a strange nation,
2 Judah became the haven of Heaven,
   Israel became God's dominion.

3 The sea had seen it and retreated,
  the course of the Jordan turned backward,
4 mountains danced like rams,
  hills skipped like lambs.

5 What caused the sea to retreat?
  the course of the Jordan to turn?
6 mountains to dance like rams?
  hills to skip like lambs?

7 The earth trembled at God's presence,
  at the presence of the Lord of Jacob,
8 who changed the rock to a pool of water,
  the flint to a fountain.

This psalm is a familiar one in the Jewish liturgy; Ashkenazi Jews chant it to a melody that shifts to a sinuous, haunting minor key with the questions in lines five and six. Psalm 114 keeps to the Psalms' characteristic manner of repeating with variation an image or statement: Israel emerges from Egypt; the House of Jacob (another name for Israel) emerges from a strange nation (another name for Egypt). The mountains dance like rams; the hills (a variation on mountains) skip like lambs, not rams. Once again, we "Find the Parts" to see how the poem works: one image answers another.

The singer of Psalm 114 proposes a metaphor, one infinitely more true than any drab, prosy statement about how things are transformed by the joy of release from bondage. He does not, of course, imagine that the hills *literally* skipped like rams: since the ancient Israelites lacked the concept of laws of nature, they did not picture those laws being suspended in an outlandish way. Instead, it all comes down to the idea of God's presence, which makes the whole world tremble: God brings water out of solid rock (as happens in the book of Exodus). Again, a magical transformation is not implied: Middle Eastern shepherds still strike rocks to release the springs within them. But the bounty that rushes forth, the timing of the gift, is all God's—an intimate truth for the self, not a natural fact.

The Psalms are the right place to end a discussion of reading poetry because, more than any other poems I can think of, they display the healing power of words with utter directness. Their personal, considered speech is like a motto or trusted formula, their memorability a staff to lean on. In some sense, they are the truest poems, the ones in which the smallest number of words do the most beneficial work. The other poets we have looked at in this chapter—Dickinson, Gunn, Whitman, Yeats, Stevens—aim for a similarly consecrated power, though their claims for poetry move in varied directions. All of them make language strange and make it accurate in equal measure; all serve the awakened self of the careful, passionate reader.

Reading Drama

Sometimes the best sources are the earliest ones. When think-ing about drama, I find it helpful to go back to its first critic, Aristotle. In the fourth century BCE, drawing on his knowl-edge of the ancient Greek drama of his day, Aristotle identified two central features of stage tragedy: recognition and reversal. Tragedy, Aristotle wrote, demands a self-recognition from its hero. "Who are you really?" the play says to its protagonist. You are exposed; all eyes are on you. You will be pushed toward an unwelcome, even shocking revelation of your identity. This is what occurs in Aristotle's favorite play, *Oedipus the King*. At the beginning of the tragedy, Oedipus sees himself as a responsible, esteemed ruler: a servant of the people, proud of his own ca-pacities. By the end, he realizes that he is an incestuous, parrici-dal monster, a source of plague—the most miserable man who has ever lived. That is a recognition, and an incomparably bru-tal one. *Oedipus the King* also demonstrates Aristotle's second category, reversal: from a successful, self-assured position, Oe-dipus plummets to an unimaginably terrible one. Sophocles's play is a detective story of a peculiar, high-ironic sort. Oedipus, who sees himself as a masterful sleuth, unknowingly tracks himself, and collaborates in his own fall. He brings the moment of recognition on himself. Sure of his abilities, always in com-mand, he knows only one way to approach a problem: he faces it brazenly, confident of victory. Oedipus's fall is not his fault, but that of the gods, who find him, as we do, an exquisitely fitting subject for tragedy. He is the perfect hero to be crushed by the most freakish of all destinies.

I will return to Aristotle's idea of recognition, but first I want to survey some of the basic facts about drama. Stage plays differ from other literary genres in that they are designed for public performance. (The one exception is the oral epic: Homer's *Iliad* and *Odyssey* were also meant to be recited before a live audience.) Most plays showcase a confrontation of characters. That is, they are not, for the most part, monologues. The fact that the actors stand before one another in an open space has basic implications for drama: people are more directly vulnerable to one another in a play than they are in any other kind of literature. Drama shows us not just competing voices (see Rule Three), but voices laid open to each other, persons stripped naked. If you have seen Ian Holm, as King Lear, facing his daughter Goneril (a performance thankfully available on video), then you know the shattering intensity of tragic drama. Each of this pair is frightening and frightened, devastated by his, by her, weakness before the other. This is my flesh, my blood, my enemy, they seem to say: this father, this daughter. When Holm as Lear tells Goneril that her sister Regan (whom Lear, in Act 1, still thinks is "kind and comfortable") will "flay thy wolfish visage," she recoils from his verbal assault, blinded by sudden tears. With Shakespeare's *Lear* we are in new, frightening territory. Never before has the frailty of a person before the ones who know and (he hopes) love him been more directly shown to us. *Lear* is an extreme example, but still a characteristic one. Drama specializes in laying bare the precarious status of a lone person surrounded by all-too-near, all-too-painful presences: the actors who hover a few feet away. Ibsen's Hedda Gabler and his Master Builder, Strindberg's Captain (in *The Dance of Death*), Beckett's Didi and Gogo (in *Waiting for Godot*), Chekhov's Masha (in *The Three Sisters*): all these protagonists, as I will explain in this chapter, suffer exposure, just as Lear and Oedipus do.

All drama employs recognition, as Aristotle knew. Finding the moments of recognition in a play means knowing how to "Ask the Right Questions" (Rule Two), to focus on the way the play brings its characters to a crisis of knowledge. The plays I will discuss in this chapter are by some of our master dramatists— Shakespeare, Chekhov, Ibsen, Strindberg, and Beckett—and each of them reflects on the peculiarly exposed state that plays thrust on their characters. The actors wear clothes, but their souls are naked. They are encircled by rivals, by loving or hostile companions, and by an audience that can peer into their inmost lives. The first lesson in how to read (or see) a play is to pay attention to its naked moments: when one character stands perplexed and shown up, at a loss before the others. There is, of course, a different kind of play, comedy, in which such exposure is avoided, and buoyant camaraderie is the engine of the plot. But even in comedy, characters are often on their own, and the joy they find may be tenuous, dependent on their own lonely fabrications of innocence or good cheer. Characters in a comedy often draw on the ability of the stage actor to improvise and, by doing so, to attain freedom, but this freedom is fragile. My examples of pure comedy are from Shakespeare, our most influential comic writer for the stage. In them, a faint aura of isolation sneaks into even the most gregarious of happy endings.

The "Basic Thought" (Rule Nine) of a play often revolves around recognition, or the exposure of characters to one another, or the momentary freedom of characters to improvise their lives. The peculiar circumstance of a stage play means that an actor may seem defenseless before the audience and before his fellow actors, and before the recognition that is imposed on him. He then takes up arms in his own service, relying on the powers of fantasy and onstage invention. But recognition, at least in tragedy, wins out; the actor must finally bend to the author's plan.

Shakespeare's *King Lear* is a drama of recognition. Lear, driven to madness by his cruel daughters, realizes that he too is a bare, forked creature, and a guilty one. Impulsively heartless to Cordelia and Kent, he mysteriously retains his authority, the clothing of majesty, and we are meant to recognize that too. Uncannily, he touches his height when he is brought low, and reaches a difficult wisdom in his mad episode on the heath with the blinded Gloucester, which is perhaps more treacherous and dizzying in its emotional and cognitive swervings than any other scene that Shakespeare wrote. Most of *Lear's* characters try to deflect the stunning quantity of pain that the play imposes: the Fool, Edgar, Kent, and Cordelia all have their moral, humorous, or Stoic defenses; their tenderness for Lear, and their care for the survival of their own psyches, requires such evasion. But Lear at the climax of his madness and his rage, out there on the heath with Gloucester, refuses to evade. He is open to recognition. Preaching to the blind Gloucester, he speaks truths that the rest of us cannot stand; most piercingly, this: "When we are born, we cry that we are come / To this great stage of fools." As the play's end approaches, Lear steps onto the stage with Cordelia dead in his arms. The scene is a torture to watch: Dr. Johnson, our greatest moral critic of literature, famously found it unbearable, and rejected it. But Lear himself refuses to turn away: "Why should a dog, a horse, a rat have life, / And thou no breath at all?"

Ever since I first read these words, they have been engraved within me, part of my response to every death of a beloved friend or family member. Like Job, the most sublime and inescapable figure in the Hebrew Bible, Lear asks the question that can never be answered: why suffering, why tragedy? Those who do not think as he does are men of stone, dead themselves in soul, ready to accept the uncaring realities that trammel us. "Look there" he cries after this—a faint beam of hope, a slender wish: "she stirs." But she does not. Here, to devastating effect, we "Notice Beginnings and Endings" (Rule Five): Cordelia, who in the play's first act said "nothing" in response to Lear's question about her love for him, now again fails to speak. Lear's weakness here is ours as well. We are in need; we so badly want a glimmer of goodness, a revived Cordelia. But Shakespeare, contradicting his sources—"contrary to the natural ideas of justice, to the hope of the reader, and, what is yet more strange, to the faith of the chronicles," as Johnson complained—kills Cordelia once and for all.

Lear's decision to indulge in fantasy, when he does indulge in it, is weak, all too human. When he yields to wishfulness he realizes it: as in his dream, during his reunion with Cordelia, of how the two of them will live together in prison. Chattering "like birds in a cage," Lear says, gossiping about court news ("who's in, who's out"), "we'll wear out, / In a wall'd prison, packs and sects of great ones / That ebb and flow by the moon." So he tells Cordelia, heartbreakingly. Lear knows this is desperate imagination, a wild desire to comfort her and protect himself when it is far, far too late. Lear's sense of reality is terrifyingly strong, even when those around him call him mad. He knows the world and himself, and he is known by the reader or viewer capable of such acknowledgement. He therefore becomes the most powerful instance of the Aristotelian trope of recognition.

Lear teaches us that drama is about exposure, and that recognition uncovers the truth of character and fate. This uncovering relies on the sense of time passing, a sense that drama puts at the center of experience. The result can be hard to take.

Edmund, cold yet beginning to stir with an unexpected shoot of sympathy, first interrupts Lear's pathetic reconciliation with Cordelia. Brutally shouting "Take them away!", Edmund defends himself against what he sees. He then relents, countermanding the pair's death sentence. But Edmund's pardon will come too late, every time that *Lear* is staged: time is implacable. Unlike any other genre, drama is in strict league with time. When we see a play, we spend exactly as long in its presence as the author, director and actors want us to. This fact means that the clock is always, almost visibly, ticking on stage. A play manipulates time: pauses can seem to last an eternity, and rapid-fire dialogue can set a breathtaking pace. As they play with time, actors sometimes seem to be working out a routine, making their characters up as they go along. I remember seeing a brilliant version, in German, of Beckett's *Waiting for Godot* by the Hungarian Jewish director George Tabori. The performance began with two actors rehearsing their roles, the tramps Didi and Gogo, and then slid quietly into the play itself. Tabori was making manifest what all drama implies: we are in the presence of actors fashioning their roles, working at their craft. Making us watch, they discover themselves as well, as they improvise an existence.

When drama plays with time, it also plays with the inventing of onstage presence: we are, as the saying goes, a captive audience, compelled to attend to what happens until the players release us. Everyone who treads the boards has the freedom to play himself, to grip us, the audience, with an alluring performance. But the actor is also laid open: hundreds, even thousands, of eyes surround him. The audience can seem a kind of destiny writ large, a court sitting in judgment on the actor's fate, especially in tragedy. The actor is a pawn, and knows it. Among tragic heroes, Hamlet is unique in his ability to master his audience utterly, and to elude Aristotelian recognition. We do not know him, he knows us; we cannot pluck out the heart of his mystery. His mastery results from his expert consciousness of what theatre is all about: he knows he is the lead actor in a revenge tragedy, and he is determined to thwart our expectations. He will not be the bloodthirsty Senecan villain, nor the Stoic philosopher, but something much more elusive. More than any other stage character, Hamlet is obsessed with the conditions of drama itself. The actor is free to stand apart from his role—to interpret it, shape it, bring it into being—and no one knows this better than Hamlet. For this reason, Hamlet will always be our most intriguing tragic hero.

The unique phenomena that occur on the stage are, of course, less palpable when you sit down to read a play than when you walk into a theater. But even when you read a play, you should stay conscious of what's so distinctive about the theatrical experience: the existence of a separate world up there on stage, one that the actors can try to sway. They are physically there as characters in a novel never are; they can tweak and refine their parts, do their best to overshadow other actors, and even protest against the workings of the play itself. Different playwrights give their actors more or less leeway, make more or less room for the actor to push against or speed the action. Drama can seem to be improvisation, or it can seem the workings of an ironclad, overmastering plot. *Oedipus the King* is the classic example of the latter kind of play, the inexorable one. Chekhov and Beckett, by contrast, often appear loose and improvisatory, even at their most claustrophobic: they leave much more up to the characters—that is, to the actors who play them—than Sophocles does. In *Waiting for Godot,* Beckett's tramps play with the plot (such as it is): bat it back and forth, dangle it in front of them, peer at it sadly, frivolously, morbidly.

The Norwegian playwright Henrik Ibsen is one of the heroic makers of modern drama. Like Shakespeare, like Sophocles, he too inflicts recognition on his characters. Ibsen has a (misleading) reputation as a stolid realist, but in fact he deals in magic. Ibsen is a mythmaker, a visionary writer, not the dull, prosy modern man he has often been thought to be. He exalts reality instead of deadening it. Virginia Woolf commented that in Ibsen's work "the paraphernalia of reality have at certain moments to become the veil through which we see infinity." Nearly all of Ibsen has the visionary strength that Woolf admired (with the exception of *The Wild Duck,* a cruel farce with a tender, defenseless presence at its center, the teenage girl Hedvig).

Ibsen once said to an interviewer, "There must be troll in what I write." In Nordic folklore, trolls are giant, uncanny, sadistically mischievous creatures who urge humans toward the sublimely perverse; they are not at all Smurf-like. For Ibsen, to have troll in what you write is to confide in the demonic aspect of human character, the doom-laden core self. Ibsen sees his characters down to the root, the primitive essence; they have an operatic simplicity, and are madly devoted to their separate fates.

Ibsen kept a live scorpion on his desk, along with a glaring portrait of the Swedish playwright August Strindberg, his great enemy. Ibsen depicted Strindberg in his *Hedda Gabler* as Lovborg, a driven, vain, shrewd genius. Together, Ibsen and Strindberg define the imaginative brilliance of Scandinavian drama.

The story of Ibsen's *The Master Builder* begins with the entrance of the play's temptress: Hilda, a woman in her twenties in hiking costume. Self-assured, strong, direct, and unanswerable, Hilda enters into the accomplished world of the master builder, Solness. Solness is imperious, impatient, a ladies' man; an egoist, but convinced that the fates will take retribution on him for his success. Hilda reminds Solness that he met her once, ten years ago (when she was "twelve or thirteen," she says), on the occasion of his first great architectural triumph, his building of a tower for the church in her home town. (The tower is *The Master Builder*'s central "Signpost" [Rule Six].) Solness embraced and kissed her then, she says, and promised to make her a princess in ten years' time. The powerful flirt Hilda declares now, "I want my kingdom. The time is up," and raps playfully on the table. Hilda, we guess, may be inventing this key reminiscence; she almost, but not quite, gets Solness to remember it too, and to believe that he has wanted her all along.

There is also a core memory at the back of Solness's life, and like Hilda's it is fantasy as much as reality. Solness confesses to Hilda that he had secretly wanted the fire that destroyed his home; the fire led indirectly to the death of his twin sons, but it also opened the way for his career as a brilliant architect. He has given up familial love for the sake of power. There is something of Wagner's lordly, vulnerable Wotan in Solness, and something of his twisted, power-hungry gnome Alberich, too: he is, as he tells Hilda, part troll. But there is troll in Hilda, too. To be guided by daemonic forces is the point for both of them; and these forces, they are convinced, dwell within them, at the self's grasping core.

"The impossible . . . seems to beckon and cry aloud to one," Solness says to Hilda, and she agrees, her eyes glinting with excitement. She compares herself to a wild bird of prey, but shows a catlike evasiveness as well. Her occasional scorn for Solness is unfeigned, and it spurs him on, just as much as her admiration does. Ibsen's play showcases the magnetic attraction of "competing voices" (see Rule Three): Hilda and Solness are meant for each other.

There is another aspect to Hilda: she is a little terrified by Solness's confession to her that he wanted the burning of his house; and she is genuinely disgusted, for a few moments, by his solipsistic ambition, even as she loves him for that ambition.

Ibsen brilliantly grants Hilda the qualms that we share with her about Solness. Even so, he makes her a masterful string-puller, whose aim we also share: to spur Solness on to a great and catastrophic feat. Her ambivalence is ours as well: we thrill to Solness's self-centered raptures, but despise him too.

The climax of his career, Solness decides, will be a castle in the air with a rock-hard foundation, built for his princess Hilda: the culmination of their strangely taunting erotic bond. We never see this castle built, but Ibsen gives us an uncanny combination of victory and loss in Solness's final act. At Hilda's instigation, he tries to overcome his vertigo so he can put a wreath on the pinnacle of the new house he has built for himself—an attempt to replicate his feat of ten years ago, when the child Hilda saw him place his wreath on the spire of the church tower he had built. This time he falls, and dies.

At the end of Act 2 of the play, on the route to this conclusion, Hilda whispers a triumphant, mostly inaudible monologue to herself; we hear only the words "frightfully thrilling." When *The Master Builder* ends, she has gotten her kingdom, and Solness is her dead subject; she has overmatched him, killed him, glorified him. Ibsen's great play finishes with a chilling moment of self-congratulation from Hilda, who is satisfied in her deepest troll nature. Solness's assistant, Ragnar, remarks, "So, after all, he could not do it." Hilda has an answer: She says, *"(as if in quiet spellbound triumph)"* "But he mounted right to the top. And I heard harps in the air. *(Waves her shawl in the air, and shrieks with wild intensity.)* My—my master builder!" Hilda knows her apotheosis here: the hero has been sacrificed, the catharsis reached, the triumph found.

A near-lunatic intensity similar to Hilda's possesses the heroine of Ibsen's sublime *Hedda Gabler,* which preceded *The Master Builder* by two years, and which also ends in disastrous triumph: Hedda's suicide, after she ruins two men, gives the final proof of her ceaselessly destructive nature. Hilda and Hedda are both born rebels, but whereas Hedda is an angry nihilist who claims her only real talent is for boring herself to death, Hilda has a true romantic vision: she wants to see Solness reach his true greatness, even if it means his death. Unlike Hedda, Hilda does not destroy herself; but both are masters, and for both, mastery and the surrender to an untamed destiny are one and the same thing. Hedda, that immortal manipulator of souls, craves a Frankenstein-like power to "mold a human destiny," and finds it when she destroys her lover, Lovborg (Ibsen's nasty, hilarious portrait of his rival Strindberg) as well as her husband, the plodding Tesman. Comparable to Shakespeare's Iago (as Harold Bloom remarks), Hedda is even more disenchanted than that considerable villain. When Hedda, expending scarcely any effort, dupes Tesman into thinking that love for him has made her burn the manuscript of Lovborg's brilliant book, she is disgusted by his credulity, not aroused (as Iago is when Othello takes the bait). Her plots are cruel whims, and it is sheer cruelty that finally possesses Hedda. Believing that Lovborg has committed suicide, Hedda exults, "At last a deed worth doing!" A true terrorist of the heart, she seeks beauty in maximum ruin. When Ibsen invents his Hilda, whose very name echoes Hedda's, he revises his earlier heroine, giving us a character just as intriguing as her precursor, but appreciably less dark, less hellishly capable. Hilda, who seems infinitely younger than Hedda, believes in her master builder, and is by turns surprised, inspired, and disheartened by his words and deeds. Hedda has no such capacity to be influenced by those around her; she is satanically bored by them, as she is by herself.

Ibsen's Hedda knows herself all too well: she has been endowed with self-recognition from the beginning. Ibsen forces knowledge on his characters; in this respect he differs from the other most crucial modern dramatist, Anton Chekhov. Chekhov lets his characters dodge the urgency of self-knowledge: they have a freedom that Ibsen's lack, even a dreaminess; when they can, they substitute fantasy for reality. Haunted by half-hidden wishes and memories, Chekhov's people escape the raw confrontations that Ibsen insists on. Yet deep down, they cannot avoid knowing who they are.

Chekhov and Ibsen are both artists of decline: in them we see, as Arnold Weinstein puts it, "a world beginning to go under." The same can be said of Shakespeare in his tragedies. But there are crucial differences among these three giants. Chekhov's characters avoid themselves; Ibsen's think through to the bottom of things, even if it means their ruin (as the Ibsen scholar Inga-Stina Ewbank notes). Chekhov shows us, perhaps better than any other writer, what it's like to be someone, as opposed to what it's like to go through something; Ibsen's heroes, by contrast, are what they undergo. Chekhov's people often wistfully, ineffectually reinvent their pasts; Ibsen's are fixed to theirs. An Ibsen protagonist is, in Bert States's words, "bound in every way to his problem." He is doomed to fulfill something in his nature, in a way that even Shakespeare's heroes are not. Macbeth succumbs to an accidental, if fateful, stimulus, his meeting with the witches on the heath. Lear acts on a dreadful whim, and pulls the world down around him. The poisonous chemistry between Othello and Iago seems a product of sheer, fatal, chance invention: Iago's malicious sprig of thought pops into his head, and all is done. In Shakespeare's tragedies, everything could have been otherwise. In Ibsen, by contrast, all has been foretold, if we could only read the signs— and Ibsen's people are nearly all bad readers. Trapped by the past, they still fail to see what's coming, what must come. Crisis excites and elevates them, and, perversely, they yield to the powers that rule over them. They are eager for experience, no matter how calamitous that experience turns out to be. Shakespeare's heroes are their own best audience; Ibsen's are so solidly locked into who they are that, incapable of playing to themselves, they need others to hear and judge them.

Shakespeare, like Mahler, will give us a strand of breezy comedy to play against a dark, heavy plot. His clowns, including the best of them, Falstaff, are sweet diversions. There is a world elsewhere in Shakespeare, a place of innocent foolery: the world of his comedies. But no such alternative place exists in Chekhov or Ibsen. All of Chekhov's characters are muted fools, and all are tragic heroes; we need only adjust the lens to see these different aspects of them. And they are all caught: tied forever to themselves, to each other, to their odd, sad situations. Situation for Chekhov is more atmospheric, less factual, than for Ibsen. Ibsen turns his plots; Chekhov's plays drift, turn round, in a setting open to time and accident. Chekhov objected to Ibsen, writes James Wood, because Ibsen is "like a man who laughs at his own jokes": he thinks only of clear dramatic ironies. Chekhov's own ironies are more elusive. Wood notices that many Chekhov characters are disappointed by their own stories: by the stories they tell and by the stories of their lives. Disappointment creates an atmosphere of yearning, of stifled hope.

In *The Three Sisters*, perhaps Chekhov's greatest achievement in drama, the three women of Chekhov's title, Olga, Irina, and Masha, are left after their father's death in a provincial town. They talk constantly of returning to Moscow, where they grew up; but they do not leave. They have a brother, Andrei, who marries an unpleasant woman from the town and fathers two children. But the sisters themselves are stuck in a drab, perpetual stasis. Masha, the most desperate of the three, is married to an implacable bore of a schoolteacher, Kulygin (though he too, good-natured and loyal, has his worthy side); the other two sisters remain single. The sisters are nearly always accompanied by a group of bored, playful army officers stationed in the town. At the end of the play the officers leave; just before this, one of them, Tuzenbach, who was about to marry Irina, is killed in a duel. Another officer, Vershinin, has an affair with Masha. The rest talk, smoke, drink, and pass the time.

Chekhov's characters play games to while away the hours, as Beckett's will do. One evocative example: Masha's lover Vershinin and Irina's fiancé Tuzenbach chat idly about the future of humanity. Vershinin says, "Let's conjecture for a moment about . . . let's say . . . the life that will come after us, in two or three hundred years." Tuzenbach's answer is a small masterpiece of aimless theorizing, shot though with strange, almost plangent need. "Very well," he says,

> People will travel in air balloons, our jackets will be cut differently, somebody will discover the sixth sense and learn how to use it, but life will remain the same. It will be hard, and full of unanswerable questions, but it will be happy. Even a thousand years from now, people will complain about life but, when it comes down to it, they'll prefer it to death, exactly as we do.
>   (translated by Nicholas Wright)

Tuzenbach reassures himself with the thought that life is always the same, but on the other hand it is always, in some invisible way, getting better. (And what a wonderful vein of fantasy he discovers in himself, with his talk of air balloons and the sixth sense!) Vershinin, pitching in, remarks that they themselves, just by existing, are at this very moment building "a new and happier life," though they won't live to see it. Many of Chekhov's characters in *The Three Sisters* specialize in a threadbare self-comforting that takes the form of bold and "progressive," but fatally vague, ideas about the destiny of humankind. They dream about the sense of purpose that comes from working (rather than remaining idle, as befits their class), but Olga's work as a schoolteacher and Irina's in a telegraph office are equally depressing and pointless. All of them see through their own flimsy moments of optimism. And yet what ails them is unclear.

Dialogue in *The Three Sisters* is awash with non sequiturs. Very late in the play, Vershinin makes his awkward farewell to the sisters. Avoiding as he must any address to his married lover Masha, he madly changes the subject, blurts out a few samples of the new scientific ideas, and then sputters to a halt:

> I should be going! In previous eras, man was a warlike creature. Invasions, battles, conquests were his favorite occupations, but that's a thing of the past, and what remains is a vast and empty void which nothing can fill, so we embark on a desperate search, which will, of course, achieve its goal in the end. The sooner the better! (*He looks at his pocket watch.*) I really do have to go.
> (translated by Nicholas Wright)

In Chekhov's universe, the grander the verbal gesture, the more vapid; Vershinin flails in the void that he so nervously invokes. Like Beckett's characters in *Waiting for Godot,* Chekhov's in *The Three Sisters* use words to dig, somewhat frantically, shallow holes: nothing too risky, nothing that will uncover too much meaning. In sadness and with easy jokes, they divert themselves; their statements explain nothing, promise nothing. Masha is less a slave to unexamined passion than the other characters in *Three Sisters;* she stands out as the bold one. She is even, at times, fearless. She despises her trivial, obtuse husband, and remains thoroughly dissatisfied with the narrow world in which she finds herself; often enough, she stoops to cruel insults. Her affair with Vershinin, which is alluded to rather than fully depicted in the play, makes us look down on her: she doesn't have the strength to bear her misery alone. Masha lacks the devastating, inhuman sense of superiority that empowers Ibsen's Hedda Gabler. Instead, her scorn seems to her a failing: one more sign of her doomed, weak nature, rather than a source of strength. Masha reflects late in the play on her anger:

> When you grab your happiness in bits and pieces, bits at a time, and then you lose it, like I have, you find that, little by little, you become . . . quite coarse and aggressive. (*She points to her breast.*) There's something in here that's seething with fury.
>
> (translated by Nicholas Wright)

The moment of self-examination passes swiftly. This is all Chekhov gives us in the way of recognition: he merely glances at Aristotelian categories (the death of Irina's fiancé Tuzenbach in the duel is a minor-key reversal, an anticlimax rather than a climax). At the play's end a stagnant set of circumstances has turned unexpectedly fatal: the officers are leaving, among them Masha's lover Vershinin; and Tuzenbach, whose proposal Irina accepted with mixed feelings, is dead. The playwright nods in the direction of traditional dramatic structure, but only fleetingly. By giving us Masha's speech, Chekhov offers, as he so frequently does, an instant of revelation that teases more than it reveals. How has Masha "grab[bed her] happiness in bits and pieces"? With Vershinin, yes, but perhaps at other times too: we are reminded of how little we have learned of her past. Why did she marry her schoolteacher husband? What dreams occupied her early life? We will never know. Early in the play, Masha proposes a sardonic toast "to dreams of happiness . . . and may we never wake up!" She has the bitter sense that only willful ignorance of the facts can bring a measure of happiness. Unable to remain ignorant and happy, she knows that her bitterness brings her no advantages.

At the end of *The Three Sisters,* Chekhov brilliantly juxta-poses the departure of the army officers, the sisters' discontent, the imperious manners of their brother Andrei's wife, and—most painfully of all—the prancing of Masha's husband in a fake moustache and beard that he took from a boy in his school. Such an effort to lighten the atmosphere is too crude, too strained and unfeeling; yet in his very obliviousness, Kulygin, the foolish husband, illustrates a way of surviving that we can-not afford to mock too severely. Annoying as he is, he still takes hold of life with more energy than the sisters, whose sensibili-ties we infinitely prefer because they are romantically dissatis-fied. Kulygin, dull and slow, is also a kind, good man. In real life, Kulygin and the sisters would be equally intolerable; an opaque hopelessness like Masha's is no more appealing than her husband's dutiful appetite for work and family, rounded off by his incongruous, failed buffoonery. Yet as we watch or read *The Three Sisters* we feel for all these people. Among writers, Chek-hov is the supreme artist of sympathy because he makes us reach out to those we would never much care for in our actual day-to-day existence. Their melancholy is ours, and their painful ef-forts to at once imagine their lives and avoid imagining them, ours as well.

Chekhov makes us sympathize with his characters. The cold and cutting Strindberg makes us, often enough, turn away from his characters in revulsion. We heartily dislike nearly all of Strindberg's heroes, though we take delight in their misan-thropic eloquence. *Miss Julie,* Strindberg's brilliant fever dream of a play, is his best known work, and illustrates the gleaming battle of proud, reckless personalities that is his forte. Even bet-ter, for me, is the first part of *The Dance of Death.* Strindberg wrote *The Dance of Death* in 1900 as two discrete plays, and Part 1 is often performed separately. Its two main characters are

Edgar the Captain, a sublime hater of everyone and everything, and his profoundly dissatisfied wife, Alice. The two are marooned together on an island with Kurt (the Captain's protégé and, eventually, Alice's lover), and a group of petty bureaucrats and military officers who never appear in the play, but whom the Captain loves to deride. When Kurt asks the Captain, "Isn't it horrible to sit alone surrounded by enemies, like you do?" he responds that his enemies have helped him: they enable him to thrive. Rancor propels his life, motivates him, juices him up.

Strindberg's dialogue in *The Dance of Death* at times resembles a biting, absurdist vaudeville routine:

> *Kurt:* But you have a big income, I remember you saying.
> *Captain:* Certainly I have a big income. But it isn't big enough.
> *Kurt:* Then it can't be big, in the usual sense—
> *Captain:* Life is strange and so are we.
>
> (translated by Michael Meyer)

When the ailing Captain discovers that he has been sent flowers by the military officers he scorns so heartily, he responds with a hilarious vigor, both sentimental and tongue-in-cheek, that rouses Alice's disgust: "Put the flowers in vases. I am not a credulous man, and humanity is scum, but this simple homage, by God, it comes from the heart." (Strindberg took delight in demonstrating the part of the Captain for his friend August Falck, who was preparing to perform the role: "with sour-sweet, fawning expressions, with gestures both jaunty and pitiful," Falck remembered, Strindberg threw himself zestfully about the room.) Asked why he once pushed Alice into the sea, the Captain deadpans, "I don't know. It just seemed to me quite natural when she stood there on the jetty that she should go in." Told by Kurt that, since he is a sick man, he should go to bed, Strindberg's Captain responds with acerbic, high-comic panache: "No, not that. Not bed. Then it's the end. Then one never gets up again. I'll sleep on the sofa tonight." The Captain may remind the reader of other towering, exuberantly funny misanthropes: the Mickey Sabbath of Philip Roth's novel *Sabbath's Theater* (who finally decides not to commit suicide because, Roth writes, "How could he leave? How could he go? Everything he hated was here") and the Roy Cohn of Tony Kushner's *Angels in America,* a power-hungry octopus who feeds off the enmity of others. Like Ibsen's Hedda, another sublime loather of mankind, the Captain is a triumph of voice.

In Strindberg's *Dance of Death,* the Captain's wife, Alice, proves a perfect match for him: she is another violent, distasteful sensibility, yet we find her, like him, strangely charming. (The pair are the true precursors of Edward Albee's George and Martha in *Who's Afraid of Virginia Woolf?*) Act 2, Scene 1 of Strindberg's play ends when Alice unbuttons her dress; Kurt bites her throat, throws her on the sofa, and rushes offstage, an action that excites Alice greatly. Perhaps even more deadly than the Captain, Alice at any rate gives him a run for his money. Part 1 of *The Dance of Death* ends with its bitter, brawling couple reconciled to the poisonous mixture of farce and nightmare that is their lives; grudgingly, they admit that they enjoy their venom-laden mudslinging. The Captain says he has been shaken by a recognition—in his sickness, he has stared death in the face—but in fact the seemingly endless duel between him and Alice will continue. "Let's go on," the Captain grunts at the play's end, knowing that the marital battlefield is necessary not just for his (and our) entertainment, but for his survival. The real recognition in Strindberg's *Dance of Death* is the fact that Alice and the Captain are forever locked in place, their lives another dire though hilarious episode in Strindberg's many-roomed inferno.

Samuel Beckett, the central English-language playwright of the post–World War II era, takes a step beyond Strindberg's vital, vicious cosmos, and moves into a strange, attenuated landscape. Hugh Kenner aptly defines "the Beckett universe" as "a shambles of phenomena within which certain symmetries and recurrences are observable, like the physical world as interpreted by early man." In Beckett's *Waiting for Godot,* we see two broken-down figures (the tramps Vladimir and Estragon, who call each other Didi and Gogo), a shabby tree, a country road; we attend to the connection between voice and sense of place (Rule Three). Of Didi and Gogo, Kenner writes that "the resources of vaudeville are at their somewhat incompetent disposal": the kick in the rear, the falling trousers. As we watch Beckett's play, we ask ourselves: Why are we here and what are we waiting for? The same thing that the tramps are waiting for: Godot, a mysterious rumor of a character who, perhaps needless to say, never shows up. As Kenner remarks, *Godot* sometimes seems more like the absence of a play than a play. Have the tramps learned their parts? At times they falter, at a loss for words. Twice in the play, once in Act 1 and once in Act 2, a bullying strongman named Pozzo appears, railing in good set terms, and accompanied by his slave Lucky. Pozzo manufactures a fiction of busy movement and shrill speeches that goes nowhere. Beckett suggests that, rather than rant like Pozzo, it's better to improvise more playfully, if feebly, like Didi and Gogo—and to wait.

Harold Bloom summarizes Beckett's debt to the influential, and thoroughly pessimistic, German philosopher Arthur Schopenhauer. Schopenhauer, Bloom writes, saw the will as "a blind pressure, a tendency entirely without ground or motive": a force that cannot be fended off, since it lives within each of us. Beckett's tramps are spurred on by an urge to do something, no matter what—though they are not frenzied like the quasi-fascistic

Pozzo, but instead wearied, distracted, persistent. They live in the precincts of Schopenhauerian frustration. "Schopenhauer dismissed the ego as an illusion, life as torment, and the universe as nothing, and he rightly credited these insights to that great modernist, the Buddha," Bloom notes; and Beckett, as the "greatest master of nothing," pledges his allegiance to Schopenhauer. Yet as Beckett's biographer Anthony Cronin remarks, there is in his plays and fictions a "strange élan," something inexplicably close to gaiety. Didi and Gogo, tired as they are, are itching to cavort a little; they have an appetite for futility. Their stunts, whose jerry-built nature suits the ramshackle state of things in *Godot*, never rise to the assured level of ritual. (Beckett's later plays are often rituals, whether tributes to waning memory like the beautiful *Ohio Impromptu*, or obsessive wringings of mind like *Not I*, with its quivering, agile mouth surrounded by blackness. I recommend the filmed versions of these two plays, starring, respectively, Jeremy Irons and Julianne Moore, in the BBC series of Beckett plays.)

There is something in *Godot*'s tramps of Chekhov's Uncle Vanya, who declares that it is a beautiful day for killing oneself. *Godot* is full of perfect one-liners: Estragon's "I'll never forget this carrot," Pozzo's "I am perhaps not particularly human, but who cares?"; Vladimir's answer to Estragon's "I tell you I wasn't doing anything": "Perhaps you weren't. But it's the way of doing it that counts, the way of doing it, if you want to go on living." Consider Didi's response to Gogo's "We always find something, eh Didi, to give us the impression we exist?": "*(Impatiently.)* Yes yes, we're magicians." The tramps do an Alphonse and Gaston routine ("No no, after you"; "No no, you first"); then an Abbott and Costello, swapping insults. Pozzo and Lucky, by contrast, are Cain and Abel, locked in violent struggle. Pozzo too has his moments of beauty: "They give birth astride of a grave, the light gleams an instant, then it's night once more." Beckett lived to tire of his tramps, as his recently published letters reveal, but we never do.

Didi and Gogo play seriously with redemption, hopelessness, and the absence of God:

> *Estragon* (stopping, brandishing his fists, at the top of his voice):
>   God have pity on me!
> *Vladimir* (vexed): And me?
> *Estragon:* On me! On me! Pity! On me!

In *Godot,* the range of competing voices (Rule Three) is remarkable. Commanded "Think, pig" by his master Pozzo, the miserable Lucky gives a cacophonous, absurd speech. This jabbering monologue ends in a clumsy, agonized pile-up of bodies when the remaining characters tackle Lucky—they are no longer able to endure his careening flood of words:

> What is more for reasons unknown in spite of the tennis on on
> the beard the flames the tears the stones so blue so calm alas alas
> on on the skull the skull the skull in Connemara in spite of the
> tennis the labors abandoned left unfinished graver still abode of
> stones.

The pointedly misnamed Lucky here resembles a prophetic voice scrambled, stuck in a groove, frantically unaware of what these stark associations might mean (Beckett adds "the tennis" to leaven the blind, blocked intensity of these lines). Lucky's headlong verbal barrage is countered by the elegiac duet of Didi and Gogo later in the play:

> *Vladimir:* You're right, we're inexhaustible.
> *Estragon:* It's so we won't think.
> *Vladimir:* We have that excuse.
> *Estragon:* It's so we won't hear.
> *Vladimir:* We have our reasons.

Estragon: All the dead voices.

Vladimir: They make a noise like wings.

Estragon: Like leaves.

Vladimir: Like sand.

Estragon: Like leaves.

Silence.

Vladimir: They all speak at once.

Estragon: Each one to itself.

Godot includes as well a fascinating parody of then-fashionable existentialist resolve, in Didi's vehement speech in Act 2:

> Let us do something, while we have the chance! It is not every day that we are needed. Not indeed that we personally are needed. Others would meet the case equally well, if not better. To all mankind they were addressed, those cries for help still ringing in our ears! But at this place, at this moment of time, all mankind is us, whether we like it or not. Let us make the most of it, before it is too late! Let us represent worthily for once the foul brood to which a cruel fate consigned us. What do you say? *(Estragon says nothing.)*

Such cries for help were issued during the Nazi takeover of Europe and the ensuing world war. Beckett himself, a brave member of the French resistance, answered the call superbly; but now all that can be done (in 1948–1949, when Beckett wrote the play, or 1952, the year of *Godot*'s premiere) is to look back and attempt, vainly, to rouse oneself. Didi's messy admixture of melodrama (foul brood, cruel fate) does not suffice to inspire action.

Didi's mock-existentialist speech gestures toward the moment of recognition that Beckett refuses to provide. And he gives no reversal either: Godot will never arrive, the tramps will keep coming back to the same spot, the show must go on. The play's action slowly runs down, then stops.

Michael Goldman captures something essential about *Godot* when he writes that we cannot decide how much of the play is genuine anguish and how much comic shtick. At times anguish seems to wrap itself in slapstick; at other times, the comic routines play the anguish for laughs. With its delicate, uncertain weighing of the proportions of grief and laughter, *Godot* participates in a long comic tradition. Beckett refines the world down to nearly nothing, whereas Shakespeare expands it, shows it in its true, many and varied colors. But in another way Shakespeare's comedies still resemble Beckett's *Godot:* both balance unhappy stasis with antic activity, and both foster the actors' improvisation. Both seek to dispel the strident, oppressive yelpings of those who try to drive time forward, like Pozzo in *Godot.* Instead, Beckett's dismal but funny lesson is that we should wait, even in unhope. "Be Patient," Rule One for readers, is a grim rule in Beckett's universe too.

Shakespearean comedy is far more hopeful than Beckett's *Godot,* but both authors promote a wry energy and the know-how that can adapt to strange chances—whether the chance is a budding comic routine (Beckett) or the sudden branching out of desire (Shakespeare). In the opening minutes of Shakespeare's *Twelfth Night,* my own favorite among his romantic comedies, we are treated to vignettes of Duke Orsino's rather lugubrious love melancholia (he is hopelessly, and ineffectually, in love with the Countess Olivia), Olivia's mourning for her dead brother, and Viola's mourning for the brother she thinks is dead (her twin Sebastian, who will return to help supply the play's happy ending). The sadness of Orsino is largely an exercise in narcissistic self-absorption; Viola's melancholy will yield, when she disguises herself as the male page Cesario, to a love-sick attachment to Orsino himself; and Olivia's mourning is quickly replaced by her mad love for the unfortunate Viola, whom she takes to be a man. These three, Orsino, Olivia, and

Viola, never in synch, sing a trio of love laments. If this plot seems to you rather tilted, even wacky, it is. *Twelfth Night* drums up a festival of zany desire, with Orsino, Olivia, and Viola, as well as Olivia's steward, Malvolio, each chasing after an un-suitable love object. Malvolio has been convinced by the "lighter people," including Uncle Toby and the clown Feste, that Olivia loves him; this crowd stir themselves up to riotous merriment at Malvolio's expense. Shakespeare makes it clear that the energetic persecution of Malvolio is another form of madness that, like the lovers', gets out of hand.

In *Twelfth Night,* the partying impulse of comedy competes with its brooding other, melancholy. Feste administers comic therapy to Olivia when she is sunk in sadness for her dead brother; a few minutes later, in the same scene, Viola-as-Cesario will rouse Olivia further, transforming her from a dignified mourner to a devil-may-care, love-crazy bachelorette. Cesario, speaking as ambassador for Orsino, summons up the fervent role-playing of the lovelorn suitor, with a passion that Orsino himself could never manage—and Olivia falls hard, and in-stantly, for the oddly feminine young man. Startled awake by desire, she forgets all unhappiness. "I am the man," Viola muses, amazed by the realization that Olivia has fallen for her—I mean him. (The fact that heroines were played by boys in Shakespeare's theatre adds an enticing soupçon.)

Olivia's rapid plunge into love is the comic counterpart of something that happens in Shakespeare's tragedies: the awaken-ing into obsessive thoughtfulness that Cassius inflicts on Bru-tus, or—much more darkly—that Iago inflicts on Othello, or Lady Macbeth on Macbeth. All these encounters (Cassius's ap-proach to Brutus, Iago's to Othello's, and Lady Macbeth's to Macbeth) correspond to a common experience, written on a stupendous scale in Shakespeare's tragedies. In the midst of talking, we may be interrupted by a friend who asks us, "Do you realize what you're saying?"—a question often tantamount to "Do you know who you are?" We are being tempted into discovering a new, essential side of our identity. We return to the question of recognition, Aristotle's key concept. Brutus becomes who he is, as Othello becomes who he is, and Macbeth too, at the instigation of their conversational partners, their tempters. In Shakespeare's comedies, too, such temptation opens up the self to new recognition. In comedy, though, the consequences are not destructive, but wholly enlivening. In *Twelfth Night,* Olivia rises to her role as bewildered, go-for-broke lover; she becomes a fresh self, jolted by Feste and then Viola / Cesario out of her earlier stagnant mood.

Comedy, unlike tragedy, is about acceptance. (What did you do to deserve this gift, fortune's favor? Nothing in particular; it is yours to enjoy.) One of Shakespeare's most moving pledges of allegiance to comedy's spirit is Helena's grateful acknowledgement when she reencounters Demetrius near the end of *A Midsummer Night's Dream:* "And I have found Demetrius like a jewel, / Mine own and not mine own." Like a passerby who stumbles over a precious stone in her path, Helena has recovered her beloved Demetrius; but he still doesn't quite seem to be her property, and this uncertainty casts a spell. (Demetrius is still under the influence of the play's magical love juice, so he's perhaps not his own, either.) Comedy means relaxing into a seemingly magical—but actual—state of things; and so Shakespeare's comic faith rises above the grudge match between the sour, puritanical Malvolio and the resentful Feste (a duel expertly played by Nigel Hawthorne and Ben Kingsley in Trevor Nunn's delightful film version of *Twelfth Night*). Such grudges impede recognition; they stand in the way of the freedom that happily coincides with chance events, with impromptu meetings and strangely intersecting desires. All these are comedy's lifeblood. Though Feste is *Twelfth Night*'s fool, though he rouses Olivia to comic life, his vengeful, pitiless stalking of Malvolio is untrue to the comic mood. Gripes and persecutory plots suit not comedy, but satire, with its malevolent mission, its crabbed consciousness. In order for *Twelfth Night*'s rejuvenating spirit to do its work, satire has to be separated from comedy, and comedy has to have the upper hand, just as it has to have the upper hand over the play's opening symphony of melancholics.

Aristotle insisted that tragedy is based on recognition and reversal: people seeing who they are for the first time; the state of things being turned upside down. In comedy, what gets recognized is not the hero's true identity, but the giddy fact of newness, the likelihood of the unprecedented. Reversals keep happening: every sorrow might be turned to its opposite, and every gaiety run aground for a while, before the comic spirit again takes the helm.

In Shakespeare, as in Sophocles, Beckett, Chekhov, Strindberg, and Ibsen, drama thrives on the openness of the people on stage to their own inventions, their ability to improvise a diversion or a momentary happiness. But drama also exposes its characters, makes them vulnerable in the face of the dramatist's at times pitiless art. There is an unavoidable actuality to the theatre, with its performers subject to the audience, the author, and each other. Always in drama, even when we read a play alone, we imagine the action in real time, in real space: a room where, for a few hours, actors face their partners, their judges—the audience. To read a play with appreciation means always coming back to the fact of a stage, and on it people like us, playing with and against time.

Reading Essays

In French, *essayer* means to try something out. In its root sense, an essay is an attempt, a trial, an experiment. When in the year 1571 Michel de Montaigne, retired at the age of thirty-eight from political life, decided to spend his days writing down his thoughts about the world, about himself, and about how the two got on together, he decided to call the genre he invented the essay. Montaigne's essays differ from the musings of ancient writers like Plutarch and Marcus Aurelius. Those classic sages are aloof, judicious. But Montaigne barges into his work; he laughs, muses, and bustles his way through an essay. He is there in every line he writes, a full-fledged human standing up amid his pages: cut these words and they would bleed, his admirer Emerson remarked. Montaigne's motto was *que sçais-je?* ("what do I know?")—an open question that prompted him to investigate the most seemingly insignificant aspects of his life, and to surprise himself by finding them pregnant with sense. He tells us, "I mostly scratch my ears, which are sometimes itchy on the inside," and he adds that scratching is "one of nature's sweetest gratifications." He likes to sit with his heels higher than his seat; when he eats he often bites his tongue, and sometimes his fingers, from haste. In his great essay "Of Experience" Montaigne writes,

> And I cannot, without an effort, sleep by day, or eat between
> meals, or breakfast, or go to bed without a long interval, of

about three hours, after supper, or make a child except before
going to sleep, or make one standing up, or endure my sweat, or
quench my thirst with pure water or pure wine, or remain bare-
headed for long, or have my hair cut after dinner.

(translated by Donald M. Frame)

What a glorious catalog of peccadilloes! Yet Montaigne refuses
to turn himself into a loveable eccentric; there is nothing special, he suggests, about his peculiarities. Our own peculiarities,
after all, are precisely as worthy as his.

Montaigne invented the essay as we know it. His own life is
right there in his pages—though, as Phillip Lopate, himself one
of our distinguished essayists, says of Montaigne, the old fox no
doubt kept much to himself. He is frank yet at times evasive,
and not at all afraid to rub the reader the wrong way. To be an
essayist, Montaigne demonstrated, is to be oneself in prose.

The essayists I consider in this chapter—Montaigne, Woolf,
Hazlitt, Lamb, James Baldwin, and André Aciman—all testify
to the importance of voice (Rule Three) and style (Rule Four).
They all "Explore Different Paths" (Rule Thirteen) in their
prose: the essayist gets to shift position, to turn around and
travel down a new road at a moment's notice. And they all challenge the reader to "Ask the Right Questions" (Rule Two): what
is essential within the seemingly casual movement of an essay?
What has the author set out to uncover, to illuminate?

There is a modesty about the essay, but also a sense that the
essayist, whether Montaigne or one of his inheritors, can get
away with things that a novelist or poet couldn't (for instance,
abrupt changes in direction, guided by the author's whim).
Sometimes loudly, sometimes quietly, the essayist cajoles us into
trusting him or her. Essays can drift, turn sharply this way or
that, run up a blind alley and stay there for a while. They depend on a reliable partnership between author and reader.

T

The personal essay differs from its more assertive sibling, the memoir. The memoir as it is usually practiced today tends toward exposure, the spilling of secrets. Memoir is also, as Sven Birkerts argues in *The Art of Time in Memoir,* a sustained investigation of why a life has turned out as it has. "Memoir returns to the past, investigating causes in the light of their known effects," Birkerts remarks. Essays investigate a different matter: voice as a source of identity, rather than identity's historical causes. Vivian Gornick, in her book *The Situation and the Story,* suggests that the personal essayist focuses on not why but who: the essayist discovers, in the course of writing, who is speaking, and so dramatizes a truth of the author's voice. The personal essay, unlike the memoir, often maneuvers around the author's experience, rather than laying it bare. Memoirs are inclined to oscillate between two fixed poles, the present and the past self, and are constrained by the strict whens and wheres of autobiographical fact. The personal essayist, by contrast, may have a whole string of selves, or (looked at another way) the same everchanging, yet strangely static self: shifting like the weather, yet always offering a constancy, a steady undercurrent. A memoir stays firmly anchored to one main subject, the author's effort to confront and answer the question that is her life. For the memoirist, something needs to be solved (even if, in the end, it can't be). The personal essay travels more freely through the world, and is not interested in solving anything. The essayist indulges, questions, and above all, experiments on himself.

Lopate, in the introduction to a marvelous anthology, *The Art of the Personal Essay,* convincingly explains the difference between the familiar and the personal essay. Both forms are rambling, diverting and diverted, tending toward the free and the frank. But the familiar essay, Lopate points out, aims at lightness of touch, shown in observational humor or pathos; the personal essay may be appreciably heavier. Familiar essays take the reader warmly in hand, and sometimes tend toward cozy servings up of idiosyncrasy. But both kinds of essay are candid and conversational, open to the flourishes of personality.

Personal essayists are often secretive, even when they confess the rough or scandalous details of their lives; they cannot be easily captured. Casual instead of rigorous, they quickly admit the unofficial, intuitive character of their approach to the world, and see an advantage in their lack of credentials. They style themselves idlers, and think themselves somehow superior to the responsible classes. They go against the grain, pride themselves on their foibles; they have an interest in play and are grateful for the work of chance.

Essayists are happily rumpled, congenial even when antisocial, and usually forgiving—outright misanthropy would be ridiculous. Their work is not a lesson; they refuse to nag. Montaigne, the first and still the best of all personal essayists, gives his readers, not an unmasking of humanity à la Erasmus or the classical moralists, but a fond, if mixed, portrait. In Montaigne's view, we bear a chameleon complexity. We are all soiled in the working, as Polonius says in *Hamlet,* and for Montaigne the dirt makes us more worthy because it makes us more interesting. Montaigne's patchwork approach to thinking and living served him well. America's most important essayist and thinker, Ralph Waldo Emerson, admired the transitory, magpie manners of Montaigne and imitated them in his own practice of reading for the lustres, the gleams that shine out from a text. We must read Emerson just the same way: searching for illumination, ready for anything.

Lopate shrewdly names cheek as the personal essayist's central personality trait. The essayist shies away, circles around the point, gives small surprises and climaxes, and backs sideways into a conclusion. Sometimes there is a drizzle of quotations, evidence of the essayist's haphazard, but loving, excursions into books. Lopate calls the personal essay "basic research on the self": you can't get any closer to an author than when you absorb the intimate, loping rhythm of the confessions in Hazlitt, Lamb, or Baldwin. The essayist, who is not a monologist like one of Beckett's moored characters but a sociable creature, keeps a confidential proximity to the reader. He (or she) can be hearty, even hilarious, when the mood takes him, but he is never chipper; enforced gaiety seems like bondage to him. Richard Rodriguez, an eminent essayist and memoirist, has commented that, though homosexual, he has never felt like a gay man, since writers are by nature not gay, but morose, and he is a writer.

In spite of all the bustle and banter that color so many essays, the essayist frequently finds himself alone, stranded in moody reflection. Then he is free to spurn the advances of a too-familiar world, as William Hazlitt does at the beginning of "On Going a Journey": "One of the pleasantest things in the world is going on a journey; but I like to go by myself. I can enjoy society in a room; but out of doors nature is company enough for me." This sounds resolute enough; and a page or so later Hazlitt goes on to say, "The soul of a journey is liberty, perfect liberty, to think, feel, do, just as one pleases." But his very next sentence casts such independence in a new and different light: "We go a journey chiefly to be free of all impediments and of all inconveniences; to leave ourselves behind, much more to get rid of others." We want to be free, not only of others, but of ourselves too. Being yourself means getting free from all the polite conversation, all the faces you put on in the social world. (What self will be found underneath, after the false courtesies are scraped away?) But Hazlitt is no hater of his fellows; when the mood strikes him, he can be ardently gregarious, ready to jump into a good conversation (as he does in "The Fight," which I will discuss in a few pages).

Virginia Woolf in "The Modern Essay" reports that the essayist simply gives us himself, or herself. She cites Max Beerbohm's *Cloud of Pinafores,* whose author is just "Max": opinionated, deft (and a trifle daft), easily stylish. In the 1890s, she writes,

> it must have surprised readers accustomed to exhortation, information, and denunciation to find themselves familiarly addressed by a voice which seemed to belong to a man no larger than themselves. He was affected by private joys and sorrows, and had no gospel to preach and no learning to impart. He was himself, simply and directly, and himself he has remained.

Beerbohm's success is a victory of personality, Woolf concludes: and a victory of style as the essence of personality. On Montaigne, Woolf speaks of "the supreme difficulty of being oneself": "We can never doubt for an instant that his book was himself," she remarks.

> He refused to teach; he refused to preach; he kept on saying that he was just like other people. All his effort was to write himself down. . . . As for reading, he could seldom read any book for more than an hour at a time, and his memory was so bad that he forgot what was in his mind as he walked from one room to another.

Woolf's essays pick out what is personal in culture and history, and hold it up for warm appreciation. ("There is no history, only biography," Emerson wrote, and Woolf would have concurred.) But Woolf also values hard, brilliant environments; she wants to estrange us. One key example is her marvelous essay "On Not Knowing Greek." In fact, the consummately literate Woolf knew Greek very well from childhood on; her point is to underline the sheer foreignness of this ancient language, which bears the imprint of a stirring and unfamiliar world. The

Greek authors, Woolf remarks, cannot be divorced from their landscape, so different from damp, foggy England. The Greeks lived in sun and bright rocks and groves of olive trees, a scene open on all sides to gods and men. (Voice and sense of place [Rule Three] are central here.) "This is the quality that first strikes us in Greek literature, the lightning-quick, sneering, out-of-doors manner," Woolf writes. She adds, "Every word is reinforced by a vigour which pours out of olive-tree and temple and the bodies of the young." Savoring the sharp, mercurial ecstasy of Greek, she virtually cries out: "Then, spare and bare as it is, no language can move more quickly, dancing, shaking, all alive, but controlled." Anyone who has ascended far enough into the heights of ancient Greek to sample the jagged sublime of Aeschylus or the serene, pure excitements of Plato will agree with Woolf's description. But even those utterly ignorant of Greek will have glimpsed an electric revelation by the end of her essay. She not only evokes a language, but makes us awestruck travelers in a long-ago world.

Woolf's "On Not Knowing Greek" dips us in a cold, alien, infinitely desirable element, the world of ancient Greece; when she displays her excited thirst for this lost Greek realm, Woolf takes us eagerly with her. In her passionate wish to share her desire with the reader, she resembles William Hazlitt, the central English Romantic essayist. Hazlitt himself exemplifies what he calls "familiar style": he instantly makes the reader his companion. Above all, Hazlitt prizes gusto (his term), the appetitive grasp that adds something essential to an observation. In "On Going a Journey," Hazlitt sprinkles his texts with aperçus: "With change of place we change our ideas; nay, our opinions and feelings"; "The world in our conceit of it is not much bigger than a nutshell"; "We measure the universe by ourselves, and even comprehend the texture of our own being only piecemeal." These fragments of wisdom act not to diminish but to elevate us: the more variable we are, the more fascinating our attempts to understand our evasions, and evade our understandings, of ourselves. Hazlitt's nutshell is like Hamlet's; it contains infinity. No matter how small the matter of a Hazlitt essay may seem, it expands to encircle the whole of life.

Listen to Hazlitt's cockcrow on the first page of "The Fight," the most exhilarating of all his essays:

> I was determined to see this fight, come what would, and see it I did, in great style. It was my *first fight*, yet it more than answered my expectations. Ladies—it is to you that I dedicate this description; nor let it seem out of character for the fair to notice the brave. Courage and modesty are the old English virtues; and may they never look cold and askance on one another! Think, ye fairest of the fair, loveliest of the lovely kind, ye practisers of soft enchantment, how many more ye kill with poisoned baits than ever fell in the ring; and listen with subdued air and without shuddering, to a tale tragic only in appearance, and sacred to the FANCY!
>
> I was going down Chancey-lane, thinking to ask at Jack Randall's where the fight was to be, when looking through the glass-door of the *Hole in the Wall*, I heard a gentleman asking the same question.

Hazlitt hams it up. He knows he is being rather silly here; but let him enjoy his opening stunt. Hazlitt had recently fallen in love with Sarah Walker, a housekeeper more than twenty years younger than he, and would soon be jilted by her, to his despair; his gentle, joshing, but for all that seriously vulnerable address to the ladies recurs later in his essay. If we read quickly and impatiently, we may find Hazlitt's plea to the female "practisers of soft enchantment" merely distracting and irrelevant; but if we follow Rule One, "Be Patient," we will see that the way he uses his tale to impress the ladies has a point: it allows

Hazlitt himself, not just the boxers in the ring, to shine in bold, ardent fashion. His storytelling prowess (his tale will, he says, be "sacred to the FANCY!") is partly tongue in cheek; but he also seriously wants to make a grand impact through the suspense-filled force of his writing.

Like a barker talking up a fight, Hazlitt, in the paragraph I have quoted, gives an improvisational flair to his broad, masculine gesture. He takes his hat off to the "fairest of the fair," asking for their favor in the name of England. Within a few pages, we will see that Hazlitt himself displays "great style," just as much as the boxers whose fight he attends; his heroic efforts to travel to the fight seem to him "the exploits of the brave." In a tangled tour de force, Hazlitt spends more of his essay on getting to the fight than on the fight itself; he ends up in a crowded coach, where he talks the hours away with his companions. Finally, Hazlitt announces the main event: "Reader, have you ever seen a fight? If not, you have a pleasure to come, at least if it is a fight like that between the Gas-man and Bill Neate." The conflict between Tom Hickman ("the Gas-man") and Neate takes on epic proportions in Hazlitt's eyes:

> In the first round every one thought it was all over. After making play a short time, the Gas-man flew at his adversary like a tiger, struck five blows in as many seconds, three first, and then following him as he staggered back, two more, right and left, and down he fell, a mighty ruin. There was a shout, and I said, 'There is no standing this.' Neate seemed like a lifeless lump of flesh and bone, round which the Gas-man's blows played with the rapidity of electricity or lightning, and you imagined he would only be lifted up to be knocked down again. It was as if Hickman held a sword or a fire in that right hand of his, and directed it against an unarmed body. They met again, and Neate

seemed, not cowed, but particularly cautious. I saw his teeth clenched together and his brows knit close against the sun. He held out both his arms at full length straight before him, like two sledge-hammers, and raised his left an inch or two higher.

Hazlitt turns his two fighters into giant antagonists, godlike specimens of endurance. Their stamina is more than human, as is their ability to resurrect themselves from the floor. Here we "Get a Sense of Style" (Rule Four). Hazlitt's sentence rhythm mimics the rain of punches that the Gas-man hurls against Neate: "three first [a staccato hit of a phrase], and then following him as he staggered back [a slow, looping respite], two more, right and left [back to the deadly-accurate patter], and down he fell, a mighty ruin [the lofty summing-up]."

Neate finally lands a devastating blow, and "The Fight" climaxes with a genuinely frightening depiction of the Gas-man's fall:

It was doubtful whether he would fall backwards or forwards; he hung suspended for a second or two, and then fell back, throwing his hands in the air, and with his face lifted up to the sky. I never saw anything more terrific than his aspect just before he fell. All traces of life, of natural expression, were gone from him. His face was like a human skull, a death's head, spouting blood. The eyes were filled with blood, the nose streamed with blood, the mouth gaped blood. He was not like an actual man, but like a preternatural, spectral appearance, or like one of the figures in Dante's *Inferno*.

Describing for us the knockout of the Gas-man, Hazlitt registers the shock of death-in-life; for a moment, stunned, he thinks he is seeing a dead man, and he reaches out for a literary source, Dante's hell. For a split second, he has entered the underworld.

Hazlitt recovers—gasping, excited, nearly disbelieving what he has seen. "The Fight" concludes with a quick note to Hazlitt's friend Toms, who was present with him at the grand battle between Neate and the Gas-man: "PS. Toms called upon me the next day, to ask me if I did not think the fight was a complete thing? I said I thought it was. I hope he will relish my account of it."

"The Fight," like the contest it describes, is indeed a complete thing: it galvanizes us, exploiting first the hot eagerness of anticipation and then the cold shocks of battle. The essay sounds all its notes together: lively, jostling anticipation, breathless violence, satisfied memory. Devoted to its occasion, it yet rises boldly above it, and becomes a proud declaration of gusto. In "The Fight," Hazlitt produced the first great example of boxing reportage (a fine tradition that peaks with A. J. Liebling's *The Sweet Science*), as well as one of the irreplaceable personal essays in English. It is harrowing, high comic, and hodgepodge all in one.

Hazlitt's friend Charles Lamb knew tragedy first hand. Lamb was gentle and shy, a stammerer and a convivial drinker. His life was forever marked by the day when, at the age of twenty-one, he came home to discover that his sister Mary, in a fit of madness, had killed their mother. Charles took care of his sister for the rest of his life; she was his comrade, almost his other self. Given his dreadful experience, Lamb was awake to terror, as Anne Fadiman makes clear in her beautiful appreciation, "The Unfuzzy Lamb." (Lamb's "Witches and Other Night Fears" is a harrowing ride for the weak-stomached reader.) Hazlitt wrote of his friend Lamb, "His jests scald like tears." (He was alluding to a particularly painful moment in *King Lear,* when Lear laments, "Mine own tears / Do scald like molten lead.") In 1795–1796, Lamb spent six weeks "very agreeably in a mad house in Hoxton": "I had many

many hours of pure happiness," he wrote to the poet Coleridge, another close friend. "Dream not Coleridge, of having tasted all the grandeur & wildness of Fancy, till you have gone mad."

Yet despite the madness, Lamb is normally mild and winning, as readers have long appreciated. Fond of his own failings, he cherishes the archaic and out-of-the-way. In "The Old and the New Schoolmaster," Lamb announces,

> In everything that relates to *science,* I am a whole Encyclopaedia behind the rest of the world. . . . I am entirely unacquainted with the modern languages; and, like a better man than myself [that is, Shakespeare], have "small Latin and less Greek." I am a stranger to the shapes and textures of the commonest trees, herbs, flowers—

and his profession of ignorance goes on to encompass astronomy, history, geography, economics and much else.

The Lamb of "The Old and the New Schoolmaster" ponders the advantage his ignorance has acquired for him. He looks down on the new schoolmaster who, not content to while away his time in a single dusty corner of knowledge like his older predecessor, must make a lesson out of everything. When he "saunters through green fields (those natural instructors), with his pupils," the up-to-date teacher must grind out a point. Lamb complains,

> He must seize every occasion—the season of the year—the time of the day—a passing cloud—a rainbow—a wagon of hay—a regiment of soldiers going by—to inculcate something useful. . . . Nothing comes to him, not spoiled by the sophisticating medium of moral uses.

Lamb's picture of the old schoolmasters, by contrast, is cherishing and charmed. They, he says,

came to their task as to a sport! Passing from infancy to age,
they dreamed away all their days as in a grammar-school. Re-
volving in a perpetual cycle of declensions, conjugations, syn-
taxes, and prosodies; renewing constantly the occupations which
had charmed their studious childhood; rehearsing continually
the part of the past; life must have slipped from them at last like
one day.

Industrious and indolent at once, the old-school grammarians
are cocooned in a pleasant dream of life, a kind of after-dinner
sleep. Lamb is deeply sympathetic to their retiring sensibility,
and envies their security. Yet, in the end, Lamb is more interested in showing the limits of the new schoolmaster than in
lauding the old one. The new schoolmaster is always a teacher:
he treats everyone he meets as a student; and, Lamb emphasizes, being a teacher is as unhealthy as being a student, because
it means being attached to an unequal form of life. According
to Lamb, the student subjected to a teacher's superior mind
does not benefit, but rather finds himself cramped:

Too frequent doses of original thinking from others, restrain
what lesser portion of that faculty you may possess of your own.
You get entangled in another man's mind, even as you lose
yourself in another man's grounds. You are walking with a tall
varlet, whose strides outpace yours to lassitude.

Emerson, in an entirely different tone, expresses some of this
truth in "Self-Reliance" when he commands the reader, "Insist
on yourself; never imitate." For Emerson, though, we are the
taller ones, hedged by the small-spirited. But the more modest
Lamb knows this too. Lamb is surely aware exactly how remarkable, how odd, how truly new his reactions are, even when he
paints them as old-fashioned and reclusive. Both authors know
that to find our originality we need to fight that of others, and

that we do so by seeing everyone in the world—no matter how venerable, or weighty, or innovative—as our equal.

Lamb's argument makes intuitive sense: for him the freest and most genuine contact, the only real intercourse, is conversation, and conversation must occur between equals or not at all. We must resist the pull toward a pedagogical model, with its asymmetry of teacher and student. Talking to oneself, dreaming, gossiping, and reminiscing are ways of instruction, too, but we wouldn't want to ruin them by putting them in a classroom.

"The Old and the New Schoolmaster" navigates between the cantankerous and the charming. Lamb vigorously pushes away the usual chatter about the advantages of knowledge (which he claims to lack) and good teaching (which he disdains). For all its iconoclasm, though, the essay achieves a winning softness due to Lamb's habit of showing himself as fond, inept and a bit lost, rather than settled in a superior way of life.

"A Bachelor's Complaint of the Behaviour of Married People," the second Lamb essay I will discuss, similarly combines a confession of inadequacy with a battle cry. Here Lamb calls himself a loser in matters of the heart. He depicts himself as a slighted, if not superfluous, third wheel at dinners with married couples. But he combines these confessions of his sad insignificance with a call to arms against the arrogant habits of the proudly married. He is a little bit nebbish, a little bit firebrand.

In "A Bachelor's Complaint" as in "The Old and New Schoolmaster," Lamb's prose reflects the sway and rhythm of conversation: he may dawdle, speed up, get distracted, or veer off course. Style and voice are united here, to subtle effect. Lamb is sunny and genial, but with a dark cloud hovering nearby. Rather miraculously, "A Bachelor's Complaint" is a good-natured essay, though it presents a lengthy grouse against most of humanity: the married, and especially the married with children. "Nothing is to me more distasteful than that entire complacency and satisfaction which beam in the countenance of a new-married couple," Lamb writes. The happy pair broadcasts a reminder that everyone else is barred from such happiness, now and for all time. Even worse are the couples with children—and here Lamb reaches his grumpy, hilarious heights:

> But what I have spoken of hitherto is nothing to the airs these creatures give themselves when they come, as they generally do, to have children. When I consider how little of a rarity children are—that every street and blind alley swarms with them—that the poorest people commonly have them in most abundance—that there are few marriages that are not blest with at least one of these bargains—how often they turn out ill, and defeat the fond hopes of their parents, taking to vicious courses, which end in poverty, disgrace, the gallows, etc.—I cannot for my life tell what cause for pride there can possibly be in having them. If they were young phoenixes, indeed, that were born but one in a year, there might be a pretext. But when they are so common . . .

Notice that delicious throwaway: "the gallows, etc."! Lamb's endless delight in his own performance infects the reader, who may well be one of those insidious proud mamas and papas Lamb rails against. As someone who became a parent, to my surprised pleasure, only late in life, I can second some of Lamb's discontent. All too often, one is not treated as fully human unless one has a child; every child is deemed special, while no mere bachelor is.

After his merciless zingers, Lamb adds on the next page a gallant qualification: "I know that a sweet child is the sweetest thing in nature, not even excepting the delicate creatures which bear them." But the damage has been done. And Lamb can't resist tacking on one more objection, this time to the way wives break up their husbands' friendships. Lamb ends "A Bachelor's

Complaint" with a jocular threat: if he's not treated better by his married friends, he says, he'll replace the Latin pseudonyms in his text with real names, "to the terror of all such desperate offenders in future." This essayist is not seriously dangerous, we know; the zest of his attacks softens their bite. We would rather spend our time with him, barbs and all, than with any number of more settled, sententious companions.

James Baldwin is more aggressive than the sharp-witted but congenial Lamb. Prickly, scornful, and exciting to watch, Baldwin may be America's greatest twentieth-century essayist. "Notes of a Native Son," first published in 1955, is, in a large sense, an argument against Baldwin's great precursor, Richard Wright, whose novel *Native Son* Baldwin had attacked in *Partisan Review* in 1949. Since Wright, already established as a central African American author, had significantly encouraged the young Baldwin in his early literary efforts, the review caused a storm (it is reprinted in the volume *Notes of a Native Son,* which has the title essay at its center). Wright in *Native Son* depicted a black protagonist, Bigger Thomas, who decides on revenge against the white world and murders two people. Incapable of equivocation, Bigger represents the integrity of violence. Bigger's lawyer Max, a Jewish communist, pleads his case at his trial, and turns the plea into a denunciation of racial oppression.

Baldwin, unlike Wright, but like Ralph Ellison in his essays and his central novel *Invisible Man,* takes a stand for equivocation and against integrity. In "Notes of a Native Son," the symbol of integrity is Baldwin's taciturn, mean father; the essay keeps returning to the father's funeral, an event at which, Baldwin says, the father's bitterness was bequeathed to his son. (David Baldwin was actually Baldwin's stepfather, though Baldwin, who never knew his biological father, always calls him his father.) The elder Baldwin was a preacher often down on his luck; Baldwin, as a teenager in his father's grip, himself preached for several years (he quit in 1941, at age seventeen, two years before his father's death). Baldwin's verdict on his father, "handsome, proud, and ingrown," is a hard one: "He could be chilling in the pulpit and indescribably cruel in his personal life and he was certainly the most bitter man I have ever met." Even this merciless sentence, though, concludes with a qualification: "yet it must be said that there was something else in him, buried in him, which lent him his tremendous power and, even, a rather crushing charm." Understandably, the elder Baldwin rages against whites; Baldwin the writer speaks of this passed-down anger as a poison, an ineradicable disease, "a kind of blind fever, a pounding in the skull and fire in the bowels." This tormenting anger is not special to Baldwin, he adds, but a common racial inheritance: "There is not a Negro alive who does not have this rage in his blood—one has the choice, merely, of living with it consciously or surrendering to it. As for me, this fever has recurred in me, and does, and will until the day I die." Baldwin, writes Darryl Pinckney, claims "the authority of the survivor, of the witness"; he feels racial history in his flesh.

As Baldwin sees it, his inheritance, like that of all African Americans, is fierce anger, undying hatred of whites. But such rage kills, and being conscious of the rage rather than surrendering to it means seeing that black and white America are also entwined; that there is a strange, even perverse, love between the two, not just enmity. Always aware of his ambivalence, Baldwin dances between a grim acceptance of hate and the knowledge that hate is blind rather than insightful, that it defends against something deeper: "I imagine that one of the reasons people cling to their hates so stubbornly is because they sense, once hate is gone, that they will be forced to deal with pain." At his father's funeral, after the eulogist describes David Baldwin as a patient and thoughtful man, Baldwin suddenly realizes that the other mourners expect themselves, when they die, to receive just as forgiving and just as fictive a tribute:

> This was perhaps the last thing human beings could give each other and it was what they demanded, after all, of the Lord. Only the Lord saw the midnight tears, only He was present when one of His children, moaning and wringing hands, paced up and down the room. When one slapped one's child in anger the recoil in the heart reverberated through heaven and became part of the pain of the universe. And when the children were hungry and sullen and distrustful and one watched them, daily, growing wilder, and further away, and running headlong into danger, it was the Lord who knew what the charged heart endured as the strap was laid to the backside; the Lord alone who knew what one *would* have said if one had had, like the Lord, the gift of the living word. It was the Lord who knew of the impossibility every parent in that room faced: how to prepare the child for the day when the child would be despised and how to *create* in the child—by what means?—a stronger antidote to this poison than one had found for oneself.

And, Baldwin continues, perhaps his father's mourners are thinking that such an antidote doesn't exist; that they must after all fight racist poison with poison. Baldwin discerns "several schisms in the mind" in his audience of mourners. They reflect on their sins, their inarticulate cruelties; they see in God both the glorious possibility of redescription, so that cruelty becomes gentleness and bondage freedom, and, more deeply, the hidden well of knowing what to say, how to explain their own inability to prepare their children for a future of being despised by white society. In the passage I have quoted, Baldwin's incredulous, pained underlining of the word "create" conveys the monumental absurdity of the task he describes. ("Create" is Baldwin's "Key Word" here [Rule Eight]: it reaches desperately toward the wished-for, and most likely impossible, escape from the suffering one causes, undergoes, or watches and absorbs helplessly.) Baldwin condemns, without hesitation, the white America of his time. Yet he does not let the Harlem of the 1940s and 1950s off the hook; he says, elsewhere in his essay, that white and black bear equal responsibility for the grim ghetto streets.

In "Notes of a Native Son," Baldwin is most like his father—most stubborn, most rash, most silent and indomitable—when, tormented by being refused service because of his race, he throws a glass and shatters a mirror in a New Jersey restaurant. He flees, his heart pounding, convinced that he is going to be murdered by an angry white mob; he escapes this fate, but is frightened by the hate-filled being he has become.

Unlike *Native Son*'s Bigger Thomas, and unlike his father, Baldwin knows in his bones a strange meeting of opposites. Baldwin began his essay with the fact that his father's last son was born on the same day that he died. And there are still more bizarre, productive conjunctions: the day of his father's funeral is also Baldwin's own birthday, as well as the day of a race riot, with a black mob looting and destroying white-owned stores ("to smash something is the ghetto's chronic need," Baldwin writes). At the funeral, he reflects on the coming together of contraries. "Life and death so close together," Baldwin remarks, "and love and hatred, and right and wrong, said something to me which I did not want to hear concerning man, concerning the life of man." What he hears is that "Hatred, which could destroy so much, never failed to destroy the man who hated and this was an immutable law." Yet love, hatred's opposite, is not particularly available in Baldwin's "Notes of a Native Son," nor is the hope for a better society. In other essays in *Notes of a Native Son,* Baldwin disdains the progressive illusions of bohemians, and treats communists, whom he seems to regard as particularly ignorant children, with Jamesian archness: "However they might extol Russia, their concept of a better world was quite helplessly American and betrayed a certain thinness of imagination, a suspect reliance on suspect and badly digested formulae, and a positively fretful romantic haste" (from "Many Thousands Gone"). Baldwin exists in a realm of perpetual qualification, contradictory reactions, and self-doubt; all he has to go on is his knowledge of his own split self. Finally (in the great essay "Encounter on the Seine: Black Meets Brown") he pronounces with grim satisfaction on the unhappy union of white and black in America: "Now he is bone of their bone, flesh of their flesh." Baldwin here echoes Laban's words to Jacob, the hardworking nephew he defrauds, and who later defrauds him, as well as Adam's to Eve. (I discuss these biblical passages in my Rule Six, "Identify Signposts.")

Like Baldwin, André Aciman explores the fraught nature of identity, its forever divided center. Aciman is an Egyptian Jew: born in Alexandria, raised in Egypt, Italy, and France, and currently living in the United States, he defines himself as an exile. In his essay "In a Double Exile," Aciman begins by invoking Elijah, the messianic guest for whom a cup of wine is set out at every Passover seder. At a key moment in the seder, someone opens the door for Elijah; it is a solemn moment, even haunted, Aciman writes: "everyone stares at the doorway, trying to make out the quiet movements of the prophet as he glides his way in and takes the empty seat among us."

No sooner has Aciman invoked this religious solemnity than he lightly turns his back on it. In his very next sentence, he writes,

> But by then my mind has already drifted many, many times, and like all disbelievers who find themselves wondering why they are attending a Seder after last year's resolution, I begin to think of

how little this ritual means to me—recalling the ten plagues,
the crossing of the Red Sea, manna from heaven.

Like the expert essayist he is, Aciman uses his drifting mind to
explore the contradictions he feels within him. He disdains
the seder as a tedious and seemingly endless ceremony, but he
knows the poignant meaning of its story, the way it calls up the
sense of survival and deliverance experienced by so many Jews
in the face of anti-Semitic tyranny. Aciman himself was forced
out of Egypt just like the Jews in the Passover story, by the
"modern pharaoh" Nasser, who stripped Jews of their posses-
sions before expelling them. (Egypt, home to 75,000 Jews in
1948, now contains fewer than sixty after the ethnic cleansing
of the 1950s and 1960s.) In the 1960s Egypt was, as in biblical
times, ruled by a tyrant; but after the exodus the freed Israelites, wandering in the desert, remember it nostalgically. And so
does Aciman. In the course of his essay, Aciman fondly thinks
back to a lazy, magical time, his youthful life in Egypt. Passover
often coincided with Easter and Ramadan, and students would
be let out of school in the afternoon so that Muslims fasting for
Ramadan could rest. The boy Aciman loved those afternoons:
"The city was always quiet then, there was hardly any home-
work, and summer was only a few weeks away." Just after Aciman offers this idyllic image of an Egypt of restful peace, with
all three of its religions in easy harmony, he crosses it with an
ominous memory: his family's last seder in Egypt, "on the eve
of our departure for Italy in 1965—a long, mirthless, desultory
affair, celebrated with weak lights and all the shutters drawn so
that no one in the street might suspect what we were up to that
night." The Acimans were, he reflects, "celebrating Passover
the way our Marrano ancestors had done under the Spanish
Inquisition: in secret, verging on shame, without conviction, in
great haste." This very lack of conviction makes Aciman's expe-

rience convincing: the ambivalent and touching way he looks
over his own feelings, and wonders whether what he loved was
real. What overshadows Aciman's essay is Jewish history with its
echoes and its repeated exiles, its perpetual visions of a real
homelessness and an imagined home. Elijah himself is perhaps,
as Aciman hints, a ghostly presence homeless among his people.
Each Jew, Aciman concludes, "is a dislodged citizen of a country that was never really his but that he has learned to long for
and cannot forget." Aciman is a great lover of Proust, and
Proustian irony pervades his uncertain nostalgia: "We may not
always know what to remember, but we know we must remember," he writes. We each carry within us a "private Egypt" that
we never really knew, a retrospective fantasy of home; we were
in exile all along, and always will be. Gently but with probing
force, Aciman declares allegiance to memory, even and especially
when memory deals in illusion; and he dramatizes this allegiance
through the turns and counterturns so characteristic of the
essayist's art.

What better text to round off a discussion of reading essays
than one of Montaigne's finest, "Of Repentance"? Montaigne
in "Of Repentance," from the third and final volume of his essays, meditates on change, the essayist's all-swaying medium. I
give the beginning of "Of Repentance," a compact credo of
Montaigne's essay-making art, in John Florio's splendid Renaissance translation:

> Others fashion man, I repeat him; and represent a particular one,
> but ill-made; and whom were I to forme a new, he should be far
> other than he is; but he is now made. And though the lines of my
> picture change and vary, yet loose they not themselves. The world
> runnes all on wheeles. All things therein move without intermis-
> sion; yea, the earth, the rockes of Caucasus, and the Pyramides of
> Aegypt, both with the publike and with their own motion.

> Constancy it selfe is nothing but a languishing and wavering dance. I cannot settle my object; it goeth so unquietly and staggering, with a natural drunkennesse; I take it in this plight, as it is at the instant I amuse myself about it, I describe not th'essence but the passage; not a passage from age to age, or as the people reckon, from seaven yeares to seaven, but from day to day, from minute to minute. My history must be fitted to the present.

What a beautiful sentence is Montaigne's "Constancy it selfe is nothing but a languishing and wavering dance." To be constant is the Stoic ambition: steadfast, reliable, secure. But the Stoics' solidity, according to Montaigne, is merely another intoxication, albeit watered down: he detects a wavering even in these men of steel. Their sought-after freedom from illusion adds up to just another illusion; everything rocks and sways, no matter how seemingly steady it might be. Montaigne is what he is: unapologetic, tacking this way and that, endlessly fascinating to himself and to us. Even his addiction to change turns about into an opposing emphasis: we cannot escape ourselves; we are not so fluid as we like to think. From his opening avowal of unceasing change, which I began by quoting, Montaigne in "Of Repentance" rapidly shifts to an insistence that we are inevitably and always the same. Surprisingly, then, "Of Repentance" argues forcefully against repentance. Finally, Montaigne admits, we cannot change our nature.

> One may disavow and disclaim vices, that surprise us, and whereto our passions transport us: but those, which by long habite are rooted in a strong, and ankred in a powerful will, are not subject to contradiction. *Repentance is but a denying of our will, and an opposition of our fantasies* which diverts us here and there.

This is the wisdom of a middle-aged man, set in his ways and disciplined to self-acceptance. He cannot hoist himself above his limits.

I offer a small collection of sentences from "Of Repentance," still in Florio's resonant translation:

> I propose a meane life, and without luster: 'Tis all one.

> I speake truth, not my belly-full, but as much as I dare . . .

> As for me, I feele not my selfe much agitated by a shocke; I commonly find my selfe in mine owne place. . . . If I am not close and neare unto my selfe, I am never farre-off: My debauches or excesses transport me not much. There is nothing extreame and strange: yet have I sound fits and vigorous lusts.

> What I doe, is ordinarily full and complete, and I march (as wee say) all in one pace. . . .

> My actions are squared to what I am and [conformed] to my condition. I cannot doe better. . . .

> Crosses and afflictions, make me doe nothing but curse them. They are for people, that cannot bee awaked but by the whip: the course of my reason is nimbler in prosperity; it is much more distracted and busied in the digesting of mischiefes, than of delights. I see much clearer in faire weather.

Montaigne does not exclude the possibility of genuine repentance altogether: he just sets the bar higher. "I acknowledge no repentance, [that] is superficiall, meane and ceremonious. It must touch me on all sides, before I can terme it repentance. It must pinch my entrailes, and afflict them as deeply and thoroughly, as God himself beholds mee." He adds a few pages later, "I hate that accidentall repentance which olde age brings with it." Old age is weakness and waning of desire. Montaigne, when he wrote "Of Repentance" in his mid-fifties (a quite advanced age for the Renaissance) finds his temptations "so mortified and crazed" (that is, cracked) that, "holding but my hand before me, I be-calme them." Rather than congratulating himself for his constancy as a Stoic would, Montaigne attributes this self-control to the natural withering of his early lusts.

As he prepares to conclude "Of Repentance," Montaigne rises to a full-throated statement of pride, simple and plain: "Were I to live againe, it should be as I have already lived. I neither deplore what is past, nor dread what is to come: and if I be not deceived, the inward parts have neerely resembled the outward." With this quietly decisive claim, Montaigne convinces us. He does not boast or brag, but says the truth. Such truthtelling, which embraces the swings of mood and thought, marks all the other essayists I have discussed, from Hazlitt, Lamb, and Woolf to Baldwin and Aciman.

Emerson, who adored Montaigne, absorbed "Of Repentance" deeply, and echoed it in several of his greatest essays, notably "Circles" and "Self-Reliance." Emerson said of Montaigne that he "sets the reader into a working mood, makes him feel his strength, & inspires hilarity." Montaigne's book is still a tonic, as it was for Emerson. There is no better introduction to the glorious ins and outs of the essay than Montaigne, who created the form. He challenges us to read ourselves as we read him: with deep, close attention to how we argue, experiment, and disagree with ourselves, not just with others. If we pay attention to Rule One ("Be Patient") we see that all good essayists follow Montaigne's lead: they do not merely wander, but rather choose their steps with an eye to the reader, their best traveling companion. The journey, with all the divergent pathways it opens, is worth the ticket.

Conclusion

In his marvelously titled "Readers against the Grain," Charles
Lamb lamented,

> We read to say that we have read. No reading can keep pace with
> the writing of this age, but we pant and toil after it as fast as we
> can. . . . Must we *magazine* it and *review* it at this sickening rate
> for ever? Shall we never again read to be *amused*? but to judge,
> to criticize, to talk about it and about it? Farewell, old honest
> delight taken in books not quite contemporary, before this
> plague-token of modern endless novelties broke out upon us—
> farewell to reading for its own sake!

What Lamb means by "reading for its own sake" is slow reading
as I've described it in *Slow Reading in a Hurried Age:* a practice
pursued with care, for pleasure and private understanding. In
my chapter "Reading Essays" I devoted attention to the sometimes wonderfully acerbic, sometimes strangely comforting
work of Lamb, whose small, odd masterpieces include "Old
China" and the mouthwatering (even for a non-meat-eater like
me) "Dissertation upon Roast Pig." He is also a surprisingly
reliable critic, several hundred years in advance, of our current
trends in reading. Lamb's mournful words, written in 1825, apply now more than ever. In our manifold, busy Information
Age, we indeed find ourselves afflicted by a colorful plague of
"modern endless novelties," things to keep up with and comment

on. Instead of reading "to be *amused*," Lamb's ideal, we read so that we can know what to say. We click away, and chatter on. Gary Shteyngart's diverting novel *Super Sad True Love Story* is set in a near future in which people, especially young ones, scorn reading entirely. They survey streams of gossipy data on their portable devices, but they don't read. In college courses, they scan "classic texts," when they have to, for information. Shteyngart's dystopia is very close to our current reality. What Lamb called "reading for its own sake" seems almost forgotten. Instead, we harvest bits of knowledge, straining verbal plankton through our electronic jaws.

Eventually, though, we tire of such restless, unprofitable activity. We want something more: slow reading. Getting close to a book—achieving a rewarding intimacy with the author—can be learned, but only by practice, as I've argued in this book.

"Readers begin young," remarks Willard Spiegelman, "and are blissfully ignorant of why they have started on this obsession." Proust described childhood days spent entirely with books as "the pleasure of the gods." Dickens's David Copperfield remembers "a summer evening, the boys at play in the churchyard, and I sitting on my bed, reading as if for life." Compare Richard Wright on youthful reading: "I had tasted what to me was life, and I would have more of it, somehow, someway." Zora Neale Hurston escaped from small-town life by reading the Norse sagas: "My soul was with the gods and my body in the village . . . I wanted to be away from drabness and stretch my limbs in some mighty struggle." Whenever we read in earnest, no matter what our age, we recover youthful passion and dreams, a perpetual earliness.

There is no better place for me to end than with one of the greatest readers of all time, Virginia Woolf. In her immortal essay "How Should One Read a Book?" she speaks out for the practice of careful, pleasurable, solitary reading. In order to read as Woolf tells us to, we must flee from the "heavily furred and gowned" authorities who would tell us the meaning of books, boiling each one down to a lesson, a slogan, a lecture. Turn your back on the dreary schoolmaster, she advises, and seek out the author instead. "Do not dictate to your author; try to become him," Woolf proclaims. "Be his fellow-worker and accomplice." Such faithfulness will be rewarded by a glimpse of the personality that shines through each moment, each small, bright crevice, of the book you read. "If you open your mind as widely as possible, then signs and hints of almost imperceptible fineness, from the twist and turn of the first sentences, will bring you into the presence of a human being unlike any other."

Every true reader should memorize the final words of Woolf's "How Should One Read a Book?" and make them his or her proud declaration of independence. No one has ever offered higher or more just praise for reading. Woolf asks,

> Are there not some pursuits that we practice because they are good in themselves, and some pleasures that are final? And is this not among them? I have sometimes dreamt, at least, that when the Day of Judgment dawns and the great conquerors and lawyers and statesmen come to receive their rewards—their crowns, their laurels, their names carved indelibly upon imperishable marble—the Almighty will turn to Peter and will say, not without a certain envy when He sees us coming with our books under our arms, "Look, these need no reward. We have nothing to give them here. They have loved reading."

Woolf counsels us in the most important lesson of all: don't feel guilty about reading. (Maureen Corrigan in her charmingly titled *Leave Me Alone: I'm Reading* confesses, "When I'm in the company of others—even my nearest and dearest—there always comes a moment when I'd rather be reading a book." Woolf would agree.) In a sublime play on the idea of the account book that God keeps for each of our lives, recording our good and bad deeds, Woolf suggests that reading enables us to keep the accounts ourselves. We have our reward right now, as we hover over that lighted page where we know ourselves more truly and more strange (in the words of Wallace Stevens). We are more heroic in our reading than the most celebrated of great men and women. "Yet who reads to bring about an end, however desirable?" Woolf asks, rising to defend reading in its integrity. Slow reading asks and promises nothing worldly, yet committed readers belong more deeply to the world than the champions of causes, the great conquerors and statesmen—who may look to us, with our books securely in hand, like mere troublers of humanity.

Emerson yearned after "books which take rank in our life with parents and lovers and passionate experiences." And Kafka noted in a letter to his friend Oskar Pollak that "some books seem like a key to unfamiliar rooms in one's own castle." When we read, we want a book that will unlock us, even break us open. In reading, as Harold Bloom suggests, we quest after something more original than ourselves—new experience, a radical break from what we know too well. This newness finds its place in us, and makes us rise to embrace it. It becomes part of us, something we can always return to by the simple act of picking up the book again. Today more than ever, we find ourselves frustrated by the shallow promises of digital technology, as it offers ever more rapid, more ingenious, and more unsatisfying ways of keeping in touch. Instead of staying up to the minute, we should step back and think about what Woolf, like so many others, celebrates: the rewards of slow reading. Getting lost in a book may be the surest way to find what we need.

Acknowledgments

I must first thank John Kulka, my editor at Harvard University Press, who guided and transformed this book as he did several of my earlier ones (including *A New Handbook of Literary Terms,* in some ways a companion volume to *Slow Reading in a Hurried Age*). I am grateful for their advice to Harold Bloom, Morris Dickstein, Mark Edmundson, Rachel Hadas, Herbert Marks, Willard Spiegelman, and especially Jenn Lewin (for a key observation about Stevens, among other things). Martin Greenup helpfully commented on my Dickinson discussion. The members of the Association of Literary Scholars, Critics, and Writers, an organization that is truly devoted to the life of reading and the survival of the common reader, were essential in my thinking about this book; I am thinking particularly of comments and talks by Greg Delanty, Mark Halliday, Christopher Ricks, and Rosanna Warren. The University of Houston's Honors College and its current and former deans, Bill Monroe and Ted Estess, as well as the Creative Writing Program, offered inspiring proof that literary study is alive and well. My colleagues, including Richard Armstrong, Susan Collins, Robert Cremins, Jamie Ferguson, Tony Hoagland, Kathleen Lee, Andy Little, Ange Mlinko, Iain Morrisson, Jesse Rainbow, Tamler Sommers, Rob Zaretsky, and Jonathan Zecher, taught me much about reading.

On occasion in this book I have briefly quoted from essays and comments on reading in two marvelous anthologies: *Reading in Bed,* edited by Steven Gilbar, and *Buried in Books,* edited by Julie Rugg. Helaine Smith's book *Homer and the Homeric Hymns* was a model for posing the most important questions about reading and interpreting.

Grateful acknowledgment is made to the following for permission to reprint previously published material: Elizabeth Bishop, excerpts from "At the Fishhouses," from *The Complete Poems: 1927–1979.* Copyright 1983 by Alice Methfessel. Reprinted by permission of Farrar, Straus and Giroux, LLC and Faber and Faber, Ltd. Translations of Psalms 131 and 114 by David Curzon from *The Jerusalem Review* 9 (1998). Copyright 1998 by David Curzon. Reprinted by permission of the author. Robert Frost, "Design," from *The Poetry of Robert Frost*, edited by Edward Connery Latham. Copyright 1969 by Robert Frost. Reprinted by permission of the Random House Group Limited. Robert Frost, "In White." Reprinted by permission of the Estate of Robert Frost. Thom Gunn, "To the Dead Owner of a Gym," from *Collected Poems.* Copyright 1994 by Thom Gunn. Reprinted by permission of Farrar, Straus and Giroux, LLC and Faber and Faber, Ltd. Samuel Menashe, "Full Fathom Five." Copyright 2005 by Samuel Menashe. Reprinted by permission of the Literary Classics of the United States, Inc., New York, NY.

My father, Louis Joseph Mikics, died as I was finishing *Slow Reading in a Hurried Age.* I owe much to his example, his generosity, and his cheerfulness and courage in the face of hardship. My mother- and father-in-law, Edith and Larry Malkin, were sustaining presences during the writing of this book. Finally, I owe most to my wife, Victoria Malkin, and my son, Ariel Malkin Mikics.